uCertify Guide for ISEB Exam BH0-006

ITIL V3 Foundation Certificate in IT Service Management

Pass your ITIL Foundation V3 Certification in first attempt

uCertify Team
www.ucertify.com

Copyright

uCertify Guide for ISEB Exam BH0-006

Foreword

IT certification exams require a lot of study and practice. Many of our customers spend weeks, if not months preparing for the exam. While most classroom training and certification preparation software do a good job of covering exam material and providing practice questions, summarization of the highlights and key study points is often missing.

This book is intended to bridge the gap between preparation and the final exam. It is designed to be an easy reference that will walk you through all the exam objectives with easy to remember key points required to successfully pass the certification exam. It reinforces the key points, while helping you focus on the exam requirements. The benefits are multifold and can help you save hours of exam review, while keeping key concepts fresh in your mind before the exam. This critical review will help you with the final exam preparation touches and give you the confidence needed for the big day.

Benefits of this exam countdown and quick review guide:

1. Focused approach to reviewing exam material – review what you must know

2. All key exam concepts highlighted and reinforced

3. Time saving – must know facts at your finger tips in one condensed version

4. Detailed explanations of all possible answers to practice questions to ensure your grasp of the topic

5. A full length simulation exam to determine your exam readiness

Table of Contents

How this book will help you

uCertify's guide for ISEB Exam BH0-006 is an invaluable supplement to those who are in the final stages of their preparation for the ISEB Exam BH0-006: ITIL V3 Foundation Certificate in IT Service Management.

This book is organized into three sections.

Section A

Section A contains general information about the book and Exam BH0-006. It describes the exam objectives, pre-requisites, exam format, test taking tips and strategies, and more.

Section B

Section B contains seven chapters. Each chapter contains a Quick Review of the material you need to know for a given objective. It reinforces concepts reviewed via pop quiz and practice questions.

- **Pop Quiz:** Short and to-the-point questions with definitive answers.

- **Practice Questions:** At the end of each chapter, a series of questions test your understanding of the topics covered in the chapter. These questions are patterned after actual exam questions and difficulty levels. Detailed explanations are provided for each question, explaining not just the correct answer, but the incorrect answers as well, to ensure a real grasp of the question.

Section C

Section C contains fifty full-length questions. These questions will test your preparation for the exam within a stipulated time period. The Answer Sheet for the exam contains a complete analysis of the question.

Finally, the Appendices includes Acronyms and Glossary followed by References and Index. This is very handy for the last minute reviews.

We wish you all the best for your exam!

Principal contributors:

Mohd. Ali Naqvi,

uCertify Team

Section A

Introduction

About uCertify

uCertify is a leading provider of IT certification exam preparation software. For over a decade, we have been preparing top quality preparation guides for over 200 IT certification exams. Our software Preparation Kits (Prepkits, as we call them), contain exhaustive study material, tips, study notes and hundreds of practice questions that culminate in a full length simulated preparation exam. Choose exams from vendors, such as Microsoft, Oracle, CompTIA, SUN, CIW, EC-Council, ADOBE, CISCO, ITIL, IBM, LPI, and ISC-2. Authored by highly experienced and certified professionals, uCertify PrepKits not only guarantee your success at getting certified, but also equip you to truly understand the subject.

As they say, "Successful people don't do different things, they do things differently." uCertify's preparation methodology is that difference. We will give you a competitive edge over the others who may be paper certified but not qualified to use the skills on the job. A customer pass rate of over 99% is the testimony to the success of our methodology. We guarantee it! Our industry best 100% money back guarantee is second to none! Check it out at:

http://www.ucertify.com/about/guarantee.html

Learn more about us at www.ucertify.com and www.prepengine.com, our smarter learning platform, which powers each of our Prepkits.

About this Book

What this book is and what it's not

This book is invaluable as a final review guide for ISEB Exam BH0-006. It is a supplement to your exam preparation, be it classroom training, practical experience, or even test preparation software. The book is designed to help you save your time while ensuring your are ready, by providing you a Quick Review of all exam objectives, without having to review all exam material. In addition, the book helps reinforce key concepts and terminology, both of which are important to review just before your exam. A big bonus is the full length exam simulation practice test that will be a good indicator of your exam readiness.

This book is not a substitute for exhaustive test preparation services, such as uCertify Prepkits or classroom training. uCertify strongly recommends that you first study the exam material extensively and gain as much practical experience as possible in the areas you are expected to have skills in. Use this book as a final review before your actual exam.

About Exam BH0-006: ITIL V3 Foundation Certificate in IT Service Management

The ISEB (ITIL V3) Foundation Certificate in IT Service Management BH0-006 exam is aimed at raising an individual's understanding of, and competence in, IT Service Management as described in the ITIL Service Strategy, ITIL Service Design, ITIL Service Transition, ITIL Service Operation, ITIL Continual Service Improvement, ITIL Introduction, and ITIL Glossary publications.

Successful completion of the Foundation certificate also fulfils the pre-requisite entry criteria for the next level of study within the ITIL qualifications scheme; the ITIL V3 Intermediate Level. The Official Accreditor has developed the Credit Profiler to help candidates calculate the number of credits they have achieved in the ITIL V3 scheme.

Benefits of Certification

IT certification is an industry wide, internationally standardized, highly recognized method that demonstrates your technical problem skills and expertise in a given area. By passing a certification exam, an individual shows to his current or potential employer that s/he recognizes the value of staying current with the latest technology. The certification process helps you gain market relevant skills culminating in an industry respected certificate in one or more areas offered for certification. While not all employers require certification, getting certified is tangible proof of your motivation and skills as an IT professional. Surveys consistently show certified professionals to earn more than their counterparts who do not have a formal certification. Most certified professional have found that their financial investment in training and certification is paid off by gains in salary, job opportunities, or expanded roles, typically over a short period of time.

Exam Registration

ISEB exams can be registered and taken at Prometric or VUE testing centers across the globe. Be sure to give yourself plenty of time to prepare for the exam before you schedule your exam day.

Name	Phone (US and Canada)	Phone Other Countries
Prometric: http://www.prometric.com	1-800-775-3926	1-410-843-8000

Exam Objectives & Skills Expected

The ISEB (ITIL V3) Foundation Certificate in IT Service Management BH0-006 exam is aimed at raising an individual's understanding of, and competence in, IT Service Management as described in the ITIL Service Strategy, ITIL Service Design, ITIL Service Transition, ITIL Service Operation, ITIL Continual Service Improvement, ITIL Introduction, and ITIL Glossary publications. Following are some important areas in which an individual should possess good knowledge before taking the (ITIL v3) BH0-006 exam:

- Describing the concept of Good Practice

- Defining and explaining the concept of a Service

- Defining and explaining the concept of Service Management

- Defining Functions and Processes

- Explaining the process model and the characteristics of processes

- Describing the structure, scope, components and interfaces of the Service Lifecycle

- Accounting for the main goals and objectives of Service Strategy

- Accounting for the main goals and objectives of Service Design

- Briefly explaining what value Service Design provides to the business

- Accounting for the main goals and objectives of Service Transition

- Briefly explaining what value Service Transition provides to the business

- Accounting for the main goals and objectives of Service Operations

- Briefly explaining what value Service Operation provides to the business

- Accounting for the main goals and objectives of Continual Service Improvement

- Defining Utility and Warranty

- Defining Resources, Capabilities, and Assets

- Defining Service Portfolio and Service Catalogue

- Defining the role of IT Governance across the Service Lifecycle

- Defining Business Case and Risk

- Defining Service Provider, Supplier, Service Level Agreement (SLA), Operational Level Agreement (OLA)

- Defining Contract, Service Design Package, Service Knowledge Management System (SKMS), and Availability

- Defining Configuration Item (CI), Configuration Management System

- Defining Service Change, Change types, Definitive Media Library (DML), and Release Unit

- Defining concept of Seven R's of Change Management; no requirement to learn list Event

- Defining Alert (SO Glossary)

- Defining Incident, Impact, Urgency, and Priority

- Defining Service Request and Problem

- Defining Workaround, Known Error, and Known Error Data Base (KEDB)

- Defining the role of communication in Service Operation

- Defining Service Assets and Release policy

- Defining key Principles and models of Service Strategy, Service Design, and Continual Service Improvement

- Defining Service Strategy and Service Design processes

- Defining Service Transition and Service Operation processes

- Explaining the role, objectives and organizational structures for the Service Desk function

- Stating the role, objectives, and organizational overlap of the Technical Management function

- Stating the role, objectives, and organizational overlap of the Application Management function

- Stating the role, objectives, and organizational overlap of the IT Operations Management function

- Accounting for the role and the responsibilities of the Process owner and Service owner

- Recognizing the RACI model and explaining its role in determining organizational structure

- Understanding how Service Automation assists with Integrating Service Management processes

Who should take this exam?

The ITIL Foundation Certificate in IT Service Management (BH0-006) exam is primarily aimed toward the following; however, the ITIL certification is open to any individuals who may have an interest in the subject:

Those who require a basic understanding of the ITIL framework

Those who need understanding of how ITIL can be used to enhance the quality of IT service management within an organization

IT professionals or others working within an organization that has adopted and adapted ITIL who need to be informed about, or contribute, to an ongoing service improvement program.

The ITIL Foundation Certificate in IT Service Management itself is not intended to enable the holders of the certificate to apply the ITIL practices for Service Management without further guidance.

Candidates can expect to gain knowledge and understanding in the following upon successful completion of the education and examination components related to this certification.

- Service Management as a practice (Comprehension)

- Service Lifecycle (Comprehension)

- Key Principles and Models(Comprehension)

- Generic Concepts (Awareness)

- Selected Processes (Awareness)

- Selected Roles (Awareness)

- Selected Functions (Awareness)

- Technology and Architecture (Awareness)

- ITIL Qualification scheme (Awareness)

FAQ for ISEB Exam BH0-006

Q. What are the pre-requisites for taking the BH0-006 exam?

A. The ITIL Version 3 (V3) Qualifications scheme provides a modular approach to the ITIL certification, and is comprised of a series of certifications focused on different aspects of ITIL Best Practice, to various degrees of depth and detail. The modular, tiered approach to certification not only offers increased flexibility to candidates relating to the disciplines or areas of ITIL that they are able to study, but generally makes ITIL certification more accessible and achievable.

Q. What is the format of the exam?

A. This exam consists of Multiple Choice questions.

Q. What does one gain from this certification?

A. ISEB's BH0-006 exam is designed to test your knowledge of the ISEB .NET Framework fundamentals. The BH0-006 exam measures your skills that include developing applications, implementing service processes, threading, application domains, embedding configuration, diagnostic, management, and installation features into a .NET Framework application, etc.

The majority of people that consider ITIL as a qualification do so for career and personal development reasons. Often this is driven by a change of job or career, where you notice that to get to the top of the CV pile, you need to have an extra qualification like ITIL (even if you have been involved in service management successfully for many years without it). In many advertised positions ITIL has become a prerequisite.

The majority of companies that implement ITIL also encourage their employees to take the exams. If your staff has accredited ITIL qualifications, then you can present your company as using ITIL. This works particularly well where you tender for or supply to any large IT organizations or outsourcing companies.

Q. Which certification does it cover?

A. Successful completion of the Foundation certificate also fulfils the pre-requisite entry criteria for the next level of study within the ITIL qualifications scheme; the ITIL V3 Intermediate Level. The Official Accreditor has developed the Credit Profiler to help candidates calculate the number of credits they have achieved in the ITIL V3 scheme.

Q. How many questions are asked in the exam?

A. You will be required to attempt 40 questions.

Q. What is the duration of the exam?

A. You are required to attempt all questions within 120 minutes.

Q. What is the passing score?

A. The passing score of the exam is 65% (26/40).

Q. What is the exam retake policy?

A. In the unfortunate case you fail an examination, you can take part in another examination session. This does not necessarily have to be at the same examination center.

For the retake of the ITIL Foundation examination, you could, for example, turn to one of the Prometric Testing Centers. There is no limit to the number of times you can retake the examination.

Q. Where can I get more practice questions?

A. Download uCertify PrepKit to have more practice questions from the download link below:

http://www.ucertify.com/exams/ITIL/BH0-006.html

Q. Where can the test BH0-006 be taken?

A. ISEB exams may be taken at Prometric OR Pearson VUE testing facilities.

Q. What is the exam fee?

A. The net price for taking test BH0-006 is US$210.

- **If booking an exam through an Accredited Training Provider:**

  If you are attending a course and exam with one of our Accredited Training Organisations, you can obtain information on the fees and charges for the ISEB Foundation Certificate in IT Service Management (ITIL® V3) qualification by contacting the Accredited Training Organisation directly.

- **If taking a Computer Based Exam:**

  - If you are taking the exam via a computer based examination centre, you can obtain information on the fees and charges for the ISEB Foundation Certificate in IT Service Management (ITIL® V3) qualification from Prometric or Pearson.

- **If sitting a Public Exam:**

  - If you are taking the exam through one of the BCS public examination dates, you can obtain information on the fees and charges for the ISEB Foundation Certificate in IT Service Management (ITIL® V3) qualification by contacting BCS.

Q. How to book the ITIL V3 Foundation exam?

A. There are two ways you can take the exam, either online through a computer based examination centre, or via one of our public examination sittings held throughout the year in London.

If you are taking training through an accredited training provider, you will obtain and submit your registration form through them.

Online Exam

Taking the exam online via a computer based examination centre provides you with your exam result immediately.

You can book an online exam either with Prometric or Pearson Vue using the links below.

- **Book with Prometric**

- **Book with Pearson Vue**

Prometric have in excess of 5000 offices in over 160 countries. Pearson Vue have in excess of 4000 offices in over 140 countries.

BCS Examination Sittings

You can register for one of our many exam dates in London using the form below.

Please be aware that payment must be made at least three weeks before the exam date, and that exam places will be confirmed once payment has been received.

If cancelling the exam within two weeks of the exam date a cancellation charge will apply. Exam fees

Candidate results are sent by post within three weeks of the exam date.

 Registration form:

http://www.bcs.org/server.php?show=conMediaFile.14309

Q. What are the job prospects after passing the ITIL V3 Foundation exam?

A. The job prospects after passing the ITIL V3 Foundation exam are as follows:

- ITIL Configuration Manager

- Problem Analyst

- Remedy ARS Developer

- Application Business Analyst

- Technical Writer - ITIL v3

- Remedy SACM Service Request Analyst

- Change Manager

- Incident Resolution Manager

- Support Analyst

- Configuration Manager

- Websphere Application Server (WAS) Administrator

- BMC Remedy Support Specialist

- Remedy Action Senior Developer

Q. What are the OGC ITIL certification providers?

A. The OGC ITIL certification providers are as follows:

- EXIN - The National Exam Institute for Informatics (Netherlands)

- ISEB - The Information Systems Examination Board (UK), part of the British Computer Society

Since the early 1990s, ISEB and ISEB have been setting up the ITIL-based certification program, developing and providing ITIL exams at three different levels: Foundation, Practitioner and Manager.

ISEB and BCS/ISEB (the British Computer Society) have from that time onwards been the only two examination providers in the world to develop formally acknowledged ITIL certifications, provide ITIL exams and accredit ITIL training providers worldwide. These rights were obtained from OGC, the British government institution and owner of the ITIL trademark.

Q. Who provides the training for ITIL certification?

A. Further information about the Foundation Certificate in IT Service Management (ITIL V3) can be obtained from the following accredited Training Providers.

ISEB strongly recommends taking an accredited training course before attempting an ISEB exam. You can feel confident that by using an accredited training course the training materials, course tutors and the organisation are of a high standard and have been independently assessed by ISEB.

Detailed statistical analysis proves that candidates attending accredited training courses have a much better chance of passing our examinations as well as adding more value to your career and for your employer.

Filter by training providers who offer online courses

UK

- Acrobat Training and Consulting Limited

  Uk based, operates worldwide

- Advance ITSM Ltd

  UK based, operates worldwide

- Afiniti Limited

  Uk based, operates worldwide

- Bishops Beech Limited

  UK based, operates worldwide

- ConnectSphere

  UK based, operates worldwide

- e-Quant Limited

  UK based, operates worldwide

- FGI Limited

  UK based, operates worldwide

- Fox IT

  UK based, operates worldwide

- Grey Matters Education Limited

  UK based, operates worldwide

- Helix Service Management Services Limited

  UK based, operates worldwide

- Hewlett Packard Education Services

  UK based, operates worldwide

- ITILplus

  UK based, operates worldwide

- ITIL® Works

  UK based, operates worldwide

- Logica

  UK based, operates worldwide

- Marval Training & Consultancy Ltd

  UK based, operates worldwide

- NES AIM Academy

  Uk based, operates worldwide

- PA Consulting

  UK based, operates worldwide

- Pink Elephant

  UK based, operates worldwide

- Purple Griffon Limited

  UK based, operates worldwide

- QA Limited

  UK based, operates worldwide

- Quanta Training Limited

  UK based, operates worldwide

- Sortium Limited

  UK based, operates worldwide

- Sysop

  UK based, operates worldwide

- Wardown Consulting Limited

  UK based, operates worldwide

International

- ALC Group PTE Ltd

  Based in Singapore, operates worldwide

- Dimension Data Learning Solutions

  Based in Australia, operates worldwide

- Dowling Consulting

Based in Australia, operates worldwide

- Foster Melliar (Pty) Limited

  Based in South Africa, operates worldwide

- Itilics Pte Ltd

  Based in Singapore, operates worldwide

- Meeza QSTP LLC

  Based in Qatar, operates worldwide

- Opsys - SM2

  Based in Belgium, operates worldwide

- ProActive Services Pty Limited

  Based in Australia, operates worldwide

- Procept Associates Limited

  Based in Canada, operates worldwide

- Process Catalyst Solutions LLC

  Based in the USA, operates worldwide

- Profecto Service Management AB

  Based in Sweden, operates worldwide

- QAI India Limited

  Based in India, operates worldwide

BCS is always here to help with your queries.

For general information about ISEB please contact:

Customer Service

Tel: + 44 (0)1793 417655

Email: isebenq@hq.bcs.org.uk

Frequently Asked Questions:

Visit the folloiwng link of questions and answers on range of ISEB qualifications.

http://isebfaq.bcs.org/faq-pro/

Test Taking Tips

- Stay calm and be relaxed.

- When you start the test, read the question and ALL its options carefully, even if you think you know the correct answer. Be prepared for the tricky questions!

- If you are taking an adaptive test, remember that you will not get a chance to change your answer once you move on, so be sure before you mark the answer. In a linear test, you will have a chance to change the answer before you hand in the exam.

- If you know the correct answer, attempt the question and move on; if you are not sure, mark your best guess and move on. If it is a linear test, you should also bookmark the question so that you can return to it later.

- Sometimes related questions help you get the right answers for the questions you were unsure of; so, it is always a good idea to bookmark the question.

- If you are unsure of the correct answer, read all the options and eliminate the options that are obviously wrong; then, choose from the options that are left.

- Once you have finished answering all the questions, check the time left. If you have time, review the book-marked questions.

- Never leave a question unanswered. All certification tests that we know are timed and count unanswered questions as wrong. If you don't have time, take a blind guess.

Before the test

- Be confident and relaxed.

- Sleep well the night before the exam.

The Big Day

It is strongly recommended that you arrive at the testing center at least 15 minutes before the exam is scheduled. Don't forget to bring two pieces of identification with you, one of which must be a photo I.D., such as a valid driver's license. You will be required to show the identification when you sign in at the testing center. The center-in-charge will explain the examination rules, after which you will be asked to sign a document that states that you fully understand and abide by the rules of the exam.

Once you are signed in, you will be directed to the exam room. Carrying anything into the room is strictly prohibited. You will be given a few blank pieces of paper and a pen on entering the room. Once you complete the exam, your score will be tabulated and you will know immediately whether you have passed or failed the exam. If you fail, you can retake it as soon as you are ready, even the same day. It is a good idea to note down all the difficult topics you faced during the exam and revise this review guide or other training material before retaking the exam. If you fail the same exam second time, you must wait at least 14 days before you will be allowed to reschedule.

The testing center-in-charge is typically available to assist with administrative aspects of the testing.

Section B
Core Contents

Chapter 1 - Service Management as a practice

Overview

The purpose of this unit is to help the candidate to define Service and to comprehend and explain the concept of Service Management as a practice. Specifically, candidates must be able to:

- Describe the concept of Good Practice.

- Define and explain the concept of a Service.

- Define and explain the concept of Service Management.

- Define Functions and Processes.

- Explain the process model and the characteristics of processes.

The recommended study period for this unit is minimum 45 minutes.

Key Points

Describe the concept of Good Practice

Good practices are commodities, usually accepted, confirmed, and effective ways of doing things, which were earlier considered best practices of pioneering organizations.

- Innovations are formed to be successful.

- Innovations applied thoroughly turn into best practices.

- Best practices copied by others become common, good practices.

- Good practices are commoditized, commonly accepted principles, or regulatory requirements.

A "practice" is defined as a way of working. Good or best practices are field-proven activities or processes, which have been successfully used by various organizations. These good practices come from a number of possible sources:

- Existing public standards, such as ISO

- Industry practices that are shared among industry practitioners

- Academics research, which discovers good practices through practical analysis

- Training and education, which identifies good practices through sharing experiences

- Internal experience in providing such services

Choose Good Practices over Proprietary ones because of the following reasons:

Good Practices, Public Standards, and Frameworks

- Broad community distribution

- Public training and certification

- Valid in diverse applications

- Peer reviewed

- Used by different parties

- Free and publicly available

- Labor market skills easy to find

Proprietary Knowledge

- Difficult to adopt

- Difficult to reproduce or transfer

- Difficult to document

- Highly customized

- Specific to business needs

- Difficult to adapt or reuse

- Owners anticipate compensation

Governance relates to decisions that define expectations, grant power, or verify performance. It consists either of a separate process or of a specific part of management or leadership processes. Sometimes, people set up a government to administer these processes and systems. It is always concerned with fairness and transparency.

Define and explain the concept of a Service

A service is a way of delivering value to customers by facilitating outcome that customers wish to get without the control of specific costs and risks. It is a series of activities designed to enhance the level of customer satisfaction.

Outcomes are probable from the performance of tasks and are limited by the existence of certain constraints. A service facilitates outcomes by enhancing the performance and by reducing the clutch of constraints. The result is an increase in the possibility of desired outcomes. Its importance varies by product, industry and customer; defective or broken merchandise can be exchanged, often only with a receipt and within a specified time frame.

A service is normally an integral part of customers' value proposition. In their book Rules to Break and Laws to Follow, Don Peppers and Martha Rogers, write that *"customers have memories. They will remember you, whether you remember them or not."* Further, *"customer trust can be destroyed at once by a major service problem, or it can be undermined one day at a time, with a thousand small demonstrations of incompetence."*

A service is a way of delivering value to customers by facilitating outcome that customers wish to get without the control of specific costs and risks. It is a series of activities designed to enhance the level of customer satisfaction.

Pop Quiz

Q1: What does a service MUST always deliver to customers?

Ans: Value

Q2: Which concept belongs to IT Service Continuity Management?

Ans: Vulnerability

Define and explain the concept of Service Management

Service Delivery is primarily concerned with proactive services the ICT must deliver to provide adequate support to business users. It focuses on the business as the customer of the ICT services (compare with: Service Support). The discipline consists of the following processes:

- Service Level Management

- Capacity Management

- IT Service Continuity Management

- Availability Management

- Financial Management

Service Support is one of the two disciplines that comprise ITIL Service Management. It is focused on users of the ICT services and is primarily concerned with ensuring that they have access to the appropriate services to support the business functions. To a business, customers, and users are the entry point to the process model. They get involved in service support by:

- Asking for changes

- Needing communication, updates

- Having difficulties, queries

- Real process delivery

The service desk is the single contact point for customers' problems. If there is a direct solution, it tries to resolve the problem. If not, it creates an incident. Incidents initiate a chain of processes: Incident Management, Problem Management, Change Management, Release Management and Configuration Management. This chain of processes is tracked using the Configuration Management Database (CMDB), which records each process, and creates output documents for traceability (Quality Management).

A user should automate service management processes because of the following reasons:

- It improves the utility and warranty of services.

- It makes adjustment of capacity of automated resources easier.

- It provides faster response to variations in demand volumes.

- It enables automated resources to better handle capacity.

- It provides fewer restrictions on time of access or time zones.

- It provides a good basis for measuring and improving service processes.

- It eliminates human errors.

- It provides better scheduling, routing, and allocation of resources.

- It needs computers that are ahead of what humans can do.

- It allows for easier capture of service process knowledge, and puts that knowledge in a reusable format.

Availability Management is the ability of an IT component to perform at an agreed level over a period of time.

Automation can have a particularly significant impact on the performance of service assets, such as management, organization, people, process, knowledge, and information.

Define Functions and Processes

Functions are units of organizations specialized to execute specific types of work and also accountable for specific outcomes. They are independent with capabilities and resources required for their performance and outcomes. Capabilities contain work methods internal to the functions. Functions have their own body of knowledge. They provide structure and stability to organizations and provide a way of structuring organizations to apply the specialization standard. Functions define roles and the related authority and responsibility for a specific performance and outcomes. Functions have a tendency to optimize their work methods locally to focus on assigned outcomes.

Processes provide transformation towards a goal. They make use of feedback for self-reinforcing and self-counteractive action to function as closed-loop systems. It is important to consider the complete process or how one process fits into another. Process definitions describe actions, dependencies, and sequence.

The characteristics of processes are as follows:

- **Processes are measurable:** They are performance driven. Managers are required to measure cost, quality, and other variables whereas practitioners are concerned with duration and productivity.

- **Processes have specific results:** The reason processes exist is to deliver a specific result. The result has to be independently identifiable and countable.

- **Processes have customers:** Every process delivers its prime results to a customer or stakeholder.

- **Processes respond to specific events:** While a process can be iterative, it should be traceable to a definite trigger.

Process management is the ensemble of activities of planning and monitoring the performance of a process. Especially in the sense of business process, often confused with reengineering. Process Management is the application of knowledge, skills, tools, techniques and systems to define, visualize, measure, control, report, and improve processes with the goal to meet customer requirements profitably. Some people are of view that it is different from Program Management in the sense that Program Management is concerned with managing a group of inter-dependent projects. However, from another view point, Process Management includes Program Management.

ISO 9001 promotes the process approach to managing an organization.

"...promotes the adoption of a process approach when developing, implementing and improving the effectiveness of a quality management system, to enhance customer satisfaction by meeting customer requirements. Source: clause 0.2 of ISO 9001:2000"

Explain the process model and the characteristics of processes

Project schedule is one of the primary outputs of the Develop Schedule process. This process includes analyzing sequences, durations, resource requirements, and schedule constraints to create the project schedule.

The characteristics of processes are as follows:

- Processes are measurable

- Processes have specific results

- Processes have customers

- Processes respond to specific events

Pop Quiz

Q1: Which is the FIRST LEVEL of the V model?

Ans: Business/Customer Needs

Q2: In which process is Risk assessment NOT a major part?

Ans: Service Level Management

Key Terms

- **Good practices** are commodities, usually accepted, confirmed, and effective ways of doing things, which were earlier considered best practices of pioneering organizations.

- A **service** is a way of delivering value to customers by facilitating outcome that customers wish to get without the control of specific costs and risks.

- **Service Delivery** is primarily concerned with proactive services the ICT must deliver to provide adequate support to business users.

- **Functions** are units of organizations specialized to execute specific types of work and also accountable for specific outcomes.

- **Processes** provide transformation towards a goal.

- **Project schedule** is one of the primary outputs of the Develop Schedule process.

Test Your Knowledge

Q1. Which of the following is concerned with fairness and transparency?

    A.   Governance

    B.   Continual Service Improvement

    C.   Service Strategy

    D.   Service Support

Q2. Which of the following is a way of delivering value to customers by facilitating outcome that customers wish to get without the control of specific costs and risks?

    A.   Functions

    B.   Processes

    C.   Service

    D.   Service Desk

Q3. Availability Management allows organizations to sustain the IT service availability to support the business at a justifiable cost. Which of the following elements of Availability Management are used to perform at an agreed level over a period of time?

Each correct answer represents a part of the solution. Choose all that apply.

    A.   Reliability

    B.   Maintainability

    C.   Serviceability

    D.   Resilience

    E.   Security

    F.   Recoverability

    G.   Error control

Q4. Which of the following is NOT a part of the project schedule?

    A.   Start dates of activities

    B.   End dates of activities

    C.   Duration of activities

D.   Cost estimates

Q5.   Why should a user Automate Service Management Processes?

Each correct answer represents a complete solution. Choose all that apply.

A.   It improves utility and warranty of services.

B.   It makes adjustment of capacity of automated resources easier.

C.   It enables automated resources to better handle capacity.

D.   It provides a good basis for measuring and improving service processes.

E.   It gathers, analyzes, stores, and shares knowledge and information within an organization.

Answer Explanation

A1.   Answer option A is correct.

Governance relates to decisions that define expectations, grant power, or verify performance. It consists either of a separate process or of a specific part of management or leadership processes. Sometimes people set up a government to administer these processes and systems. It is always concerned with fairness and transparency. In case of a business or a non-profit organization, governance relates to consistent management, cohesive policies, processes, and decision-rights for a given area of responsibility.

Answer option B is incorrect. Continual Service Improvement (CSI) align and realign IT Services to changing business needs by identifying and implementing improvements to the IT services that support the Business Processes. The perspective of CSI on improvement is the business perspective of service quality, even though CSI aims to improve process effectiveness, efficiency and cost effectiveness of the IT processes through the whole lifecycle. To manage improvement, CSI should clearly define what should be controlled and measured.

Assistance is provided for linking improvement efforts and outcomes with Service Strategy, Design, and Transition. A closed-loop feedback system, based on the Plan-Do-Check-Act (PDCA) model specified in ISO/IEC 20000, is established and capable of receiving inputs for change from any planning perspective. CSI needs to be treated just like any other service practice. There needs to be upfront planning, training and awareness, ongoing scheduling, roles created, ownership assigned, and activities identified to be successful. CSI must be planned and scheduled as process with defined activities, inputs, outputs, roles and reporting.

Answer option C is incorrect. Service Strategy is the center and origin point of the ITIL Service Lifecycle. It provides guidance on how to design, develop, and implement service management not only as an organizational capability but also as a strategic asset. Service Strategy provides guidance on clarification and prioritization of service provider investments in services. More generally, Service Strategy focuses on helping IT organizations improve and develop over the long term. In both cases, Service Strategy relies largely upon a market-driven approach.

Service Strategy is useful in the framework of Service Design, Service Transition, Service Operation, and Continual Service Improvement. Service Strategy ensures that organizations are in a position to deal with the costs and risks associated with their Service Portfolios.

Service Strategy is set up for operational effectiveness as well as for distinctive performance. Decisions made with respect to Service Strategy have broad consequences including those with delayed effect.

Answer option D is incorrect. Service Support is one of the two disciplines that comprise ITIL Service Management. It is focused on users of the ICT services and is primarily concerned with ensuring that they have access to the appropriate services to support the business functions. To a business, customers, and users are the entry point to the process model. They get involved in service support by:

- Asking for changes

- Needing communication, updates

- Having difficulties, queries

- Real process delivery

The service desk is the single contact point for customers' problems. If there is a direct solution, it tries to resolve the problem. If not, it creates an incident. Incidents initiate a chain of processes: Incident Management, Problem Management, Change Management, Release Management and Configuration Management. This chain of processes is tracked using the Configuration Management Database (CMDB), which records each process, and creates output documents for traceability (Quality Management).

A2. Answer option C is correct.

A service is a way of delivering value to customers by facilitating outcome that customers wish to get without the control of specific costs and risks. It is a series of activities designed to enhance the level of customer satisfaction.

Outcomes are probable from the performance of tasks and are limited by the existence of certain constraints. A service facilitates outcomes by enhancing the performance and by reducing the clutch of constraints. The result is an increase in the possibility of desired outcomes. Its importance varies by product, industry and customer; defective or broken merchandise can be exchanged, often only with a receipt and within a specified time frame.

A service is normally an integral part of customers' value proposition. In their book Rules to Break and Laws to Follow, Don Peppers and Martha Rogers, write that *"customers have memories. They will remember you, whether you remember them or not."* Further, *"customer trust can be destroyed at once by a major service problem, or it can be undermined one day at a time, with a thousand small demonstrations of incompetence."*

Answer option A is incorrect. Functions are units of organizations specialized to execute specific types of work and also accountable for specific outcomes. They are independent with capabilities and resources required for their performance and outcomes. Capabilities contain work methods internal to the functions. Functions have their own body of knowledge. They provide structure and stability to organizations and provide a way of structuring organizations to apply the specialization standard. Functions define roles and the related authority and responsibility for a specific performance and outcomes. Functions have a tendency to optimize their work methods locally to focus on assigned outcomes.

Answer option B is incorrect. Processes provide transformation towards a goal. They make use of feedback for self-reinforcing and self-counteractive action to function as closed-loop systems. It is important to consider the complete process or how one process fits into another. Process definitions describe actions, dependencies, and sequence.

Answer option D is incorrect. Service Desk is a primary IT capability called for in IT Service Management (ITSM) as defined by the Information Technology Infrastructure Library (ITIL). It is intended to provide a Single Point of Contact ("SPOC") to meet the communication needs of both Users and IT, and to satisfy both Customer and IT Provider objectives. ("User" refers to the actual user of the service, while "Customer" refers to the entity that is paying for service)

A3.   Answer options A, B, C, D, E, and F are correct.

Availability Management allows organizations to sustain the IT service availability to support the business at a justifiable cost. The high-level activities are Realize Availability Requirements, Compile Availability Plan, Monitor Availability, and Monitor Maintenance Obligations. Availability is usually calculated based on a model involving the Availability Ratio and techniques such as Fault Tree Analysis.

Availability Management is the ability of an IT component to perform at an agreed level over a period of time.

Reliability: How reliable is the service? Ability of an IT component to perform at an agreed level at described conditions.

Maintainability: The ability of an IT component to remain in, or be restored to an operational state.

Serviceability: The ability of an external supplier to maintain the availability of component or function under a third party contract.

Resilience: A measure of freedom from operational failure and a method of keeping services reliable. One popular method of resilience is redundancy.

Security: A service may have associated data. Security refers to the confidentiality, integrity, and availability of that data. Availability gives us the clear overview of the end to end availability of the system.

Recoverability: The time it should take to restore a component back to its operational state after a failure.

Answer option G is incorrect. The Error Control Process is an iterative process to diagnose known errors until they are eliminated by the successful implementation of a change under the control of the Change Management process.

A4.   Answer option D is correct.

Project schedule is one of the primary outputs of the Develop Schedule process. This process includes analyzing sequences, durations, resource requirements, and schedule constraints to create the project schedule.

Answer options A, B, and C are incorrect. The project schedule details these information as well as the resource assignments.

A5.   Answer options A, B, C, and D are correct.

A user should automate service management processes because of the following reasons:

- It improves the utility and warranty of services.

- It makes adjustment of capacity of automated resources easier.

    o   It provides faster response to variations in demand volumes.

- It enables automated resources to better handle capacity.

    o   It provides fewer restrictions on time of access or time zones.

- It provides a good basis for measuring and improving service processes.

    o   It eliminates human errors.

- It provides better scheduling, routing, and allocation of resources.

  o It needs computers that are ahead of what humans can do.

- It allows for easier capture of service process knowledge, and puts that knowledge in a reusable format.

Note: *Automation can have a particularly significant impact on the performance of service assets, such as management, organization, people, process, knowledge, and information.*

Answer option E is incorrect. Knowledge Management is used to gather, analyze, store, and share knowledge and information within an organization. The primary purpose of Knowledge Management is to improve efficiency by reducing the need to rediscover knowledge. It is part of Service Transition and the owner of Knowledge Management is the Knowledge Manager. ITIL V3, however, defines Knowledge Management as the one central process responsible for providing knowledge to all other IT Service Management processes.

Note: *Knowledge Management is dealt with in many other Service Management processes. The Knowledge Management process itself ensures that all information used within Service Management, stored in the Service Knowledge Management System, is consistent and readily available.*

Chapter 2 - The Service Lifecycle

Overview

The purpose of this unit is to help the candidate to understand the value of the Service Lifecycle, how the processes integrate with each other, throughout the Lifecycle and explain the objectives and business value for each phase in the Lifecycle Specifically, candidates must be able to:

- Describe the structure, scope, components and interfaces of the Service

- Lifecycle

- Account for the main goals and objectives of Service Strategy

- Account for the main goals and objectives of Service Design

- Briefly explain what value Service Design provides to the business

- Account for the main goals and objectives of Service Transition

- Briefly explain what value Service Transition provides to the business

- Account for the main goals and objectives of Service Operations

- Briefly explain what value Service Operation provides to the business

- Account for the main goals and objectives of Continual Service

- Improvement

It is recommended that this training is covered within other units.

The recommended study period for this unit is minimum 1.0 hours.

Key Points

Describe the structure, scope, components and interfaces of the Service Lifecycle

As the center and origin point of the ITIL Service Lifecycle, the ITIL Service Strategy volume provides guidance on clarification and prioritization of service-provider investments in services. More generally, Service Strategy focuses on helping IT organizations improve and develop over the long term. In both cases, Service Strategy relies largely upon a market-driven approach. Key topics covered include service value definition, **business-case** development, service assets, market analysis, and service provider types. Following is the list of covered processes:

- Service Portfolio Management

- Demand Management

- IT Financial Management

- Supplier Management

The ITIL Service Design volume provides good-practice guidance on the design of IT services, processes, and other aspects of the service management effort. Significantly, design within ITIL is understood to encompass all elements relevant to technology service delivery, rather than focusing solely on design of the technology itself. As such, Service Design addresses how a planned service solution interacts with the larger business and technical environments, service management systems required to support the service, processes which interact with the service, technology, and architecture required to support the service, and the supply chain required to support the planned service. Within ITIL v2, design work for an IT service is aggregated into a single Service Design Package (SDP). Service Design Packages, along with other information about services, are managed within the service catalogs. Folloiwng is the list of covered processes:

- Service Catalogue Management

- Service Level Management

- Risk Management

- Capacity Management

- Availability Management

- IT Service Continuity Management

- Information Security Management

- Compliance Management

- IT Architecture Management

- Supplier Management

Service transition, as described by the ITIL Service Transition volume, relates to the delivery of services required by a business into live/operational use, and often encompasses the "project" side of IT rather than "BAU" (Business as usual). This area also covers topics such as managing changes to the "BAU" environment. Following is the list of processes:

- Service Asset and Configuration Management

- Service Validation and Testing

- Evaluation

- Release Management

- Change Management

- Knowledge Management

Best practice for achieving the delivery of agreed levels of services both to end-users and the customers. Service operation, as described in the ITIL Service Operation volume, is the part of the lifecycle where the services and value is actually directly delivered. Also the monitoring of problems and balance between service reliability and cost etc are considered. The functions include technical management, application management, operations management and Service Desk as well as, responsibilities for staff engaging in Service Operation. Following is the List of processes:

- Event Management

- Incident Management

- Problem Management

- Request Fulfillment

- Access Management

Aligning and realigning IT services to changing business needs (because standstill implies decline).

Continual Service Improvement, defined in the ITIL Continual Service Improvement volume, aims to align and realign IT Services to changing business needs by identifying and implementing improvements to the IT services that support the Business Processes. The perspective of CSI on improvement is the business perspective of service quality, even though CSI aims to improve process effectiveness, efficiency and cost effectiveness of the IT processes through the whole lifecycle. To manage improvement, CSI should clearly define what should be controlled and measured.

CSI needs to be treated just like any other service practice. There needs to be upfront planning, training and awareness, ongoing scheduling, roles created, ownership assigned, and activities identified to be successful. CSI must be planned and scheduled as process with defined activities, inputs, outputs, roles and reporting. Following is the List of processes:

- Service Level Management

- Service Measurement and Reporting

- Continual Service Improvement

Account for the main goals and objectives of Service Strategy

Successful Service providers must have the capability to think, plan, act and enhance their activities strategically. ITIL V3 guidance, specifically in the V3 Service Strategy Core text, provides guidance on the achievement of strategic goals or objectives that require the use of strategic assets.

The ultimate goal is to transform IT service management into a strategic asset that adds real value to the Service Provider. ITIL Service Strategy helps Service Providers to answer the following:

- What IT Services should we provide?

- Whom should we provide these services to?

- How do we genuinely differentiate from competitors?

- How do we create lasting business value for our customers?

- How can we make a case for ROI and other investments?

- How should we best define and measure service quality?

- How do we choose between different paths for improving service quality?

- How do we efficiently (re)allocate resources across a portfolio of services?

- How do we resolve conflicting demands for shared resources?

ITIL Service Strategy contains guidance and knowledge from many other disciplines such as operations, engineering, marketing,finance, program management, organizational development, supplier management and process dynamics.

A broad, but direct approach from experienced and qualified professionals is necessary to obtain and take action on the above questions. The answers must form the starting point for a 'body of knowledge' to be created and acted on.

The objectives of Service Strategy Process are as follows:

- To provide guidance on how to design, develop, and implement Service Management.

- To ensure that IT organizations are in a position to achieve operational effectiveness and to offer distinctive services to their customers.

- To make the IT organizations think and act in a strategic manner.

Note: *Service Strategy Process is part of IT Service Management.*

Strategy as a perspective is used to define the governing set of beliefs, values, and wisdom of purpose shared by the entire organization. It sets the overall direction in which the service provider progresses to execute their purpose and builds their performance anatomy. Some real-world examples are as follows:

- Focus on users and all else will follow.

- It is all about growth, innovation, and the dependency of technology.

- Consumer connectivity first, any time, anywhere.

- Our purpose is to improve the quality of life of the communities we serve.

- We will be the best service provider in our industry.

Strategy as a position is used to express individuality in the minds of customers. It often means, competing in the similar space as others but with a different value proposition that is eye-catching to the customer. No matter whether it is about offering a wide range of services to a specific type of customer, or being the lowest-cost alternative, it is a strategic position. There are three broad types of positions, which are as follows:

- Variety-based positions

- Needs-based positions

- Access-based positions

Service Strategy considers the business outcomes and value creation as its principles.

The Four Ps of strategy are the entry points to service strategy in the ITIL lifecycle. The entry points to service strategy are referred to as "the Four Ps".

Pop Quiz

Q1: Which are the TWO main components of ITIL Service Management?

Ans: Service Support and Service Delivery

Q2: Which is the CORE of the Service Lifecycle?

Ans: Service Strategy

Account for the main goals and objectives of Service Design

The ITIL Service Design volume provides good-practice guidance on the design of IT services, processes, and other aspects of the service management effort. Significantly, design within ITIL is understood to encompass all elements relevant to technology service delivery, instead of focusing solely on design of the technology itself. As such, Service Design addresses how a planned service solution interacts with the larger business and technical environments, service management systems required to support the service, processes which interact with the service, technology, and architecture required to support the service, and the supply chain required to support the planned service. Within ITIL, design work for an IT service is aggregated into a single Service Design Package (SDP). Service Design Packages (SDP), along with other information about services, is managed within the Service Catalog.

Briefly explain what value Service Design provides to the business

ITIL Service Design is used to design and develop IT services. Its scope includes the design of new services, as well as changes and improvements to existing ones.

- Business Transaction Management (BTM) is an approach to managing IT from a business transaction perspective. BTM aims to guarantee service quality for users conducting business transactions while simultaneously optimizing the IT applications and infrastructure across which those transactions execute. At the heart of BTM lies the ability to capture and to track all transactions, across all IT tiers, automatically and continuously.

- BTM is ideally suited to managing performance and availability problems because it clearly identifies exactly where transactions are held up. But for IT, problem management is just the tip of the iceberg. BTM also enables proactive problem prevention as well as the generation of business service intelligence for optimization of resource provisioning and virtualization.

Account for the main goals and objectives of Service Transition

ITIL Service Transition is used to build and deploy IT services. It also makes sure that changes to services and Service Management processes are carried out in a coordinated way.

Service Transition contains the detailed description of Service Asset and Configuration Management, Transition Planning and Support, Release and deployment Management, Change Management, Knowledge Management, as well as the key roles of staff engaging in Service Transition.

Briefly explain what value Service Transition provides to the business

Service Transition is a pivotal aspect of ITIL Version 3, as it enables the execution of the vision mandated in ITIL Service Design to turn into a reality.

The task would be impossible to achieve without specific policies and principles. So, in order for ITIL service transition to work efficiently and effectively, you should be fully aware of the following fourteen CSI policies:

Implementing a formal policy:

To prevent any miscommunication and disappointing results, it is imperative that a formal policy for ITIL service transition is discussed and agreed on by all parties involved.

Implementing all changes to services through service transition:

Changes concerning the service catalogue or service portfolio are implemented by Change Management, which are managed directly by the ITIL service transition process.

Adopt a similar framework and standards:

To avoid any risk of confusion – or even complications in the service transition process, it is best to make use of both a common framework and ITSM standards that can easily be used by all operations and service owners.

Maximising the usage of established processes and systems:

Service transition aims to find processes that can be useful for more than one service process or purpose. As these processes are made with the business operations in mind, ongoing operational efficiency is usually a key target - as changes are made across the service transition process.

Aligning ITIL service transition plans with the business needs:

In order to satisfy the customer's service demands and maximize the value of any changes, it should be noted that the service transition's plans are synchronized with the business organization's requirements.

Establishing and maintaining relationships with stakeholders:

Try to connect and establish a working relationship with customers, users, suppliers and customer representatives to maintain a clear view of the changes and how they will impact and affect the company overall.

Establishing effective controls and disciplines:

To ensure a seamless transition of service changes and deployments, it is best to find the most effective controls and disciplines for the whole service lifecycle.

Providing systems for knowledge transfer and decision support:

The ITIL service transition process aims to develop systems and processes that would make it easier to control future processes and minimize any service errors. Through detailed documentation and quality data collection, service operations will run better and more efficiently.

Plan release and deployment packages:

Service transition offers - in advance – many specific techniques to handle a release, or a deployment of a service change in which efforts are put into finding the most cost effective and efficient way to progress.

Anticipating and managing course corrections:

Anticipate the inevitable occurrence of changes and certain alterations across the service lifecycle, and also have a team trained that can manage and make instant course corrections that limits any deviation from the original service design framework.

Proactively manage resources across service transition:

Service transition aims to provide the shared services of skilled and specialist resources that would help fix problems easier to avoid longer disruptions in the service lifecycle.

Ensuring early involvement in the service lifecycle:

Start participating in the earliest stages of service design, so as to provide insight and detect possible flaws for the service. This also helps to ensure that the various service processes will encounter fewer complications once delivered to service operations.

Assure the quality of the new or changed service:

ITIL's service transition process aims to make sure that the quality and efficiency of the prescribed changes are in agreement with the service design requirements.

Proactively improve quality during service transition:

To be aware of the needs of the service operation and pro-actively check for flaws in any of the changed services - as progress occurs through service transition.

By doing this, it is more cost efficient for the business to fix issues and problems as early as possible – rather than within Service Operations which impacts real users, customers and presents a big risk to any SLA.

Account for the main goals and objectives of Service Operations

ITIL Service Operation is used to make sure that IT services are delivered effectively and efficiently. This includes fulfilling user requests, resolving service failures, fixing problems, as well as carrying out routine operational tasks.

Event management, Incident management, Problem management, Request fulfillment, Access Management, and Service desk are part of Service Operation stage of the Service Lifecycle.

The purpose of Service Operation is to coordinate and carry out the activities and processes required to deliver and manage services at agreed levels to business users and customers. Service Operation is also responsible for the ongoing management of the technology that is used to deliver and support services.

Well-designed and well-implemented processes will be of little value if the day-to-day operation of those processes is not properly conducted, controlled and managed. Nor will service improvements be possible if day-to-day activities to monitor performance, assess metrics and gather data are not systematically conducted during Service Operation.

Service Operation includes the execution of all ongoing activities required to deliver and support services. The scope of Service Operation includes:

- **The services themselves:** Any activity that forms part of a service is included in Service Operation, whether it is performed by the Service Provider, an external supplier or the user or customer of that service

Service Management processes. The ongoing management and execution of many Service Management processes are performed in Service Operation, even though a number of ITIL processes (such as Change and Capacity Management) originate at the Service Design or Service Transition stage of the Service Lifecycle, they are in use continually in Service Operation. Some processes are not included specifically in Service Operation, such as Strategy Definition, the actual design process itself. These processes focus more on longer-term planning and improvement activities, which are outside the direct scope of Service Operation; however, Service Operation provides input and influences these regularly as part of the lifecycle of Service Management.

- **Technology:** All services require some form of technology to deliver them. Managing this technology is not a separate issue, but an integral part of the management of the services themselves. Therefore a large part of this publication is concerned with the management of the infrastructure used to deliver services.

- **People:** Regardless of what services, processes and technology are managed, they are all about people. It is people who drive the demand for the organization's services and products and it is people who decide how this will be done. Ultimately, it is people who manage the technology, processes and services. Failure to recognize this will result (and has resulted) in the failure of Service Management projects.

Each stage in the ITIL Service Lifecycle provides value to business. For example, service value is modelled in Service Strategy; the cost of the service is designed, predicted and validated in Service Design and Service Transition; and measures for optimization are identified in Continual Service Improvement. The operation of service is where these plans, designs and optimizations are executed and measured. From a customer viewpoint, Service Operation is where actual value is seen.

Pop Quiz

Q1: Which is the core structure of ITIL?

Ans: A Service Lifecycle

Q2: Which stage of the Service Lifecycle is MOST concerned with defining policies and objectives?

Ans: Service Strategy

Briefly explain what value Service Operation provides to the business

The primary goals of Service Operation are as follows:

- Enable responsive, stable and repeatable IT Service Delivery

- Provide robust end-to-end working practices

- Deliver improved Processes such as Incident and Problem Management

- Deliver new Processes such as: Event Management and Service Request Fulfilment

- Promote more adaptive, responsive and agile Service Operation functions

- Help shape and define Service Strategy, Service Design, Service Transition and Continual

- Service Improvement (the core of the new ITIL V3 Service Lifecycle Model)

Service Operation purpose is as follows:

- To coordinate and deliver key activities and processes required to provide and manage services at agreed levels to the business, users and customers

- To manage the technology and toolsets that are used to deliver and support services

- To manage, measure, control and feedback improvements in the day to day operations

- To monitor performance, assess metrics and gather data to input into the Continual Service Improvement Process Area

What is the value of Service Operation to a business?

The required value of what any given service should provide to the business is actually modelled in Service Strategy and that model manifests itself in a more structured way within Service Design.

The structure and cost of the Service is then designed and validated in Service Design and Service Transition. The actual measures for required levels of optimization are identified in Continual Service

Improvement.

What are the principles of Service Operation?

The first principle of Service Operation is concerned with finding the right balance between:

- The Internal IT view versus the external business view

- Ongoing stability versus responsiveness

- Quality Improvements versus Cost to deliver the Service and Reactive working versus proactive working

- The themes of 'Reactivity', 'proactivity' and 'control' are all important.

What is the Scope of Service Operation?

- Processes and working practices

- The physical organization of Service Operation

- Execution of all ongoing activities required to deliver and support service

- Service Management processes Technology and supporting toolsets

- Management of the infrastructure used to deliver services

- The people who manage the technology, processes and services

Account for the main goals and objectives of Continual Service Improvement

ITIL Continual Service Improvement (CSI) is used to use methods from quality management in order to learn from past successes and failures. The CSI process implements a closed-loop feedback system as specified in ISO 20000 as a means to continually improve the effectiveness and efficiency of IT services and processes.

The basic steps involved in Continuity Management are as follows:

- Prioritizing the businesses to be recovered by conducting a Business Impact Analysis (BIA)

- Performing a Risk Assessment (aka Risk Analysis) for each of the IT Services to identify the assets, threats, vulnerabilities, and countermeasures for each service

- Evaluating the options for recovery

- Producing the Contingency Plan

- Testing, reviewing, and revising the plan on a regular basis

---

Pop Quiz

Q1: Which is mainly concerned with the design of changed services?

Ans:. Service Design

Q2: How frequently should CAB meetings be held?

Ans: As required

The Demand Management process is the first and foremost concerned with understanding Patterns of Business Activity (PBA). Demand Management is about understanding where the demand is coming from.

Continual Service Improvement is looking for the ways to improve process efficiency and cost effectiveness.

The Service Improvement Plan (SIP) refers to the steps that must be taken if there is a major gap in the projected delivery quality of a service and the actual delivery.

The Four Ps of strategy are the entry points to service strategy in the ITIL lifecycle. The entry points to service strategy are referred to as "the Four Ps". They identify the different forms a service strategy may take, which are as follows:

Perspective: It is used to describe a vision and direction. It is a way of interacting with customers or the way in which services are provided.

Position: It is used to describe the decision to adopt a well-defined attitude, such as the following.

- Should the provider compete on the basis of value or low cost?

- Should the services be specialized or broad sets?

- Should the value be biased towards utility or warranty?

An internal service provider (Type I) restricted to serving one business unit may adopt a position based on "product know-how" or "customer responsiveness".

Plan: It is used to describe the way of transitioning from 'as is' to 'to be'. A plan might detail, "How do we offer high-value or low-cost services?" Or in the case of our law firm CIO, "How do we achieve and offer our specialized services?"

Pattern: It is used to describe a series of steady decisions and actions over time. A service provider who constantly offers particular services with deep expertise is adopting a "high-value" or "high-end" service strategy. A service provider who constantly offers reliable services is adopting a "high-warranty" strategy.

Pop Quiz

Q1: Which concept is part of IT Service Continuity Management?

Ans: Vulnerability

Key Terms

- **Strategy as a perspective** is used to define the governing set of beliefs, values, and wisdom of purpose shared by the entire organization.

- **Strategy as a position** is used to express individuality in the minds of customers.

- **Service Strategy** considers the business outcomes and value creation as its principles.

- The **Four Ps** of strategy are the entry points to service strategy in the ITIL lifecycle.

- The **ITIL Service Design** volume provides good-practice guidance on the design of IT services, processes, and other aspects of the service management effort.

- **ITIL Service Design** is used to design and develop IT services.

- **Business Transaction Management** (BTM) is an approach to managing IT from a business transaction perspective.

- **ITIL Service Transition** is used to build and deploy IT services.

- **ITIL Service Operation** is used to make sure that IT services are delivered effectively and efficiently.

- ITIL **Continual Service Improvement** (CSI) is used to use methods from quality management in order to learn from past successes and failures.

Test Your Knowledge

Q1. Kelly is the project sponsor of Robert's project. She has requested several changes for the project scope and these changes have, of course, been approved. Robert needs to incorporate the project scope changes into the activity list. Where else should Robert reflect these project changes?

    A.   Cost baseline

    B.   Quality control mechanism

    C.   Project final report

    D.   Scope baseline

Q2. The entry points to Service Strategy are referred to as "the Four Ps". They identify the different forms a service strategy may take. Which of the following is a correct list of the 'Four Ps'?

    A.   People, Potential, Products, and Performance

    B.   People, Products, Partners, and Profit

    C.   Perspective, Position, Plan, and Pattern

    D.   Potential, Preparation, Performance, and Profit

Q3. Which of the following contains information on the costs for providing services and provides insight into the profitability of services and customers?

    A.   Cost Data for Service Provisioning

    B.   Budget Allocation

    C.   Indirect Cost Allocation Table

    D.   Financial Analysis

Q4. Which of the following parts of the Service Lifecycle is looking for the ways to improve process efficiency and cost effectiveness?

    A.   Continual Service Improvement

    B.   Service Transition

    C.   Service Design

    D.   Service Operation

Q5. Which of the following sub-processes of Service Portfolio Management is used to define the overall goals that the service provider should follow in its development based on the outcome of Strategic Service Assessment?

A.   Strategic Planning

B.   Service Strategy Definition

C.   Service Portfolio Update

D.   Strategic Service Assessment

Answer Explanation

A1.   Answer option D is correct.

All scope changes should also be updated in the project scope baseline. The scope baseline is the project scope statement, work breakdown structure (WBS), and the WBS dictionary.

Answer option A is incorrect. If the changes affect cost, then the cost baseline would also be updated. The question did not specify that there was a change in the project cost.

Answer option B is incorrect. Quality control does not change. It always reflects the demands of the project scope.

Answer option C is incorrect. The project final report evaluates the success and failures of the project scope.

A2.   Answer option C is correct.

The Four Ps of strategy are the entry points to service strategy in the ITIL lifecycle. The entry points to service strategy are referred to as "the Four Ps". They identify the different forms a service strategy may take, which are as follows:

Perspective: It is used to describe a vision and direction. It is a way of interacting with customers or the way in which services are provided.

Position: It is used to describe the decision to adopt a well-defined attitude, such as the following. *Should the provider compete on the basis of value or low cost? Should the services be specialized or broad sets? Should the value be biased towards utility or warranty?*

An internal service provider (Type I) restricted to serving one business unit may adopt a position based on "product know-how" or "customer responsiveness".

Plan: It is used to describe the way of transitioning from 'as is' to 'to be'. A plan might detail, "How do we offer high-value or low-cost services?" Or in the case of our law firm CIO, "How do we achieve and offer our specialized services?"

Pattern: It is used to describe a series of steady decisions and actions over time. A service provider who constantly offers particular services with deep expertise is adopting a "high-value" or "high-end" service strategy. A service provider who constantly offers reliable services is adopting a "high-warranty" strategy.

Answer options A, B, and D are incorrect. These are the incorrect lists.

A3. Answer option D is correct.

Financial Analysis is a significant input to the Portfolio Management process. It contains information on the costs for providing services and provides insight into the profitability of services and customers.

Answer option A is incorrect. Cost Data for Service Provisioning provides the cost for providing a service, calculated by Financial Management as a basis for calculating the price a customer is anticipated to pay for a service.

Answer option B is incorrect. A budget is allocated by the Financial Manager to implement a Change. Budget Allocations are issued in response to the Budget Requests originating from any Service Management process in combination with Requests for Change.

Answer option C is incorrect. Indirect Cost Allocation Table is used to allocate indirect costs that are shared among various services. It also defines the rules how those costs are spread among the services.

Answer option A is incorrect. The Abort method is used to raise a ThreadAbortException in the thread on which it is invoked, to begin the process of terminating the thread. Whenever you call this method, it normally terminates the thread.

Answer option C is incorrect. The Suspend method either suspends the thread, or if the thread is already suspended, it has no effect. This method is obsolete now.

Answer option D is incorrect. The Sleep method is used to block the current thread for the specified number of milliseconds.

A4. Answer option A is correct.

Continual Service Improvement (CSI) align and realign IT Services to changing business needs by identifying and implementing improvements to the IT services that support the Business Processes. The perspective of CSI on improvement is the business perspective of service quality, even though CSI aims to improve process effectiveness, efficiency and cost effectiveness of the IT processes through the whole lifecycle. To manage improvement, CSI should clearly define what should be controlled and measured.

Assistance is provided for linking improvement efforts and outcomes with Service Strategy, Design, and Transition. A closed-loop feedback system, based on the Plan-Do-Check-Act (PDCA) model specified in ISO/IEC 20000, is established and is capable of receiving inputs for change from any planning perspective. CSI needs to be treated just like any other service practice. There needs to be upfront planning, training and awareness, ongoing scheduling, roles created, ownership assigned, and activities identified to be successful. CSI must be planned and scheduled as process with defined activities, inputs, outputs, roles and reporting.

Answer option B is incorrect. Service Transition relates to the delivery of services required by the business into live/operational use, and often encompasses the "project" side of IT rather than Business As Usual (BAU). It provides guidance for the development and improvement of capabilities for transitioning new and changed services into operations. Service Transition provides assistance on how the necessities of Service strategy determined in Service design, thus the necessities are effectively understood in Service operation while controlling the risks of failure and disruption.

Service Transition provides assistance on managing the complication related to changes in services and service management processes, preventing undesired consequences while allowing for improvement. Assistance is provided on transferring the control of services between customers and service providers.

Answer option C is incorrect. Service Design provides good practice guidance on the design of IT services, processes, and other aspects of the service management effort. It covers design principles and methods for converting strategic objectives into portfolios of services and service assets. The scope of Service Design is not limited to new services. Significantly, design within ITIL is understood to encompass all elements relevant to technology service delivery, rather than focusing solely on design of the technology itself.

As such, Service Design addresses how a planned service solution interacts with the larger business and technical environments. Service management systems require supporting the service and processes, which interacts with the service, technology, and architecture required to support the service, and the supply chain required to support the planned service. Within ITIL, design work for an IT service is aggregated into a single Service Design Package (SDP). Service Design Packages (SDP), along with other information about services, is managed within the Service Catalog.

Answer option D is incorrect. Service Operation is the best practice for achieving the delivery of agreed levels of services both to end-users and the customers (where "customers" refer to those individuals who pay for the service and negotiate the SLAs). Service Operation is the part of the lifecycle where the services and values are actually directly delivered. Also, the monitoring of problems and balance between service reliability and cost, etc. are considered.

Strategic objectives are eventually recognized through Service Operation, thus making it a critical capability. Assistance is provided on ways to sustain steadiness in service operations, allowing for changes in design, scale, scope, and service levels. Organizations are provided with detailed process course of action, methods, and tools for use in two major control perspectives, which are as follows:

1. Reactive

2. Proactive

A5.   Answer option B is correct.

The Service Strategy Definition sub-process of Service Portfolio Management is used to define the overall goals that the service provider should follow in its development, and to recognize what services will be offered to what customers, or customer segments, based on the outcome of Strategic Service Assessment.

Answer option A is incorrect. The Strategic Planning sub-process of Service Portfolio Management is used to define, initiate, and control the programs and projects needed to carry out Service Strategy.

Answer option C is incorrect. The Service Portfolio Update sub-process of Service Portfolio Management is used to regulate the contents of the Service Portfolio, reflecting changes in the Service Strategy, or changes to the services' status.

Answer option D is incorrect. The Strategic Service Assessment sub-process of Service Portfolio Management is used to assess the present situation of the service provider within its current market spaces. This comprises an assessment of current service offerings, customer requirements, and competing offers from other service providers.

Chapter 3 - Generic concepts and definitions

Overview

The purpose of this unit is to help the candidate to define some of the key terminology and explain the key concepts of Service Management. Specifically, candidates must be able to define and explain the following key concepts:

- Utility and Warranty

- Resources, Capabilities and Assets

- Service Portfolio

- Service Catalogue (Business Service Catalogue and Technical Service Catalogue)

- The role of IT Governance across the Service Lifecycle

- Business Case

- Risk

- Service Provider (the candidate is not expected to know the detail of each of the three types of Service Providers)

- Supplier

- Service Level Agreement (SLA)

- Operational Level Agreement (OLA)

- Contract

- Service Design Package

- Availability

- Service Knowledge Management System (SKMS)

- Configuration Item (CI)

- Configuration Management System

- Definitive Media Library (DML)

- Service Change

- Change types (Normal, Standard, and Emergency)

- Release Unit

- Concept of Seven R's of Change Management

- Event

- Alert (SO Glossary)

- Incident

- Impact, Urgency, and Priority

- Service Request

- Problem

- Workaround

- Known Error

- Known Error Data Base (KEDB)

- The role of communication in Service Operation

- Service Assets

- Release policy

  It is recommended that this unit is covered as part of the training in the other units.

  The recommended study period for this unit is minimum 1.0 hours.

Key Points

Utility and Warranty

The two elements of a service's business value from customers' perspective are Utility and Warranty.

Utility

- It provides the functionality offered by a product or service as the customers' view it.

- It specifies what the customers get.

- It provides fitness for purpose.

- It increases performance average.

Warranty

- It promises that the product or service will meet the approved requirements.

- It specifies how it is delivered.

- It provides fitness for use:

- Three characteristics of warranty are as follows:

- It is provided in terms of the availability or capacity of services.

- It ensures that customers' assets continue to get utility.

- It looks after the security for value creating potential of the customers' assets.

- It reduces performance variations.

Resources, Capabilities and Assets

Capabilities are types of assets, and organizations utilize them to construct value in the form of goods and services. They specify an organization's ability to control, coordinate, and deploy resources to produce value. They are usually experience-driven, knowledge-intensive, information-based, and firmly embedded within an organization's people, systems, processes, and technologies.

Resources are types of assets and they are direct inputs for production. Organizations use them to create value in the form of goods and services. Management, organization, people, and knowledge are used to transform resources. It is comparatively easy to obtain resources compared to capabilities.

Service management capabilities are influenced by the following challenges:

- Intangible nature of the output and intermediary products of service processes.

- Demand is tightly coupled with customer's assets.

- High-level of contact for producers and consumers of services.

- Perishable nature of service output and service capacity.

Pop Quiz

Q1: Which process contains the Performance and Resource Managements?

Ans: Capacity Management

Q2: What is the main purpose of the Service Portfolio in terms of describing services?

Ans: Business Value

Service Portfolio

The service pipeline is one of the three phases of Service Portfolio. It is a future based concept that defines the strategic future direction for the service provider. It is the concept that defines the variety of services that are currently under development in Service Portfolio. The pipeline is an excellent indicator on the overall strength of the service provider, as it shows the services that are under development for customers or markets.

A service catalog is a list of services that an organization provides, often to its employees or customers. Each service within the catalog typically includes the following:

- A description of the service

- Timeframes or Service Level Agreement (SLA) for fulfilling the service

- Who is entitled to request/view the service

- Costs (if any)

- How to fulfill the service

Retired services are not available for use by present customers. However, if the customers give a strong business case, the service providers can restore the phased out service. Although these services are fully terminated, information and data added while services were under operation are stored in the knowledge base of the company. Retiring the services is a normal event in a service lifecycle.

Service Portfolio represents a complete list of the services managed by a service provider; some of these services are visible to the customers, while others are not. It contains present contractual commitments, new service development, and ongoing service improvement plans initiated by Continual Service Improvement. It also includes third-party services, which are an integral part of service offerings to customers. Service Portfolio is divided into three phases, which are as follows:

- Service Pipeline

- Service Catalogue

- Retired Services

Service Catalogue

Business Service Catalogue includes details of all of the IT services delivered to customers. It also includes the IT services together with relationships to the business units and the business processes that rely on the IT services. Business Service Catalogue is the customers' perspective of the Service Catalogue.

Technical Service Catalogue includes details of all the IT services delivered to customers. It also includes the IT services together with relationship to the supporting services, shared services, components, and Configuration Items (CIs). Technical Service Catalogue is the technical perspective of the Service Catalogue and is not available to customers.

Pop Quiz

Q1: Which key feature is used to record all IT services?

Ans: Service Catalogue

Q2: What is contained in a Customer Service Catalogue?

Ans: Details of all operational services

The role of IT Governance across the Service Lifecycle

Information system governance, also known as IT Governance, is used by the management to regulate the Information Systems, to accomplish its objectives; so, IT governance forms an integral part of corporate governance. To monitor and develop an information system, ITIL and COBIT methods are used.

There are narrower and broader definitions of IT governance. Weill and Ross focus on "*Specifying the decision rights and accountability framework to encourage desirable behaviour in the use of IT.*"

In contrast, the IT Governance Institute expands the definition to include foundational mechanisms: "*... the leadership and organisational structures and processes that ensure that the organisation's IT sustains and extends the organisation's strategies and objectives.*"

While AS8015, the Australian Standard for Corporate Governance of ICT, defines Corporate Governance of ICT as "*The system by which the current and future use of ICT is directed and controlled. It involves evaluating and directing the plans for the use of ICT to support the organisation and monitoring this use to achieve plans. It includes the strategy and policies for using ICT within an organisation.*"

The elements required to implement a good IT governance framework are as follows:

- Structure: It is concerned with who is making the decisions, what structural organizations will be created, who will take part in these organizations, and what responsibilities will they assume.

- Process: It is concerned with how the IT investment decisions are made, what are the decision making processes for planning investments, evaluating investments, approving investments, and prioritizing investments.

- Communication: It is concerned with how will the results of these processes and decisions be calculated, observed, and communicated, what methods will be used to communicate IT investment decisions to the executive management, board of directors, business management, IT management, employees, and shareholders.

The responsibilities performed by the core team of IT governance are as follows:

- Define plan and deliverables.

- Undertake core tasks.

- Report on process.

- Organize team and roles (architects, project managers, process owners).

Business Case

The Business Case is a justification for an important item of expenditure. It includes information about cost, benefits, options, issues, risks, and potential problems. It is a decision support and planning tool that projects the expected outcome of a business action. It uses qualitative terms. A typically business case structure is as follows:

- Introduction: It provides business objectives address.

- Methods and assumptions: It specifies the boundaries of the business case.

- Business impacts: It provides financial and non-financial business case results.

- Risks and contingencies

- Recommendations: It specifies specific actions.

The Business Case is a justification for an important item of expenditure. It includes information about cost, benefits, options, issues, risks, and potential problems.

Risk

Risk concerns the deviation of one or more results of one or more future events from their expected value. Technically, the value of those results may be positive or negative. However, general usage tends to focus only on potential harm that may arise from a future event, which may accrue either from incurring a cost ("downside risk") or by failing to attain some benefit ("upside risk").

There are different definitions of risk for each of several applications. The widely inconsistent and ambiguous use of the word is one of several current criticisms of the methods to manage risk.

In one definition, "risks" are simply future issues that can be avoided or mitigated, rather than present problems that must be immediately addressed.

In risk management, the term "hazard" is used to mean an event that could cause harm and the term "risk" is used to mean simply the probability of something happening.

OHSAS (Occupational Health & Safety Advisory Services) defines risk as the product of the probability of a hazard resulting in an adverse event, times the severity of the event.

In statistics, risk is often mapped to the probability of some event seen as undesirable. Usually, the probability of that event and some assessment of its expected harm must be combined into a believable scenario (an outcome), which combines the set of risk, regret, and reward probabilities into an expected value for that outcome.

Risk versus uncertainty

Risk: Combination of the likelihood of an occurrence of a hazardous event or exposure(s) and the severity of injury or ill health that can be caused by the event or exposure(s).

In his seminal work Risk, Uncertainty, and Profit, Frank Knight (1921) established the distinction between risk and uncertainty.

"... Uncertainty must be taken in a sense radically distinct from the familiar notion of Risk, from which it has never been properly separated. The term "risk," as loosely used in everyday speech and in economic discussion, really covers two things which, functionally at least, in their causal relations to the phenomena of economic organization, are categorically different. ... The essential fact is that "risk" means in some cases a quantity susceptible of measurement, while at other times it is something distinctly not of this character; and there are far-reaching and crucial differences in the bearings of the phenomenon depending on which of the two is really present and operating. ... It will appear that a measurable uncertainty, or "risk" proper, as we shall use the term, is so far different from an unmeasurable one that it is not in effect an uncertainty at all. We ... accordingly restrict the term "uncertainty" to cases of the non-quantitive type."

Thus, Knightian uncertainty is immeasurable, not possible to calculate, while in the Knightian sense risk is measureable.

Another distinction between risk and uncertainty is proposed in How to Measure Anything: Finding the Value of Intangibles in Business and The Failure of Risk Management: Why It's Broken and How to Fix It by Doug Hubbard:

Uncertainty: The lack of complete certainty, that is, the existence of more than one possibility. The "true" outcome/state/result/value is not known.

Measurement of uncertainty: A set of probabilities assigned to a set of possibilities. Example: "There is a 60% chance this market will double in five years"

Risk: A state of uncertainty where some of the possibilities involve a loss, catastrophe, or other undesirable outcome.

Measurement of risk: A set of possibilities each with quantified probabilities and quantified losses. Example: "There is a 40% chance the proposed oil well will be dry with a loss of $12 million in exploratory drilling costs".

In this sense, Hubbard uses the terms so that one may have uncertainty without risk but not risk without uncertainty. We can be uncertain about the winner of a contest, but unless we have some personal stake in it, we have no risk. If we bet money on the outcome of the contest, then we have a risk. In both cases there are more than one outcome. The measure of uncertainty refers only to the probabilities assigned to outcomes, while the measure of risk requires both probabilities for outcomes and losses quantified for outcomes.

Information technology risk, or IT risk, IT-related risk, is a risk related to information technology. This relatively new term due to an increasing awareness that information security is simply one facet of a multitude of risks that are relevant to IT and the real world processes it supports.

The increasing dependencies of modern society on information and computers networks (both in private and public sectors, including military) has led to new terms like IT risk and Cyberwarfare.

Nominal group technique requires participants to be together in the same room. Each participant jots down risks in the project on piece of papers. Each piece of paper lists only one risk. These risks are posted on a board and analyzed by the participants. It is then ranked and prioritized in writing.

Pop Quiz

Q1: Which term is responsible for low risk, frequently occurring, and low cost changes?

Ans: Request Fulfillment

Q2: Which ITIL process is responsible for analyzing risks and counter measures?

Ans: IT Service Continuity Management

Service Provider

A Service Provider is an organization that supplies services to one or more internal or external customers. When the Service Provider is predominantly providing Services it is often reffered to as the "IT Service Provider".

The business unit and the service unit are the two fundamental parties in the service management environment. The business units represent the service recipient side, which is responsible for the implementation of business processes. The service units are the service providers.

The two units don't necessarily have to be part of the same organization or the same legal unit. ITIL draws a distinction between three types of business models for service providers:

- Type 1: Internal Service Provider

- Type 2: Shared Service Provider

- Type 3: External Service Provider

Although most aspects of service management apply for all types, it is important to differentiate between them. The domains of customers, contracts, competition, market, income, and strategy have a slightly different meaning for the different types.

Pop Quiz

Q1: Who owns the specific costs and risks related with providing a service?

Ans: The Service Provider

Q2: Which is used to record agreements regarding Security Management?

Ans: Service Level Agreement (SLA)

Supplier

A third party is responsible for supplying goods or services that are required to deliver IT services.

- Hardware and software vendors

- Netwrok and telecom providers

- Outsourcing organizations

Service Level Agreement (SLA)

Service Level Agreement (frequently abbreviated as SLA) is part of a service contract where the level of service is formally defined. In practice, the term SLA is sometimes used to refer to the contracted delivery time (of the service) or performance.

Description

Service Level Agreement (SLA) is a negotiated agreement between two parties where one is the customer and the other is the service provider. This can be legally binding a formal or informal 'contract'. Contracts between the Service Provider and other third parties are often (incorrectly) called SLAs, as the level of service has been set by the (principal) customer there can be no 'agreement' between third parties (these agreements are simply a 'contract'). Operating Level Agreements or OLA(s) however, may be used by internal groups to support SLA(s).

The SLA records a common understanding about services, priorities, responsibilities, guarantees, and warranties. Each area of service scope should have the 'level of service' defined. The SLA may specify the levels of availability, serviceability, performance, operation, or other attributes of the service, such as billing. The 'level of service' can also be specified as 'target' and 'minimum', which allows customers to be informed what to expect (the minimum), whilst providing a measurable (average) target value that shows the level of organization performance. In some contracts penalties may be agreed in the case of non compliance of the SLA (but see 'internal' customers below). It is important to note that the 'agreement' relates to the services the customer receives, and not how the service provider delivers that service.

SLAs have been used since late 1980s by fixed line telecom operators as part of their contracts with their corporate customers. This practice has spread such that now it is common for a customer to engage a service provider by including a service-level agreement in a wide range of service contracts, in practically all industries and markets. Internal departments in larger organization (such as IT, HR and Real Estate) have adopted the idea of using service-level agreements with their 'internal' customers (users) in other departments within the same organization. One benefit of this can be to enable the quality of service to be benchmarked with that agreed across multiple locations or between different business units. This internal benchmarking can also be used to market test and provide a value comparison between an in-house department and an external service provider.

Service Level Agreements are by their nature 'output' based - the result of the service as received by the customer is the subject of the 'agreement'. The (expert) service provider can demonstrate their value by organizing themselves with ingenuity, capability, and knowledge to deliver the service required, perhaps in an innovative way. Organizations can also specify the way the service is to be delivered, through a specification (a service-level specification) and using subordinate 'objectives' other than those related to the level of service. This type of agreement is known as an 'input' SLA. This latter type of requirement has become obsolete as organizations become more demanding and shift the delivery methodology risk on to the service provider.

Common metrics

Service Level Agreements can contain numerous service performance metrics with corresponding service level objectives. A common case in IT Service Management is a call center or service desk. Metrics commonly agreed to in these cases include:

ABA (Abandonment Rate): It is the percentage of calls abandoned while waiting to be answered.

ASA (Average Speed to Answer): It is the average time (usually in seconds) it takes for a call to be answered by the service desk.

TSF (Time Service Factor): It is the percentage of calls answered within a definite timeframe, e.g. 80% in 20 seconds.

FCR (First Call Resolution): It is the percentage of incoming calls that can be resolved without the use of a callback, or without having the caller call back the helpdesk to finish resolving the case.

TAT (Turn Around Time): It is the time taken to complete a certain task.

Uptime Agreements are another very common metric, often used for data services, such as shared hosting, virtual private servers and dedicated servers. Common agreements include percentage of network uptime, power uptime, amount of scheduled maintenance windows, etc.

Many SLAs track to the ITIL specifications when applied to IT services.

Typical contents

SLAs commonly include segments to address the following:

A definition of services; performance measurement; problem management; customer duties; warranties; disaster recovery; termination of agreement.

From a business perspective, you may need to look at Service Level Management (SLM) if you need to differentiate the service (i.e. to Gold, Silver, or Bronze) and have a differentiated price for each level of service. Key points are to write the SLA in the language that the user understands and to have regular service reviews.

In Cloud Computing

Cloud computing, (also Grid computing and service-oriented architecture), use the concept of service level agreements to control the use and receipt of (computing) resources from and by third parties.

Any SLA management strategy considers two well differentiated phases: the negotiation of the contract and the monitoring of its fulfillment in run-time. Thus, SLA Management encompasses the SLA contract definition (basic schema with the QoS (quality of service) parameters), SLA negotiation, SLA monitoring and SLA enforcement according to defined policies.

The main point is to build a new layer upon the grid, cloud or SOA middleware that is able to create negotiation mechanism between providers and consumer of services. A European Union funded Framework 7 research project, SLA@SOI, is researching aspects of multi-level, multi-provider SLAs within service oriented infrastructure and cloud computing.

In outsourcing

Outsourcing involves the transfer of responsibility from an organization to a supplier. The management of this new arrangement is through a contract that may include a Service Level Agreement (SLA). The contract may involve financial penalties and the right to terminate if SLAs are consistently missed. Setting, tracking and managing SLAs is an important part of Outsourcing Relationship Management (ORM) discipline. It is typical that specific SLAs are negotiated up front as part of the outsourcing contract and they are utilized as one of the primary tools of outsourcing governance.

Pop Quiz

Q1: In which program are activities documented with the plan of improving an IT service?

Ans: Service Improvement Program

The responsibilities of Service Level Management are as follows:

- Ensuring that the agreed IT services are delivered when and where they are supposed to be.

- Liaising with Availability Management, Capacity Management, Incident Management, and Problem Management to ensure that the required levels and quality of service are achieved within the resources agreed with the Financial Management.

- Producing and maintaining a Service Catalog (a list of standard IT service options and agreements made available to customers).

- Ensuring that appropriate IT Service Continuity plans have been made to support the business and its continuity requirements.

The Service Level Manager relies on other areas of the Service Delivery process to provide the necessary support which ensures that the agreed services are provided in a cost effective, secure, and efficient manner.

Customer Relationship Management (CRM) consists of the processes a company uses to track and organize its contacts with its current and prospective customers. CRM software is used to support these processes; information about customers and customer interactions can be entered, stored, and accessed by employees in different company departments. Typical CRM goals are to improve services provided to customers, and to use customer contact information for targeted marketing.

SLA Monitoring Chart (SLAM) is used to see an outline of actual service achievements against targets. It monitors existing agreements.

Service Level Agreement (frequently abbreviated as SLA) is a part of a service contract where the level of service is formally defined. In practice, the term SLA is sometimes used to refer to the contracted delivery time (of the service) or performance.

ITIL defines 3 types of Service Level Agreement (SLA) structures.

The Service Level Management will work with the Business delegate (Business Owner) to document the Service Level Requirements.

Service Level Management provides for continual identification, monitoring, and review of the levels of IT services specified in the service level agreements (SLAs).

Pop Quiz

Q1: Which process is used to review OLAs on a regular basis?

Ans: Service Level Management

Operational Level Agreement (OLA)

An agreement is a meeting of minds between two or more legally competent parties, about their relative duties and rights regarding current or future performance. When people feel or think the same way about something, they agree. Sometimes it is important to write down or make a promise to what has been agreed upon. This is called an agreement. Agreements are common in law and business. For example, when a person takes a loan or hires someone to work, an agreement is usually signed so everyone understands what must be done and in what time it must be done.

Underpinning Contract (UC) is a contract between an IT service provider and a third party. In another way, it is an agreement between the IT organization and an external provider about the delivery of one or more services. The third party provides services that support the delivery of a service to a customer. The Underpinning Contract defines targets and responsibilities that are required to meet agreed Service Level targets in an SLA.

An Operational Level Agreement (OLA) defines the interdependent relationships among the internal support groups of an organization working to support a Service Level Agreement. The agreement describes the responsibilities of each internal support group toward other support groups, including the process and timeframe for delivery of their services. The objective of the OLA is to present a clear, concise, and measurable description of the service provider's internal support relationships. OLA is sometimes expanded to other phrases but they all have the same meaning:

- Organizational Level Agreement

- Operating Level Agreement

- Operations Level Agreement

An Operational Level Agreement (OLA) defines the interdependent relationships among the internal support groups of an organization working to support a Service Level Agreement.

An Operational Level Agreement (OLA) defines the interdependent relationships among the internal support groups of an organization working to support a Service Level Agreement.

Contract

The Supplier Manager is responsible for ensuring that value for money is obtained from all suppliers.

Force majeure is a common clause in contracts, which essentially frees both parties from liability or obligation when an extraordinary event or circumstance beyond the control of the parties, such as a war, strike, riot, crime, or an event described by the legal term "act of God" (e.g., flooding, earthquake, volcano), prevents one or both parties from fulfilling their obligations under the contract.

IT Facilities Management is used to manage Contracts relating to an outsourced data center.

Pop Quiz

Q1: Who manages contracts relating to an outsourced Data Centre?

Ans: Facilities Management

Q2: In which role will you are MOST expected to be involved in the management of Underpinning Contracts?

Ans: Supplier Manager

Service Design Package

The Service Design Package builds upon the Service Level Requirements. It further specifies the requirements from the viewpoint of the client and defines how these are actually fulfilled from a technical and organizational point of view. It is assumed that a bundle of Supporting Services is combined in order to deliver a Business Service for the client. In this context, the IT organization may opt to supply the Supporting Service with its own resources, or to use an external service supplier.

The Service Design Package is passed from Service Design to the Service Transition process and details all information required in order to develop the service solution, including a preliminary (intended) time-schedule for the Service Transition phase.

The Service Design Package contains the following information (the actual level of detail will vary, depending on the type of service):

Service Design Package - Part 1: Header

1. Name of the service

2. Clearance information (with location and date)

    1. Clearance of the Service Design Manager

    2. Clearance of the Service Design Package by Service Management (confirmation that the requirements as laid out in this document are able to be fulfilled and where necessary, specification of any preconditions which must be fulfilled before the service can go operational)

        1. Capacity Manager

        2. Availability Manager

        3. IT Service Continuity Manager

        4. Security Manager

5. Compliance Manager

6. Financial Manager

Service Design Package - Part 2: Detailed Requirements Specification as a Basis for Service Transition

This part builds upon the Service Level Requirements and specifies in more detail what conditions the new service and its underlying applications and infrastructure must fulfill, providing all information which is needed for building the new service.

1. Service level requirements (reference to the SLR document, where service level requirements are defined)

2. Functional requirements (the SLR document contains a summary description of the desired customer outcome; however, functional requirements may need to be specified in greater detail, especially if new applications/ systems are to be developed)

3. IT security requirements which are relevant for the service

4. Compliance requirements which are relevant for the service

5. Architectural constraints (e.g. specific technology or vendors)

6. Interface requirements (e.g. if a new system needs to communicate with other systems)

7. Migration requirements (e.g. if data are to be migrated from an existing to a new application)

8. Operational requirements (e.g. requirements for backup and restore mechanisms, compatibility with existing system monitoring tools)

9. Required access rights (which users or user groups will require access to the service, and what levels of access must be provided)

Service Design Package - Part 3: Technical and Organizational Implementation Blueprint

This part details what must be done during Service Transition to meet the specified requirements.

1. Transition strategy (a brief outline of the selected approach to implementing the new service)

    1. Testing strategy

    2. Deployment strategy

    3. Migration concept

    4. Back-out strategy in the case of a failed deployment

2. Decomposition of the Business Service into Infrastructure Services

    1. Internal Infrastructure Services on which this service is based

        1. Names of the infrastructure services

        2. Service providers (responsible Service Owners)

        3. References to Operational Level Agreements (OLAs)

        4. Required changes to OLAs, if existing OLAs are not sufficient for the service to be established

    2. Externally supplied Supporting Services on which this service is based

        1. Names of the external services

        2. Name of the supplier

        3. Responsible Supplier Manager

        4. References to Underpinning Contracts (UCs)

        5. Required changes to UCs, if existing UCs do not support the introduction of the new service

3. Details on technical changes required to build, test, deploy and operate the service

    1. Development/ customization of base applications for the service (e.g. if the service to be introduced is based on the SAP system or a custom application)

    2. Supporting tools

        1. Development/ customization of migration tools

        2. Development/ customization of testing tools

        3. Development/ customization of deployment tools

        4. Development/ customization of back-out tools in the case of a failed release deployment

    3. Infrastructure modifications required to build, test, deploy and operate the service

        1. Infrastructure components to be purchased and installed

        2. Infrastructure components to be (re-)configured

    4. Required changes to facilities

4. Organizational changes required to implement and operate the service

1. Personnel resources to be added

    1. Specification of required resources

    2. Strategy for acquiring the resources

2. Skills to be developed

    1. Specification of the required skills

    2. Strategy for acquiring the skills

3. Changes to processes

    1. List of IT processes which must be changed or created, including process owners

    2. Detailed specification of required changes to IT processes, e.g. in the form of process designs

5. Operational concept, e.g.

    1. Routine administrative tasks to be carried out

    2. Rules for archiving and backup

Service Design Package - Part 4: Planning Information

This part sets an intended time frame for the service implementation and estimates the required resources; this information may be updated later by Change, Release or Project Management.

1. Preliminary Service Transition Plan

    1. Major project phases and milestones

    2. Intended time schedule

    3. Required staff resources

2. Required budget for service implementation (itemized)

Availability

Availability is the most basic aspect of assuring value to customers. It gives surety to the customer that services will be available for use under agreed terms and conditions. The availability of a service is its most happily perceived attribute from a user's perspective. A service is available only if users can access it in an agreed approach. Perceptions and preferences vary by customer and by business context. Availability of a service is more delicate than a binary evaluation of available and unavailable. The time period for which the customer can wait to avail the service should be determined and factored into service design.

- Mean Time To Repair (MTTR) is the average time taken to repair a Configuration Item or IT Service after a failure. It represents the average time required to repair a failed component or device. Expressed mathematically, it is the total corrective maintenance time divided by the total number of corrective maintenance actions during a given period of time. It generally does not include lead time for parts not readily available or other Administrative or Logistic Downtime (ALDT).

- MTTR is often part of a maintenance contract, where a system whose MTTR is 24 hours is generally more valuable than for one of 7 days if mean time between failures is equal, because its Operational Availability is higher. MTTR is every now and then incorrectly used to mean Mean Time to Restore Service.

- Mean Time Between Service Incidents (MTBSI) is a metric used to measure and report reliability. MTBSI is the mean time starting from when a system or IT service fails, until it next fails. MTBSI is equivalent to MTBF + MTRS. Mean Time Between Service Incidents (MTBSI) is used in Service Design of ITIL.

- Mean Time To Failure (MTTF) is an approximate of the average, or mean time until a component's first failure, or disruption in the operation of the product, process, procedure, or design takes place. MTTF presumes that the product CANNOT be repaired and the product CANNOT continue any of its regular operations.

In many designs and components, MTTF is especially near to the MTBF, which is a bit longer than MTTF. This is due to the fact that MTBF adds the repair time of the designs or components. MTBF is the average time between failures to include the average repair time, or MTTR.

The Availability Measurements are as follows:

- MTTR

- MTBF

- MTBSI

- MTTF

As a project is unique and is created for producing a unique product, the product verification will not be affected by the information added to the lesson learned document.

Availability Management allows organizations to sustain the IT service availability to support the business at a justifiable cost. The high-level activities are Realize Availability Requirements, Compile Availability Plan, Monitor Availability, and Monitor Maintenance Obligations.

Mean Time Between Failures (MTBF) is the predicted elapsed time between inherent failures of a system during operation. MTBF can be calculated as the arithmetic mean time between failures of a system. MTBF is typically part of a model that assumes the failed system is immediately repaired, as a part of a renewal process. This is in contrast to the Mean Time To Failure (MTTF), which measures average time between failure with the modeling assumption that the failed system is not repaired.

Overview:

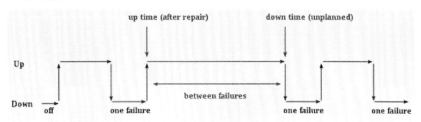

Time Between Failures = { down time - up time}

For each observation, downtime is the instantaneous time it went down, which is after (i.e. greater than) the moment it went up, uptime. The difference (downtime - uptime) is the amount of time it was operating between these two events. MTBF value prediction is an important element in the development of products. Reliability engineers/design engineers, often utilize Reliability Software to calculate products' MTBF according to various methods/standards. However, these "prediction" methods are not intended to reflect fielded MTBF as is commonly believed. The intent of these tools is to focus design efforts on the weak links in the design.

Formal definition of MTBF:

Referring to the figure above, MTBF is the sum of the operational periods divided by the number of observed failures.

$$\text{Mean time between failures} = \text{MTBF} = \frac{\Sigma(\text{downtime} - \text{uptime})}{\text{number of failures}}.$$

The MTBF is often denoted by the Greek letter ?, or

$$\text{MTBF} = \theta.$$

The MTBF can be defined in terms of the expected value of the density function (t)

$$\text{MTBF} = \int_0^\infty t f(t)\, dt$$

with

$$\int_0^\infty f(t)\, dt = 1.$$

Common MTBF Misconceptions:

MTBF is commonly confused with a component's useful life, even though the two concepts are not related in any way. For example, a battery may have a useful life of four hours, and an MTBF of 100,000 hours. These figures indicate that in a population of 100,000 batteries, there will be approximately one battery failure every hour during a single battery's four-hour life span.

Another common misconception about the MTBF is that it specifies the time (on average) when the probability of failure equals the probability of not having a failure (i.e. a reliability of 50%). This is only true for certain symmetric distributions.

In many cases, such as the (non-symmetric) exponential distribution, this is not the case. In particular, for an exponential failure distribution, the probability that an item will fail at or before the MTBF is approximately 0.63 (i.e. the reliability at the MTBF is 37%). For typical distributions with some variance, MTBF only represents a top-level aggregate statistic, and thus is not suitable for predicting specific time to failure, the uncertainty arising from the variability in the time-to-failure distribution.

Another misconception is to assume that the MTBF value is higher in a system that implements component redundancy. Component redundancy can increase the system MTBF, however, it will decrease the hardware MTBF, since the greater number of components in a system, the more frequent a hardware component will experience failure, leading to a reduction in the system's hardware MTBF.

Variations of MTBF:

There are many variations of MTBF, such as mean time between system aborts (MTBSA) or mean time between critical failures (MTBCF) or mean time between unit replacement (MTBUR). Such nomenclature is used when it is desirable to differentiate among types of failures, such as critical and non-critical failures. Mean Time To Failure (MTTF) is sometimes used instead of MTBF in cases where a system is replaced after a failure, since MTBF denotes time between failures in a system, which is repaired.

Pop Quiz

Q1: Which is the significant element for Security?

Ans: Availability Management

Q2: Which ITIL process uses Mean Time Between Failures (MTBF)?

Ans: Availability Management

Service Knowledge Management System (SKMS)

The Service Knowledge Management System is the central repository of the IT organization's data, information, and knowledge. It extends the concept of the infrastructure-focused Configuration Management System to include further information on services, capabilities, and initiatives.

The Service Knowledge Management System is used to store, manage, update, and present all information that an IT service provider needs to manage the full lifecycle of IT services. The SKMS contains knowledge of the following:

- Staff experience levels

- User numbers and behaviour

- Organization's performance

- Suppliers' and partners' requirements

Pop Quiz

Q1: What is SOA in Availability Management?

Ans: Service Outage Analysis

Q2: Items of information stored in the CMDB relating to a specific Configuration Item (CI) are called _____.

Ans: Attributes

Configuration Item (CI)

A Configuration item (CI) is an IT asset or a combination of IT assets that may depend and have relationships with other IT processes. A CI will have attributes which may be hierarchical and relationships that will be assigned by the configuration manager in the CM database.

The Configuration Item (CI) attributes are as follows:

Technical: It is data that describes the CI's capabilities which include software version and model numbers, hardware and manufacturer specifications, and other technical details like networking speeds, and data storage size. Keyboards, mice and cables are considered consumables.

Ownership: It is part of financial asset management, ownership attributes, warranty, location, and responsible person for the CI.

Relationship: It is the relationship among hardware items, software, and users.

A CI that has the same essential functionality as another CI but a bit different in some small manner.

The term Configuration Item (CI) refers to the fundamental structural unit of a configuration management system. Examples of CIs include individual requirements documents, software, models, plans, and people.

A Configuration item (CI) is an IT asset or a combination of IT assets that may depend and have relationships with other IT processes. A CI will have attributes which may be hierarchical and relationships that will be assigned by the configuration manager in the CM database.

Configuration Management System

Configuration Management (CM) is an Information Technology Infrastructure Library (ITIL) IT Service Management (ITSM) process. It tracks all of the individual Configuration Items (CI) in an IT system, which may be as simple as a single server, or as complex as the entire IT department. In large organizations a configuration manager may be appointed to oversee and manage the CM process.

Configuration Management Database is the fundamental component of the ITIL Configuration Management (CM). CMDB represents the authorized configuration of the significant components of the IT environment. It helps an organization understand the relationships between these components and track their configuration.

CMDB implementations often involve federation, the inclusion of data into the CMDB from other sources, such as Asset Management, in such a way that the source of the data retains control of the data. Federation is usually distinguished from ETL (extract, transform, and load) solutions in which data is copied into the CMDB.

Pop Quiz

Q1: Which item is a Configuration Item?

Ans: Documentation

Q2: Which discipline performs Planning, Implementation, Controlling, Status Accounting, and Verification activities?

Ans: Configuration Management

The Change Advisory Board (CAB) is a group of people that advise the Change Manager in the assessment, prioritization, and scheduling of changes. This board is made up of representatives from all areas within AccessPlus who will be affected by the change, including third party suppliers as appropriate. This board is chaired by the Change Manager who is the only permanent CAB member.

A key part of managing changes in IT is to have a Change Advisory Board (CAB). A CAB offers multiple perspectives necessary to ensure proper decision making. The CAB is tasked with reviewing and prioritizing requested changes, monitoring the change process and providing managerial feedback.

A CAB is an integral part of a defined change management process designed to balance the need for change with the need to minimize inherent risks. As such, it has requests coming in from management, customers, users, and IT. Plus the changes may involve hardware, software, configuration settings, patches, etc.

A CAB can also be used outside of the IT world as the Change Process at a high level can be applied to any system.

Configuration Management is used for the following:

- To account for all IT assets

- To provide precise information support to other ITIL disciplines

- To provide a solid base for Incident, Problem, Change, and Release Management

- To verify configuration records and correct any exceptions

Configuration Management Database is the fundamental component of the ITIL Configuration Management (CM). CMDB represents the authorized configuration of the significant components of the IT environment.

Pop Quiz

Q1: Which process uses Status Accounting as its important part?

Ans: Configuration Management

Q2: A change that must be made quickly is called?

Ans: An urgent change

Definitive Media Library (DML)

The Definitive Software Library (DSL) is one or more locations in which the definitive and approved versions of all software Configuration Items (CIs) are securely stored. It may also contain associated CIs, such as licenses and documentation. It is a single logical storage area even if there are multiple locations. All software in the DSL is under the control of Change and Release Management and recorded in the CMDB. Only software from the DSL is acceptable for use in a Release.

The Definitive Media Library (DML) is a secure library where software that has been properly reviewed and authorized is stored. Technically, Configuration Items (CIs) are what is stored in the DML after they meet up organizational standards. It is a single logical storage area even if there are multiple locations. All software in the DML is under the control of Change and Release Management and is recorded in the Configuration Management System.

The Definitive Media Library (DML) is a secure library where software that has been properly reviewed and authorized is stored. Technically, Configuration Items (CIs) are what is stored in the DML after they meet up organizational standards.

Service Change

The Change Manager authorizes and documents all changes in the IT Infrastructure and its components (CIs) to maintain a least amount of interruptive effects after the running operation. The succession of the individual stages is planned and communicated to recognize any overlapping as early as possible. In the case of further-reaching changes, he involves the Change Advisory Board (CAB).

The Problem Manager takes on research for the core causes of Incidents, and therefore he ensures the durable elimination of interruptions. If possible, he makes short-term solutions (Workarounds) available to Incident Management. The Problem Manager develops ultimate solutions for Known Errors. He also engages in the prevention of interruptions (Pro-active Problem Management), i.e. via a trend-analysis of vital services or historical Incidents.

Pop Quiz

Q1: In which database the statuses of changes are recorded?

Ans: Configuration Management Database

Q2: In which the planning of changes is kept up to date?

Ans: Forward Schedule of Changes (FSC)

The Service Improvement Plan (SIP) refers to the steps that must be taken if there is a major gap in the projected delivery quality of a service and the actual delivery. SIP is a model that belongs to the Service Level Management (SLM) process. SLM is mainly defined in the Service Design of ITIL v3, but like many processes in v3, SLM is also documented in other volumes. SIP is particularly documented in Continual Service Improvement (CSI). SIP is also referred to when capital budgeting is being discussed with reference to preference decisions.

Forward Schedule of Change (FSC) holds information of all the changes approved for implementation and their projected implementation dates. FSC should be approved by the customers, Service Level Management, Service Desk, and Availability Management. When FSC is approved, Service Desk should communicate to the user community using the most effective methods available.

The objective of FSC is to notify the recipients of the UPCOMING Changes. A simple form of FSC would be like RFC No, Change Summary, Planned date of implementation, and status of the RFC. FSC should be accessible to everyone inside the organization. FSC acts like the change calendar for external users. It allows the IT and business people to schedule their RFC accordingly.

The Change Manager authorizes and documents all changes in the IT Infrastructure and its components (CIs) to maintain a least amount of interruptive effects after the running operation.

Forward Schedule of Change (FSC) holds information of all the changes approved for implementation and their projected implementation dates.

Change types (Normal, Standard, and Emergency)

Emergency Change Advisory Board (ECAB) is a sub-set of the Change Advisory Board who makes decisions about high impact Emergency Changes.

Acceptance of defects, rework to correct defects, and process changes are the results of completing quality control activities.

An ITIL normal change refers to changes that must follow the complete change management process. By definition a normal change will proceed through all steps of the change management process and will eventually be reviewed by the Change Advisory Board (CAB). The CAB will provide advice regarding the change to the person who is deemed responsible to approve or reject normal changes.

Change types

A change request is a formal communication seeking an alteration to one or more configuration Items (CI). This change requires could take several forms:

- Request for Change document

- Service desk call

- Project initiation document

An emergency changes is a change that must be introduced as soon as possible. The Change Management process will have a specific procedure to deal with emergency changes. These changes often can't wait until the next normally scheduled change meeting

A standard change is a pre approved change that is low in risk, relatively common, and follows a procedure or work instruction. It is not necessary to submit an RFC to implement a standard change.

If it is an emergency change, or a standard change, then we are dealing with a normal change. The addition, modification, or removal of anything that could have an affect on IT services.

The normal change is one of three change types that are defined in ITIL version 3. The ITIL standard change, the normal change and the emergency change.

A new change record can be generated in a number of ways:

- An IT staff member can generate a change by hand through Change > Create New or clicking New from the change record list.

- Any user can request a change through the Service Catalog.

- A change can be requested from an incident.

- A change can be requested from a problem.

- If a user tries to create a generic task, the task interceptor will first ask them to mention what sort of task they would like to create. In this way, tasks are always assigned a handling process.

- If an appropriate inbound email action is configured, it can be generated from an email.

- If an assignment rule applies, the change will be assigned to the proper user or group. Otherwise, it can be assigned by hand.

- Email Notifications will keep involved parties informed about updates to the change reques

Release Unit

A Delta release is also known as partial release. It contains the elements of a hardware or software Configuration Item (CI) that have changed or are new since the previous Full/Delta release. The changes are added to the existing version of the CI. In delta release, it is not always possible to analyze how changes will influence the rest of the live environment.

The release management levels are as follows:

- **Major release:** It typically introduces new capabilities/functions. A major release might accumulate all the changes from preceding minor releases. Major releases advance the version number by a full increment. For example, from version 7.70 to version 8.

- **Minor release:** It integrates a number of fixes for known problems into the baseline, or trusted state, of an item. A minor release typically increments the version number at the first decimal place. For example, version 7.10 will change to version 7.20.

- **Emergency release:** It is a quick fix to repair unpredicted problems or short-term measures to prevent the disruption of important services. An emergency release increments the version number at the second decimal place. For example, from 7.1 to 7.11.

A full release contains all the elements of a software or hardware Configuration Item (CI), even though the elements have not changed. In full release, the influence of the changes is more carefully analyzed and less expected to cause incidents during implementation.

A package release moves the changes to different Configuration Item (CI) into a single release. A package release might contain changes to hardware and software CI and can contain delta and full releases. A package release reduces disturbance in the IT environment.

The steps in the release management process are as follows:

- **Build and configure:** The components of the release are collected in a controlled laboratory environment.

- **Test and Accept:** Before the distribution, testing by an independent group takes place. The independent group can be business staff, users, and other IT staff.

- **Schedule and Plan:** The rollout of the release should be planned and scheduled carefully. The plan should add a list of all CIs to be added or removed and a schedule of activities at every location involved in the rollout.

- **Communicate and prepare:** Release management should communicate the rollout plan. Each contributor requires knowing what preparations to make. Users, managers, and technicians who will implement the release must know what and when it will happen.

- **Distribute and Install:** When the planned date for installation comes, the release can be installed according to the prepared plan. Software must be distributed to the installation site. Installers must pursue a prepared script of activities to complete the installation.

A back-out plan documents all actions to be taken to reinstate the service if the related Change or Release fails or partially fails. A back-out plan might offer a full or partial reversal. However, in extreme situations, a back-out plan might just call for the IT Service Continuity Plan to be called.

There are three types of releases to reflect different ways to build and deploy changes to hardware and software CIs.

The release management levels are Major, Minor, and Emergency.

The different types of Release units are as follows:

- Delta Release

- Full Release

- Packaged Release

Pop Quiz

Q1: In which package does a structured set of Release units can be defined?

Ans: A Release Package

Q2: The scope of a Release can be best described by _____.

Ans: DSL configuration

Concept of Seven R's of Change Management; no requirement to learn list Event

The Change Management terminologies are as follows:

- Change: It is the addition, modification, or removal of CIs.

- Request for Change (RFC): It is a form used to record details of a request for a change and is sent as an input to Change Management by the Change Requestor.

- Forward Schedule of Changes (FSC): It is a schedule that contains details of all forthcoming Changes.

- Service Request Management (SRM) is the underlying workflow and processes that enable an IT procurement or service request to be reliably submitted, routed, approved, monitored, and delivered. SRM is the process of managing a service request through its lifecycle from submission through delivery and follow-up.

- SRM may be manual or automated. In a manual system, a user calls a help desk to request a service, and a help desk personnel creates a service ticket to route the service request. In an automated system, the user submits a request through an online service catalog, and the application software automatically routes the request through the appropriate processes for approval and service delivery. These systems typically enable users to track the status of their service requests, and also enable the management to monitor service delivery levels for quality control purposes.

- Change Management terminologies are Change, Request for Change (RFC), and Forward Schedule of Changes (FSC).

- Change Management is used to ensure that standardized methods and procedures are used for efficient handling of all changes.

Incident

An incident is any event which is not part of the standard operation of a service and which causes, or may cause, an interruption to, or a reduction in, the quality of service. The stated ITIL objective is to restore normal operations as quickly as possible with the least possible impact on either the business or the user, at a cost-effective price.

ISO 20000 defines an incident as:

"Any event which is not part of the standard operation of a service and which causes or may cause an interruption to, or a reduction in, the quality of that service."

Incidents can be classified into three primary categories, which are as follows:

- Software

- Hardware

- Service requests

Note that service requests are not always regarded as an incident, but rather a request for change. However, the handling of failures and the handling of service requests are similar, and therefore, are included in the definition and scope of the process of incident management.

Incidents may match with existing 'Known Problems' (without a known root cause) or 'Known Errors' (with a root cause) under the control of Problem Management and registered in the Known Error Database (KeDB). Where existing work-arounds have been developed, it is suggested that accessing these will allow the Service Desk to provide a quick first-line fix. Where an incident is not the result of a Known Problem or Known Error, it may either be an isolated or individual occurrence or may (once the initial issue has been addressed) require that Problem Management becomes involved, possibly resulting in a new problem record being raised.

There are two types of floats available: Free float and Total float.

An "Incident" is any event which is not part of the standard operation of the service and which causes, or may cause, an interlude or a decline in the quality of the service.

Incident Management records relationships between service components.

Pop Quiz

Q1: For which process is the purpose of priorities based on the impact and importance of an essential activity?

Ans: Change Management

Q2: Who should carry out advance testing once a change has been built under an ITIL Change Management process?

Ans: Independent tester

Impact, Urgency, and Priority

As ITIL defines it, Incident priority is primarily formed out of it's Impact and Urgency. There are also additional elements, like size, scope, complexity and resources required for resolution. So, most consultants recommend the simple matrix which will automatically calculate incident priority out of the simple value of Impact x Urgency.

One of the best practices that ITIL brings to the party within Incident (case) Management is prioritization.

ITIL calls out 3 separate attributes: impact, urgency, and priority.

- **Impact:** the measure of how business critical it is.

- **Urgency:** a necessary speed of resolving an incident.

- **Priority:** formulated from the combination of impact and urgency. Some formulate it as Priority = Urgency + Impact. Others use Priority = Urgency * Impact.

They key difference that ITIL presents with the concept of Priority versus the classic usage of Severity is that severity alone does not provide enough context for Prioritization. The urgency factor needs to be added to severity in order to provide an accurate understanding of how to prioritize activity.

Service Request

A Service Request is a request from a user for information, advice, a standard change, or access to an IT service. For example, to reset a password, or to provide standard IT services for a new user. Service Requests are usually handled by a service desk or a request fulfillment group, and do not require an RFC to be submitted.

Pop Quiz

Q1: What is the first step to register an incident?

Ans: Assign an incident number

Q2: Which process is accountable for frequently occurring changes where risk and cost are low?

Ans: Request Fulfillment

Problem

The Problem Control Process aims to handle problems in an efficient way. Problem control identifies the root cause of incidents and reports it to the service desk. Other activities are as follows:

- Problem identification and recording

- Problem classification

- Problem investigation and diagnosis

The standard technique for identifying the root cause of a problem is to use an Ishikawa diagram, also referred to as a cause-and-effect diagram, tree diagram, or fishbone diagram. A brainstorming session, in which group members offer product improvement ideas, typically results in an Ishikawa diagram. For problem-solving, the goal is to find causes and effects of the problem.

The Problem Management Process is intended to reduce the number and severity of incidents and problems of the business, and report it in documentation to be available for the first-line and second line of the help desk. The proactive process identifies and resolves problems before incidents occur. These activities are as follows:

- Trend analysis

- Targeting support action

These two provides information to the organization.

Problem Management is used to resolve the root cause of incidents and thus to minimize the adverse impact of incidents and problems on business that are caused by errors within the IT infrastructure, and to prevent recurrence of incidents related to these errors.

Kaizen (kai-change, zen-good) is a Japanese philosophy for improving processes continuously. Kaizen is a daily activity, the purpose of which goes beyond simple productivity improvement.

Problem Management is used to resolve the root cause of incidents, and thus to minimize the adverse impact of incidents and problems on business that are caused by errors within the IT infrastructure, and to prevent recurrence of incidents related to these errors.

Pop Quiz

Q1: At what point does an Incident turn in to a problem?

Ans: Never

Q2: Which activity is used to take place after recording and registering an incident?

Ans: Classification

Ishikawa diagrams are also called fishbone diagrams or cause-and-effect diagrams. They are diagrams that show the causes of a certain event. Common uses of the Ishikawa diagram are product design and quality defect prevention, to identify potential factors causing an overall effect. Each cause or reason for imperfection is a source of variation. Causes are usually grouped into major categories to identify these sources of variation. The categories typically include:

- **People:** Anyone involved with the process.

- **Methods:** How the process is performed and the specific requirements for doing it, such as policies, procedures, rules, regulations, and laws.

- **Machines:** Any equipment, computers, tools, etc., are required to accomplish the job.

- **Materials:** Raw materials, parts, pens, paper, etc., are used to produce the final product.

- **Measurements:** Data generated from the process that are used to evaluate its quality.

- **Environment:** The conditions, such as location, time, temperature, and culture in which the process operates.

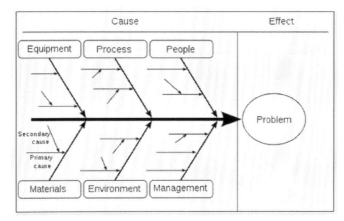

Ishikawa diagram, in fishbone shape, showing factors of Equipment, Process, People, Materials, Environment and Management, all affecting the overall problem. Smaller arrows connect the sub-causes to major causes.

Overview:

Ishikawa diagrams were proposed by Kaoru Ishikawa in the 1960s, who pioneered quality management processes in the Kawasaki shipyards and in the process became one of the founding fathers of modern management.

It was first used in the 1960s, and is considered one of the seven basic tools of quality management, along with the histogram, Pareto chart, check sheet, control chart, flowchart, and scatter diagram. It is known as a fishbone diagram because of its shape, similar to the side view of a fish skeleton.

Mazda Motors famously used an Ishikawa diagram in the development of the Miata sports car, where the required result was "Jinba Ittai" or "Horse and Rider as One". The main causes included such aspects as "touch" and "braking" with the lesser causes including highly granular factors such as "50/50 weight distribution" and "able to rest elbow on top of driver's door". Every factor identified in the diagram was included in the final design.

Causes:

Causes in the diagram are often categorized, such as to the 4 M's, described below. Cause-and-effect diagrams can reveal key relationships among various variables, and the possible causes provide additional insight into process behavior.

Causes can be derived from brainstorming sessions. These groups can then be labeled as categories of the fishbone. They will typically be one of the traditional categories mentioned above but may be something unique to the application in a specific case. Causes can be traced back to root causes with the 5 Whys technique.

Typical categories are as follows:

- The 4 M's (Used in manufacturing)
- Machine (Equipment)
- Method (Process/Inspection)
- Material (Raw, Consumables, etc.)
- Man power
- The 8 P's (Used in service industry)
- Price
- Product
- Place/Plant
- Promotion
- People
- Process
- Physical Evidence
- Productivity & Quality
- The 4 S's (Used in service industry)
- Surroundings
- Suppliers
- Systems
- Skills

- More M's

- Mother Nature (Environment)

- Man Power (physical work)

- Mind Power (Brain Work): Kaizens, Suggestions

- Measurement (Inspection)

- Maintenance

- Money Power

- Management

The 5 Whys is a question-asking method used to explore the cause/effect relationships underlying a particular problem. Ultimately, the goal of applying the 5 Whys method is to determine a root cause of a defect or problem.

The following example demonstrates the basic process:

- My car will not start. (the problem)

- Why? - The battery is dead. (first why)

- Why? - The alternator is not functioning. (second why)

- Why? - The alternator belt has broken. (third why)

- Why? - The alternator belt was well beyond its useful service life and has never been replaced. (fourth why)

- Why? - I have not been maintaining my car according to the recommended service schedule. (fifth why, a root cause)

The questioning for this example could be taken further to a sixth, seventh, or even greater level. This would be legitimate, as the "five" in 5 Whys is not gospel; rather, it is postulated that five iterations of asking why is generally sufficient to get to a root cause. The real key is to encourage the troubleshooter to avoid assumptions and logic traps and instead to trace the chain of causality in direct increments from the effect through any layers of abstraction to a root cause that still has some connection to the original problem.

History:

The technique was originally developed by Sakichi Toyoda and was later used within Toyota Motor Corporation during the evolution of their manufacturing methodologies. It is a critical component of problem solving training delivered as part of the induction into the Toyota Production System. The architect of the Toyota Production System, Taiichi Ohno, described the 5 whys method as *"... the basis of Toyota's scientific approach ... by repeating why five times, the nature of the problem as well as its solution becomes clear."* The tool has seen widespread use beyond Toyota, and is now used within Kaizen, lean manufacturing, and Six Sigma.

Criticism:

While the 5 Whys is a powerful tool for engineers or technically savvy individuals to help get to the true causes of problems, it has been criticized by Teruyuki Minoura, former managing director of global purchasing for Toyota, as being too basic a tool to analyze root causes to the depth that is needed to ensure that the causes are fixed. Reasons for this criticism include:

- Tendency for investigators to stop at symptoms rather than going on to lower level root causes.

- Inability to go beyond the investigator's current knowledge - can't find causes that they don't already know.

- Lack of support to help the investigator to ask the right "why" questions.

- Results aren't repeatable - different people using 5 Whys come up with different causes for the same problem.

- The tendency to isolate a single root cause, whereas each question could elicit many different root causes.

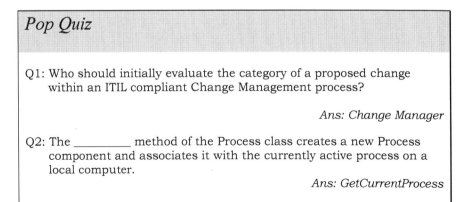

Pop Quiz

Q1: Who should initially evaluate the category of a proposed change within an ITIL compliant Change Management process?

Ans: Change Manager

Q2: The _____ method of the Process class creates a new Process component and associates it with the currently active process on a local computer.

Ans: GetCurrentProcess

These can be significant problems when the method is applied through deduction only. On-the-spot verification of the answer to the current "why" question, before proceeding to the next, is recommended as a good practice to avoid these issues.

Workaround

A workaround is a bypass of a known problem in a system. A workaround is a temporary fix that implies that a genuine solution to the problem is needed. Frequently workarounds are as creative as true solutions, involving outside the box thinking in their creation.

They are considered weak in that they will not respond well to further pressure from a system beyond the original design. In implementing a workaround it is important to flag the change so as to later implement a proper solution. Placing pressure on a workaround may result in later failures in the system.

The Problem Record contains all details of a problem, documenting the history of the problem from detection to resolution. The details of a workaround are always documented in the Problem Record.

Pop Quiz

Q1: Which concept is part of Change Management?

Ans: Post Implementation Review

Q2: An Unabsorbed cost is best described as _____

Ans: A capital cost

Known Error

The Problem Management process is responsible for producing a RFC output. Error Control activities focus on resolving Known Errors through the Change Management process.

The Error Control Process is an iterative process to diagnose known errors until they are eliminated by the successful implementation of a change under the control of the Change Management process.

A known error is a condition identified by successful diagnosis of the root cause of a problem, and the subsequent development of a Work-around.

Known Error Data Base (KEDB)

The database containing the recorded solutions of all internal and possibly some external Known Errors, sometimes called a KEL.

A database contains the recorded solutions of all internal and possibly some external Known Errors. ITIL defines a Known Error as a faulty CI. (Could be faulty due to mis-configuration, or 'cause there's smoke coming out of the back!). So there it is gloriously simple. Known Errors get found and then you put a record in the Known Errors Database. If an RFC needs to be raised to fix the CI, you do so, and if you have a workaround you attach the details to the Know Error's record.

Pop Quiz

Q1: What are the MAJOR types of Service Asset?

Ans: Resources and Capabilities

Q2: Who is responsible for Incident Management?

Ans: Service Desk

The role of communication in Service Operation

ICT Operations Management provides the day-to-day technical supervision of the ICT infrastructure. Often confused with the role of Incident Management from Service Support, Operations is more technical and is concerned not solely with Incidents reported by users, but with Events generated by or recorded by the Infrastructure.

ICT Operations may often work closely alongside Incident Management and the Service Desk, which are not-necessarily technical, to provide an 'Operations Bridge'. Operations should primarily work from documented processes and procedures and should be concerned with a number of specific sub-processes, such as: Output Management, Job Scheduling, Backup and Restore, Network Monitoring/Management, System Monitoring/Management, Database Monitoring/Management, and Storage Monitoring/Management. Operations are responsible for the following:

- A stable, secure ICT infrastructure

- A current, up to date Operational Documentation Library ("ODL")

- A log of all operational Events

- Maintenance of operational monitoring and management tools

- Operational Scripts

- Operational Procedures

ICT Deployment provides a framework for the successful management of design, build, test, and roll-out (deploy) projects within an overall ICT program. It includes many project management disciplines in common with PRINCE2, but has a broader focus to include the necessary integration of Release Management and both functional and non functional testing.

ICT Technical Support is the specialist technical function for infrastructure within ICT. Primarily as a support to other processes, both in Infrastructure Management and Service Management, Technical Support provides a number of specialist functions, which are as follows:

- Research and Evaluation

- Market Intelligence (particularly for Design and Planning and Capacity Management)

- Proof of Concept and Pilot engineering

- Specialist technical expertise (particularly for Operations and Problem Management)

- Creation of documentation (perhaps for the Operational Documentation Library or Known Error Database)

Pop Quiz

Q1: What is required by Major Incidents?

Ans: Separate procedures

Q2: Which data is least expected to be used in the Incident Control Process?

Ans: Cost of faulty item

Service Assets

Resources and Capabilities are strategic assets of each service provider to enable goods or services to be produced. The resources are a direct input parameter for the service delivery. These could be finances, infrastructure, applications, and information. On the other hand the management, the organization, people and their knowledge are necessary for the conversion of these resources.

Capabilities are skills and help the organization to develop and control the resources in order to generate added value. Typically these capabilities are based on experience and information, are knowledge intensive and therefore closely linked to an organization's people, the systems, processes and technologies and have to be enhanced over the course of time. Capabilities are part of the non-tangible assets of an organization (human capital).

Combined resources and capabilities constitute the basis for the value of a service.

The capabilities of an organization cannot produce any value without appropriate and adequate resources. The productive capacity of a service provider depends on the availability of the resources. The capabilities are needed to enhance, implement and coordinate the productive capacity.

Release policy

The Release categories consist of the new or changed software and/or hardware required to implement approved changes. The different types of Release categories are as follows:

Major software releases and hardware upgrades, normally containing large amounts of new functionality, some of which may make intervening fixes to problems redundant. A major upgrade or release usually supersedes all preceding minor upgrades, releases and emergency fixes.

Minor software releases and hardware upgrades, normally containing small enhancements and fixes, some of which may have already been issued as emergency fixes. A minor upgrade or release usually supersedes all preceding emergency fixes.

Emergency software and hardware fixes, normally containing the corrections to a small number of known problems.

Quiz

Q1: Which configuration is used to define the scope of a Release?

Ans: The DSL configuration

The different types of Release units are as follows:

- **Delta Release:** It is a release of only that part of software which has been changed. For example, security patches.

- **Full Release:** It means the entire software program is deployed. For example, a new version of an existing application.

- **Packaged Release:** It is a combination of many changes. For example, an operating system image which also contains specific applications.

Pop Quiz

Q1: Which request is used to replace something within the IT infrastructure?

Ans: Request for change

Q2: Which task is a Problem Management responsibility?

Ans: Approve all modifications done to the Known Error database

---

The Release categories consist of the new or changed software and/or hardware required to implement approved changes.

There are three building blocks of high performance service providers, which are as follows:

Market focus and position: The spotlight is on optimal scale within a market space. A market space is defined by a set of outcomes that customers want. It is the "where and how to compete" facet of a service strategy. High-performance service providers (even Type I and II providers) have amazing clearness when it comes to setting the strategic direction. They understand the dynamics of their market space and customers, and manage through appropriate strategies.

Distinctive capabilities: The spotlight is on creating and exploiting a set of unique capabilities that deliver a promised customer experience. It is about understanding the vital interchange between resources, capabilities, and value creation and capture. To create value, a service provider develops a formula for doing business that successfully translates a big idea regarding customer needs into a distinctive and cost-effective set of connected capabilities and resources to gratify those needs.

Performance anatomy: The spotlight is on creating cultural and organizational characteristics that swing service providers on the way to their goal of out-executing competing alternatives. Performance anatomy includes a set of organizational world views that are measurable by organizational leadership.

Pop Quiz

Q1: Which analysis is an illustration of Proactive Problem management?

Ans: A trend analysis

Q2: Which ITIL process is related with a Post Implementation Review?

Ans: Problem Management

Key Terms

- The two elements of a service's business value from customers' perspective are **Utility and Warranty**.

- Capabilities are types of assets, and organizations utilize them to construct value in the form of goods and services.

- **Resources** are types of assets and they are direct inputs for production.

- The **service pipeline** is one of the three phases of Service Portfolio.

- A **service catalog** is a list of services that an organization provides, often to its employees or customers.

- **Business Service** Catalogue includes details of all of the IT services delivered to customers.

- The **Business Case** is a justification for an important item of expenditure.

- **Risk concerns** the deviation of one or more results of one or more future events from their expected value.

- **Service Level Agreement** (frequently abbreviated as SLA) is a part of a service contract where the level of service is formally defined.

- An **agreement** is a meeting of minds between two or more legally competent parties, about their relative duties and rights regarding current or future performance.

- The **Supplier Manager** is responsible for ensuring that value for money is obtained from all suppliers.

- **Availability** is the most basic aspect of assuring value to customers.

- The **Service Knowledge Management System** is the central repository of the IT organization's data, information and knowledge.

- A **Configuration item** (CI) is an IT asset or a combination of IT assets that may depend and have relationships with other IT processes.

- **Configuration Management** (CM) is an Information Technology Infrastructure Library (ITIL) IT Service Management (ITSM) process.

- The **Definitive Software Library** (DSL) is one or more locations in which the definitive and approved versions of all software Configuration Items (CIs) are securely stored.

- The **Change Manager** authorizes and documents all changes in the IT Infrastructure and its components (CIs) to maintain a least amount of interruptive effects after the running operation.

- **Emergency Change Advisory Board** (ECAB) is a sub-set of the Change Advisory Board who makes decisions about high impact Emergency Changes.

- An **incident** is any event which is not part of the standard operation of a service and which causes, or may cause, an interruption to, or a reduction in, the quality of service.

- A **Service Request** is a request from a user for information, advice, a standard change, or access to an IT service.

- The **Problem Control** Process aims to handle problems in an efficient way.

- A **workaround** is a bypass of a known problem in a system.

- **ICT Operations Management** provides the day-to-day technical supervision of the ICT infrastructure.

- The **Reducing Balance method** of depreciation uses a set percentage for the asset value reduction every year.

Test Your Knowledge

Q1. Service management capabilities are influenced by the which of the following challenges that differentiate services from other systems of value creation such as manufacturing, mining, and agriculture:

1. Intangible nature of the output and intermediary products of service processes.

2. Demand is tightly coupled with customer's assets.

3. High-level of contact for producers and consumers of services.

4. Perishable nature of service output and service capacity.

Each correct answer represents a complete solution. Choose two.

A. 1 and 2 only

B. 1, 2, 3, and 4

C. 2, 3, and 4 only

D. 2 and 4

Q2. You work as a Project Manager for uCertify Inc. You are leading the analysis of a new project that may be initiated by your company. The analysis is a focus on the return on investment (ROI) for new programs that may be created if the project is initiated. What type of document are you creating for your company?

A. Project scope statement

B. Project charter

C. Business case

D. Statement of work

Q3. You have just completed scope verification for your project. This process creates three deliverables for the organization. Which one of the following is NOT an output of the scope verification process?

A. Accepted deliverables

B. Requested changes

C. Recommended corrective actions

D. Risk identification

Q4.   An assistant from the HR Department calls you to ask the Service Hours & Maintenance Slots for your ERP system. In which document will you most probably find this information?

   A.   Release Policy

   B.   Service Level Agreement

   C.   Service Level Requirements

   D.   Underpinning Contract

Q5.   Which of the following statements is the BEST description of an Operational Level Agreement (OLA)?

   A.   It is an agreement between the service provider and an external organization.

   B.   It is a document that describes business services to operational staff.

   C.   It is an agreement between the service provider and another part of the same organization.

   D.   It is a document that describes to a customer how services will be operated on a day-to-day basis.

Answer Explanation

A1.   Answer options B and D are correct.

Service management capabilities are influenced by the following challenges:

1. Intangible nature of the output and intermediary products of service processes: It is difficult to measure, control, and validate.

2. Demand is tightly coupled with customer's assets: It specifies that users' and other customers' assets such as processes, applications, documents, and transactions turn up with demand and excite service production.

3. High-level of contact for producers and consumers of services: It specifies minute or no buffer between the customer, the front-office, and back-office.

4. Perishable nature of service output and service capacity: It specifies that there is value for the customer in receiving assurance that the service will continue to be supplied with consistent quality. Providers require protecting a steady supply of demand from customers.

Answer options A and C are incorrect. Service management capabilities are influenced by all the mentioned points, i.e. 1, 2, 3, and 4.

A2.   Answer option C is correct.

You are likely creating a business case as the focus is on the return on investment if the project is initiated. The Business Case is a justification for an important item of expenditure. It includes information about cost, benefits, options, issues, risks, and potential problems. It is a decision support and planning tool that projects the expected outcome of a business action. It uses qualitative terms. A typically business case structure is as follows:

Introduction: It provides business objectives address.

Methods and assumptions: It specifies the boundaries of the business case.

Business impacts: It provides financial and non-financial business case results.

Risks and contingencies

Recommendations: It specifies specific actions.

Answer option A is incorrect. The project has not yet been initiated so this cannot be a project scope statement.

Answer option B is incorrect. The project charter is not the best answer in this instance because the focus of the study is on the return on investment for the project.

Answer option D is incorrect. A statement of work is not the best answer as that document defines the work that needs to be completed, where the work will take place, and other program- or project-specific information.

A3.   Answer option D is correct.

Risk identification is NOT an output of the verify scope process. Verify scope is a process of formalizing acceptance of the completed project deliverables. It is an inspection-driven process the stakeholders will complete to inspect the project scope deliverables. It is typically performed at the end of the phase and at the end of the project.

Answer option A is incorrect. Accepted deliverables is the primary goal of the verify scope process.

Answer option B is incorrect. Change requests can come from the verify scope process.

Answer option C is incorrect. Recommended corrective actions can come from the verify scope process.

A4.   Answer option B is correct.

You will most probably find this information in the Service Level Agreement document. Amongst other information, SLA contains information about the agreed Service Hours and maintenance slots for any particular Service.

Service Level Agreement (frequently abbreviated as SLA) is a part of a service contract where the level of service is formally defined. In practice, the term SLA is sometimes used to refer to the contracted delivery time (of the service) or performance.

Service Level Agreement (SLA) is a negotiated agreement between two parties where one is the customer and the other is the service provider. This can be a legally binding formal or informal 'contract'. Contracts between the Service Provider and other third parties are often (incorrectly) called SLAs, as the level of service has been set by the (principal) customer there can be no 'agreement' between third parties (these agreements are simply a 'contract'). Operating Level Agreements or OLA(s) however, may be used by internal groups to support SLA(s).

Answer option A is incorrect. Release Policy is a set of rules for deploying releases into the live operational environment, defining different approaches for releases depending on their urgency and impact.

Answer option C is incorrect. The Service Level Requirements document contains the requirements for a service from the client viewpoint, defining detailed service level targets, mutual responsibilities, and other requirements specific to a certain group of customers.

Answer option D is incorrect. Underpinning Contract (UC) is a contract between an IT service provider and a third party. In another way, it is an agreement between the IT organization and an external provider about the delivery of one or more services. The third party provides services that support the delivery of a service to a customer. The Underpinning Contract defines targets and responsibilities that are required to meet agreed Service Level targets in an SLA.

A5. Answer option C is correct.

An Operational Level Agreement (OLA) defines the interdependent relationships among the internal support groups of an organization working to support a Service Level Agreement. The agreement describes the responsibilities of each internal support group toward other support groups, including the process and timeframe for delivery of their services. The objective of the OLA is to present a clear, concise, and measurable description of the service provider's internal support relationships. OLA is sometimes expanded to other phrases but they all have the same meaning:

- Organizational Level Agreement
- Operating Level Agreement
- Operations Level Agreement

Answer options A, B, and D are incorrect. It is important to recognize that OLA(s) are not a substitute for an SLA (Service Level Agreement). The purpose of the OLA is very much to help ensure that the underpinning activities that are performed by a number of support team components are clearly aligned to provide the intended SLA.

If the underpinning OLA(s) are not in place, it is often very difficult for organizations to go back and engineer agreements between the support teams to deliver the SLA. OLA(s) have to be seen as the foundation of good practice and common agreement, the sum of which may contribute to an SLA.

Chapter 4 - Key Principles and Models

Overview

The purpose of this unit is to help the candidate to comprehend and account for the key principles and models of Service Management and to balance some of the opposing forces within Service Management. Specifically, candidates must be able to:

- Service Strategy

- Describe basics of Value Creation through Services

- Service Design

- Understand the importance of People, Processes, Products and Partners

- for Service Management

- Understand the five major aspects of Service Design:

  - Service Portfolio Design

  - Identification of Business Requirements, definition of Service

  - Requirements and design of Services

  - Technology and architectural design

  - Process design

  - Measurement design

- Continual Service Improvement

  - Explain the Plan, Do, Check and Act (PDCA) Model to control and manage   quality

  - Explain the Continual Service Improvement Model

  - Understand the role of measurement for Continual Service Improvement and explain the following key elements:

  - The role of KPIs in the Improvement Process

  - Baselines

- Types of metrics (technology metrics, process metrics, service metrics)

The recommended study period for this unit is minimum 1.5 hours.

Key Points

Service Strategy

The IT Steering Group (ISG) is a formal group that is accountable for ensuring that the Business and the IT Service provider strategies and plans are very much associated with each other. It takes in senior representatives from the Business and the IT Service provider. IT Steering Group (ISG) sets the direction and strategy for IT Services. It includes members of senior management from business and IT. It reviews the business and IT strategies in order to make sure that they are aligned. It also sets priorities of service development programs/ projects.

The Service Portfolio Manager decides on a strategy to serve customers in co-operation with the IT Steering Group, and develops the service provider's offerings and capabilities.

Service Design

The Capacity Manager is responsible for ensuring that services and infrastructure are competent to deliver the agreed capacity and performance targets in a cost effective and timely manner. He considers all resources required to deliver the service, and plans for short, medium, and long term business requirements.

The Application Analysts and Architects are responsible for matching requirements to application specifications. They are responsible for designing applications required to provide a service. They include the specification of technologies, application architectures, and data structures as a basis for application development or customization. The specific activities are as follows:

- Working with users, sponsors, and all other stakeholders to decide the developing needs.

- Performing cost-benefit analyses to decide the means to meet up the declared requirement.

- Input into the design of configuration data required to handle and track the application effectively.

- Developing Operational Models that will make sure optimal use of resources and the appropriate level of performance.

- Ensuring that applications are designed to be efficiently managed given the organization's technology architecture, available skills, and tools.

- Developing and maintaining standards for application sizing, performance, modeling, etc.

- Generating a set of acceptance test requirements, mutually with the designers, test engineers, and the users.

- Working with Technical Management to decide the utmost level of system requirements necessary to meet up the business requirements within financial plan and technology constraints.

Technical Analysts/Architects is a term that refers to any staff member in Technical Management who performs the activities, excluding the daily operational actions. The Technical Analyst/Architect is responsible for designing infrastructure components and systems required to provide a service. This includes the specification of technologies and products as a basis for their procurement and customization. The roles of Technical Analysts/Architects are as follows:

- Working with Application Management and other areas in Technical Management to decide the utmost level of system requirements necessary to meet the requirements within budget and technology constraints.

- Working with users, sponsors, Application Management, and all other stakeholders to decide their developing needs.

- Performing cost-benefit analyses to decide the appropriate means to meet the declared requirements.

- Developing Operational Models that will ensure optimal use of resources and the appropriate level of performance.

- Ensuring the consistent performance of the infrastructure to deliver the required level of service to the business.

- Defining all tasks required to manage the infrastructure and ensuring that these tasks are performed appropriately.

- Input into the design of configuration data required to administer and track the application effectively.

The Service Owner is responsible for delivering a particular service within the agreed service levels. He acts as the counterpart of the Service Level Manager when negotiating Operational Level Agreements (OLAs). Often, the Service Owner will lead a team of technical specialists or an internal support unit.

Technical Analysts/Architects is a term that is referring to any staff member in Technical Management who performs the activities, excluding the daily operational actions. The Technical Analyst/Architect is responsible for designing infrastructure components and systems required to provide a service. This includes the specification of technologies and products as a basis for their procurement and customization.

The IT Security Manager is responsible for ensuring the confidentiality, integrity, and availability of an organization's assets, information, data, and IT services.

The IT Architect defines a blueprint for the future development of the technological landscape, taking into account the service strategy and newly available technologies.

Continual Service Improvement

There are four commonly used terms when discussing service improvement outcomes, which are as follows:

- **Improvements:** It is the outcome that is once compared to the earlier state, which shows a computable increase in a desirable metric or decrease in an undesirable metric.

- **Benefits:** It is the profit achieved through realization of improvements.

- **Return On Investment (ROI):** It is the difference between the benefit achieved and the amount spent to achieve that benefit, it is expressed as a percentage.

- **Value On Investment (VOI):** It is the extra value produced by establishment of benefits that include long-term outcomes. ROI is a sub-component of VOI.

The Service Improvement Plan (SIP) is a formal plan to implement improvements to services and IT processes. The SIP is used to manage and log improvement initiatives triggered by Continual Service Improvement. Generally, improvement initiatives are either of the following:

- Internal initiatives pursued by the service provider on his own behalf, for example to improve processes or make better use of resources.

- Initiatives which require the customer's cooperation, for example if some of the agreed service levels are found to be no longer adequate.

A Service Improvement Plan (SIP) has costs associated with executing the following activities:

- Staff resources trained in the right skill sets to support ITSM processes

- Tools for monitoring, gathering, processing, analyzing, and presenting data

- Constant internal/external assessments studies

- Service improvements either to services or service management process

- Management time to review, recommend, and monitor CSI progress

- Communication and understanding campaigns to change behaviors and ultimately culture

- Training and development on CSI activities

Baselines are important beginning points for highlighting improvement. They work as markers or starting points for future evaluation. Baselines are also used to set up an initial data point to decide whether a service or process needs to be improved. As a result, it is essential that baselines are documented, recognized, and accepted throughout the organization. They have to be established at each level, strategic goals and objectives, tactical process maturity, operational metrics, and KPIs. If a baseline is not initially created then the first measurement efforts will become the baseline.

There are four reasons to monitor and measure value to business, which are as follows:

- **Validate:** It is used for monitoring and measuring to validate earlier decisions.

- **Direct:** It is used for monitoring and measuring to set path for activities in order to meet up targets. It is the most common reason for monitoring and measuring.

- **Justify:** It is used for monitoring and measuring to justify with realistic evidence or proof that a course of action is needed.

- **Intervene:** It is used for monitoring and measuring to identify a point of intervention including successive changes and corrective actions.

The DIKW Hierarchy, also known variously as the "Wisdom Hierarchy", the "Knowledge Hierarchy", the "Information Hierarchy", or the "Knowledge Pyramid". It refers loosely to a class of models for representing purported structural and/or functional relationships between data, information, knowledge, and wisdom. Typically information is defined in terms of data, knowledge in terms of information, and wisdom in terms of knowledge.

> **Note**: Not all versions of the DIKW model reference all four components (earlier versions not including data, later versions omitting or downplaying wisdom), and some include additional components. In addition to a hierarchy and a pyramid, the DIKW model has also been characterized as a chain, as a framework, and as a continuum.

- Benchmarking is also recognized as Best Practice Benchmarking or Process Benchmarking. It is a process used in management and mostly useful for strategic management. It is the process of comparing the business processes and performance metrics including cost, cycle time, productivity, or quality to another that is widely considered to be an industry standard benchmark or best practice. It allows organizations to develop plans on how to implement best practice with the aim of increasing some aspect of performance.

- Benchmarking might be a one-time event, although it is frequently treated as a continual process in which organizations continually seek out to challenge their practices. It allows organizations to develop plans on how to make improvements or adapt specific best practices, usually with the aim of increasing some aspect of performance.

- Capability Maturity Model Integration (CMMI) was created by Software Engineering Institute (SEI). CMMI in software engineering and organizational development is a process improvement approach that provides organizations with the essential elements for effective process improvement. It can be used to guide process improvement across a project, a division, or an entire organization. CMMI can help integrate traditionally separate organizational functions, set process improvement goals and priorities, provide guidance for quality processes, and provide a point of reference for appraising current processes. CMMI is now the de facto standard for measuring the maturity of any process. Organizations can be assessed against the CMMI model using Standard CMMI Appraisal Method for Process Improvement (SCAMPI).

- Six Sigma is a business management strategy, initially implemented by Motorola. As of 2009 it enjoys widespread application in many sectors of industry, although its application is not without controversy.

Six Sigma seeks to improve the quality of process outputs by identifying and removing the causes of defects and variability in manufacturing and business processes. It uses a set of quality management methods, including statistical methods, and creates a special infrastructure of people within the organization ("Black Belts", "Green Belts", etc.) who are experts in these methods. Each Six Sigma project carried out within an organization follows a defined sequence of steps and has quantified financial targets (cost reduction or profit increase). The often used Six Sigma symbol is as follows:

The phases of the DMAIC project methodology are as follows:

- Define high-level project goals and the current process.

- Measure key aspects of the current process and collect relevant data.

- Analyze data to verify cause-and-effect relationships. Determine what the relationships are, and attempt to ensure that all factors have been considered.

- Improve or optimize the process based upon data analysis using techniques like Design of experiments.

- Control to ensure that any deviations from target are corrected before they result in defects. Set up pilot runs to establish process capability, move on to production, set up control mechanisms, and continuously monitor the process.

The phases of the DMADV project methodology are as follows:

- Define design goals that are consistent with customer demands and the enterprise strategy.

- Measure and identify CTQs (characteristics that are Critical To Quality), product capabilities, production process capability, and risks.

- Analyze to develop and design alternatives, create a high-level design, and evaluate design capability to select the best design.

- Design details, optimize the design, and plan for design verification. This phase may require simulations.

- Verify the design, set up pilot runs, implement the production process and hand it over to the process owners.

Pop Quiz

Q1: What is the FIRST STEP in the 7 Step Improvement Process?

Ans: Define what you must measure

Q2: Which is NOT a step in the Continual Service Improvement model?

Ans: Is there a budget?

- COBIT stands for Control Objectives for Information and Related Technology. COBIT is a set of best practices (framework) for information technology (IT) management created by the Information Systems Audit and Control Association (ISACA), and the IT Governance Institute (ITGI) in 1996. COBIT provides managers, auditors, and IT users with a set of generally accepted measures, indicators, processes, and best practices to assist them in maximizing the benefits derived through the use of information technology and developing appropriate IT governance and control in a company.

The processes defined by COBIT to support CSI are as follows:

- ME1: Monitor and evaluate IT performance

- ME2: Monitor and evaluate internal control

- ME3: Ensure regulatory compliance

- ME4: Provide IT governance

The COBIT process domain 'Monitor and Evaluate' (ME) defines the processes required to evaluate current IT performance, IT controls, and regulatory compliance. These processes consider many factors that can compel the need for improvement, factors, such as a need to improve performance and handle risks more effectively through better regulatory compliance.

The business questions for CSI are as follows:

- Where are we now? This is a question that each and every business should start asking as it creates a baseline of data for services presently being delivered.

- What do we want? This is a question that is frequently asked in terms of business requirements such as 100% availability.

- What do we actually need? This is a question that asks when Service Level Management starts discussing with the business they might understand.

- What can we afford? This is a question that often moves the business from looking at what people want, to what people actually need.

- What will we get? This is a question that is often defined in a SLA. It defines the service and service levels.

- What did we get? This is a question that is documented through monitoring, reporting, and reviewing of service level achievements.

These are some key questions that will assist the business in making decisions about whether a CSI initiative is warranted or not. These questions are frequently asked from a business and IT perspective. In case of not understanding some of these questions can lead to challenges, supposed poor service or in a number of cases actual deprived service.

The types of metrics are as follows:

- **Technology metrics:** These are often associated with component and application-based metrics.

- **Process metrics:** These are used in the form of CSFs, KPIs, and activity metrics for the service management processes. These metrics are used to find out the overall health of a process. KPIs can assist to answer four key questions that are about quality, performance, value, and compliance of following the process. CSI can use these metrics as input in identifying improvement opportunities for every process.

- **Service metrics:** These metrics are the results of the end-to-end service. Component metrics are used to compute the service metrics.

It is essential to consider that these three types of metrics an organization will need to support CSI activities and other process activities.

Continual Service Improvement (CSI) align and realign IT Services to changing business needs by identifying and implementing improvements to the IT services that support the Business Processes. The perspective of CSI on improvement is the business perspective of service quality, even though CSI aims to improve process effectiveness, efficiency and cost effectiveness of the IT processes through the whole lifecycle. To manage improvement, CSI should clearly define what should be controlled and measured.

Assistance is provided for linking improvement efforts and outcomes with Service Strategy, Design, and Transition. A closed-loop feedback system, based on the Plan-Do-Check-Act (PDCA) model specified in ISO/IEC 20000, is established and capable of receiving inputs for change from any planning perspective. CSI needs to be treated just like any other service practice. There needs to be upfront planning, training and awareness, ongoing scheduling, roles created, ownership assigned, and activities identified to be successful. CSI must be planned and scheduled as process with defined activities, inputs, outputs, roles, and reporting.

The Continual Service Improvement (CSI) Manager is responsible for managing improvements to IT Service Management processes and IT services. He will continually measure the performance of the service provider and design improvements to processes, services and infrastructure in order to increase efficiency, effectiveness, and cost effectiveness.

Service Evaluation is used to evaluate service quality on a regular basis. This includes identifying areas where the targeted service levels are not reached and holding regular talks with business to make sure that the agreed service levels are still in line with business needs. It is part of Continual Service Improvement and the owner of Service Evaluation is the CSI Manager. The sub-processes of Service Evaluation are as follows:

- Complaints Management

- Customer Satisfaction Survey

- Service Review

Process Evaluation is used to evaluate processes on a regular basis. This includes identifying areas where the targeted process metrics are not reached, and holding regular bench markings, audits, maturity assessments, and reviews. It is part of Continual Service Improvement and the owner of Process Evaluation is the Process Manager. The sub-processes of Process Evaluation are as follows:

- Process Management Support

- Process Benchmarking

- Process Maturity Assessment

- Process Audit

- Process Controlling and Review

- Definition of Improvement Initiatives is used to define specific initiatives aimed at improving services and processes, based on the results of service and process evaluation. The resulting initiatives are either internal initiatives pursued by the service provider on his own behalf, or initiatives which require the customer's cooperation. It is part of Continual Service Improvement and the owner of Definition of Improvement Initiatives is the CSI Manager.

- CSI Monitoring is used to verify whether improvement initiatives are proceeding according to plan, and to introduce corrective measures where necessary. It is part of Continual Service Improvement and the owner of CSI Monitoring is the CSI Manager.

- Benchmarking is a moderately expensive process, but most organizations find that it more than pays for itself.

  Process benchmarking is a method through which the initiating firm focuses its observation and investigation of business processes with a goal of identifying and observing the best practices from one or more benchmark firms.

  Operational benchmarking includes everything from staffing and productivity to office flow and analysis of procedures performed.

  Improvements, Benefits, Return On Investment (ROI), and Value On Investment are commonly used terms when discussing service improvement outcomes.

  A Service Improvement Plan (SIP) has costs associated with executing the activities.

  Baselines are important beginning points for highlighting improvement. They work as markers or starting points for future evaluation.

  There are four reasons to monitor and measure value to business: Validate, Direct, Justify, and Intervene.

  Benchmarking is also recognized as Best Practice Benchmarking or Process Benchmarking. It is a process used in management and mostly useful for strategic management. It is the process of comparing the business processes and performance metrics including cost, cycle time, productivity, or quality.

  Capability Maturity Model Integration (CMMI) was created by Software Engineering Institute (SEI). CMMI in software engineering and organizational development is a process improvement approach that provides organizations with the essential elements for effective process improvement.

The phases of the DMAIC project methodology are Define, Measure, Analyze, Improve, and Control.

The types of metrics are as follows:

- Technology metrics

- Process metrics

- Service metrics

Process Evaluation is used to evaluate processes on a regular basis. This includes identifying areas where the targeted process metrics are not reached, and holding regular bench markings, audits, maturity assessments, and reviews.

Process Benchmarking is used to evaluate processes in relation to comparable organizations, with the aim of identifying shortcomings and developing plans for process improvement.

A schedule baseline provides a method to track project progress during project execution against what was planned.

CSI Monitoring is used to verify if improvement initiatives are proceeding according to plan, and to introduce corrective measures where necessary.

Continual Service Improvement (CSI) aligns and realigns IT Services to changing business needs by identifying and implementing improvements to the IT services that support the Business Processes.

The most commonly used terms when discussing service improvement outcomes are Improvement, Benefits, ROI, and VOI.

The basic steps involved in Continuity Management are as follows:

- Prioritizing the businesses to be recovered by conducting a Business Impact Analysis (BIA).

- Performing a Risk Assessment (aka Risk Analysis) for each of the IT Services to identify the assets, threats, vulnerabilities, and countermeasures for each service.

- Evaluating the options for recovery.

- Producing the Contingency Plan.

- Testing, reviewing, and revising the plan on a regular basis.

PDCA (Plan-Do-Check-Act) Model

PDCA (Plan-Do-Check-Act) is an iterative four-step problem-solving process typically used in business process improvement. It is also known as the Deming Cycle, Shewhart cycle, Deming Wheel, or Plan-Do-Study-Act.

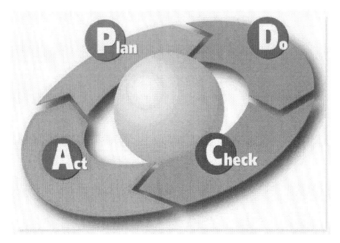

Plan:

It establishes the objectives and processes necessary to deliver results in accordance with the expected output. By making the expected output the focus, it differs from other techniques in the sense that the completeness and accuracy of the specification is also part of the improvement.

Do:

It implements the new processes, often on a small scale if possible.

Check:

It measures the new processes and compares the results against the expected results to ascertain any differences.

Act:

It analyzes the differences to determine their cause. Each will be part of either one or more of the P-D-C-A steps. Determine where to apply changes that will include improvement. When a pass through these four steps does not result in the need to improve, refine the scope to which PDCA is applied until there is a plan that involves improvement.

Use:

The PDCA cycle is designed to be used as a dynamic model. The completion of one turn of the cycle flows into the beginning of the next. Following in the spirit of continuous quality improvement, the process can always be reanalyzed and a new test of change can begin.

Additional Information:

PDCA was made popular by Dr. W. Edwards Deming, who is considered by many to be the father of modern quality control; however it was always referred to by him as the "Shewhart cycle." Later in Deming's career, he modified PDCA to "Plan-Do-Study-Act" (PDSA) so as to better describe his recommendations.

The concept of PDCA comes out of the Scientific Method, as developed from the work of Francis Bacon. The scientific method can be written as "hypothesis", "experiment", "evaluation" or Plan, Do, and Check. Shewhart described manufacture under "control" under statistical control as a three step process of specification, production, and inspection. He also specifically related this to the Scientific Method of hypothesis, experiment, and evaluation.

Shewhart says that a statistician "must help to change the demand [for goods] by showing how to close up the tolerance range and to improve the quality of goods." Clearly, Shewhart intended the analyst to take action based on the conclusions of the evaluation.

According to Deming during his lectures in Japan in the early 1950's the Japanese participants shortened the steps to the now traditional Plan, Do, Check, Act. Deming preferred Plan, Do, Study, Act because 'Study' has connotations in English closer to Shewhart's intent than "Check."

A fundamental principle of the scientific method and PDSA is iteration, once a hypothesis is confirmed, executing the cycle again will extend the knowledge further. Repeating the PDSA cycle can bring us closer to the goal, usually a perfect operation, and output.

In Six Sigma programs, the PDSA cycle is called "Define-Measure-Analyze-Improve-Control" (DMAIC). The iterative nature of the cycle must be explicitly added to the DMAIC procedure.

PDSA should be repeatedly implemented in spirals of increasing knowledge of the system that converge on the ultimate goal, each cycle closer than the previous. One can envision an open coil spring, with each loop being one cycle of the Scientific Method (PDSA), and each complete cycle indicating an increase in our knowledge of the system under study. This approach is based on the belief that our knowledge and skills are limited, but improving. Especially at the start of a project, key information may not be known; the PDSA provides feedback to justify our guesses and increase our knowledge. Rather than enter "analysis paralysis" to get it perfect the first time, it is better to be approximately right than exactly wrong. With the improved knowledge, we may choose to refine or alter the goal. Certainly, the PDSA approach can bring us closer to whatever goal we choose.

The power of Deming's concept lies in its apparent simplicity. The concept of feedback in the Scientific Method, in the abstract sense, is today firmly rooted in education. While apparently easy to understand, it is often difficult to accomplish on an on-going basis due to the intellectual difficulty of judging one's proposals on the basis of measured results. Many people have an emotional fear of being shown "wrong," even by objective measurements. To avoid such comparisons, we may instead cite complacency, distractions, loss of focus, lack of commitment, re-assigned priorities, lack of resources, etc.

CSI 7-Step Improvement Process

The CSI 7-step Improvement Process is as follows:

Define what should be measured:

At the start of the Service Lifecycle, Service Strategy and Service Design should have identified this information. Later, CSI can start its cycle yet again at *"Where are we now?"* It identifies the perfect situation for both the Business and IT.

Define what can be measured:

It is related to the CSI activities of *"Where do we want to be?"* once the new service level requirements of the business, IT capabilities, and available budgets are identified. CSI can perform a breach analysis to identify the opportunities for improvement and answering the question "How do we get there?"

Gathering the data:

In order to answer the *"Did we get there?"* question, data must be gathered first. Data is gathered based on goals and objectives recognized. The data is raw and no conclusions are drawn at this point.

Processing the data:

The data is processed in alignment with the given CSFs and KPIs. This way timeframes are coordinated, unaligned data is streamlined and made consistent, and gaps in the data are recognized. This step processes data from multiple dissimilar sources into an *'apples to apples'* contrast.

Analyzing the data:

The data becomes information as it is analyzed to recognize service gaps, trends, and the impact on business. It is the analyzing step that is often unnoticed or forgotten in the rush to present the data to management.

Presenting and using the information:

The answer to *"Did we get there?"* is formatted and communicated in the way required to present to the various stakeholders an accurate results of the improvement efforts. Knowledge is presented to the business in a way that reflects their needs and assists them in shaping the next steps.

Implementing corrective action:

In order to optimize, improve, and correct services, the gained knowledge is used. Managers can identify issues and provide solutions. Following this step the organization establishes a new baseline and the cycle begins a further.

Pop Quiz

Q1: Which is the first activity of the CSI model?

Ans: Understand the vision of the business

Key Terms

- The **IT Steering Group** (ISG) is a formal group that is accountable for ensuring that the Business and the IT Service provider strategies and plans are very much associated with each other.

- The **Capacity Manager** is responsible for ensuring that services and infrastructure are competent to deliver the agreed capacity and performance targets in a cost effective and timely manner.

- **Technical Analysts/Architects** is a term that refers to any staff member in Technical Management who performs the activities, excluding the daily operational actions.

- The **Service Improvement Plan** (SIP) is a formal plan to implement improvements to services and IT processes.

- **Baselines** are important beginning points for highlighting improvement.

- **COBIT** stands for Control Objectives for Information and Related Technology. COBIT is a set of best practices (framework) for information technology (IT) management created by the Information Systems Audit and Control Association (ISACA), and the IT Governance Institute (ITGI) in 1996.

- **Continual Service Improvement** (CSI) align and realign IT Services to changing business needs by identifying and implementing improvements to the IT services that support the Business Processes. PDCA (Plan-Do-Check-Act) is an iterative four-step problem-solving process typically used in business process improvement.

- **PDCA** (Plan-Do-Check-Act) is an iterative four-step problem-solving process typically used in business process improvement.

Test Your Knowledge

Q1.   Which volume provides guidance on clarification and prioritization of service-provider investments in services?

   A.   Service Strategy

   B.   Service Design

   C.   Service Operation

   D.   Service Management

Q2.   Which process of the Service Strategy is used to decide on a strategy to serve customers, and to develop the service provider's offerings and capabilities?

   A.   Financial Management

   B.   Demand Management

   C.   Service Portfolio Management

   D.   Supplier Management

Q3.   With which of the following activities are the Service Improvement Plan (SIP) costs associated?

   1.   Staff resources trained in the right skill sets to support ITSM processes

   2.   Tools for monitoring, gathering, processing, analyzing, and presenting data

   3.   Application Development and Customization

   4.   Constant internal assessments studies

   5.   Service improvements either to services or service management process

   6.   Training and development on CSI activities

   Each correct answer represents a complete solution. Choose all that apply.

   A.   3, 4, 5, and 6 only

   B.   1 and 2

C.   1, 2, 4, 5, and 6 only

D.   2, 4, and 6 only

E.   1, 3, 5, and 6 only

Q4.   Which of the following have to be established at each level, strategic goals and objectives, tactical process maturity, operational metrics, and KPIs?

A.   IT Architecture Management

B.   Capability Maturity Model Integration

C.   Baselines

D.   Capabilities

Q5.   Which of the following is a process improvement approach that provides organizations with the essential elements for effective process improvement and guides process improvement across a project, a division, or an entire organization?

A.   COBIT

B.   Capability Maturity Model Integration

C.   Service Portfolio

D.   Six Sigma

Answer Explanation

A1.   Answer option A is correct.

As the center and origin point of the ITIL Service Lifecycle, the ITIL Service Strategy volume provides guidance on clarification and prioritization of service-provider investments in services. More generally, Service Strategy focuses on helping IT organizations improve and develop over the long term.

Answer option B is incorrect. Service Design provides good practice guidance on the design of IT services, processes, and other aspects of the service management effort. It covers design principles and methods for converting strategic objectives into portfolios of services and service assets.

Answer option C is incorrect. Service Operation is the best practice for achieving the delivery of agreed levels of services both to end-users and the customers (where customers refer to those individuals who pay for the service and negotiate the SLAs). Service Operation is the part of the lifecycle where the services and value are actually directly delivered.

Answer option D is incorrect. Service Management is not a volume. However, Service Management is integrated into Supply Chain Management as the joint between the actual sales and the customer. The aim of high performance Service Management is to optimize the service-intensive supply chains, which are usually more complex than the typical finished-goods supply chain.

A2.   Answer option C is correct.

Service Portfolio Management is used to decide on a strategy to serve customers, and to develop the service provider's offerings and capabilities. It is part of Service Strategy. The Owner of Service Portfolio Management Process is the Service Portfolio Manager. Managing services as a portfolio is a new concept in ITIL V3. ITIL V3 introduces strategic thinking about how the Service Portfolio should be developed in the future. The following are the Sub-Processes of Service Portfolio Management:

- Strategic Service Assessment

- Service Strategy Definition

- Service Portfolio Update

- Strategic Planning

Answer option A is incorrect. Financial Management is used to manage the service provider's budgeting, accounting, and charging requirements.

Answer option B is incorrect. Demand management is a planning methodology use to manage forecasted demand.

Answer option D is incorrect. Supplier Management is used to ensure that all contracts with suppliers support the needs of the business, and that all suppliers meet their contractual commitments.

A3. Answer options B and C are correct.

A Service Improvement Plan (SIP) has costs associated with executing the following activities:

- Staff resources trained in the right skill sets to support ITSM processes

- Tools for monitoring, gathering, processing, analyzing, and presenting data

- Constant internal/external assessments studies

- Service improvements either to services or service management process

- Management time to review, recommend, and monitor CSI progress

- Communication and understanding campaigns to change behaviors and ultimately culture

- Training and development on CSI activities

Answer options A, D, and E are incorrect. Application Development and Customization is used to make available applications and systems which provide the required functionality for IT services. It includes the development and maintenance of custom applications as well as the customization of products from software vendors. It is part of Service Transition and the owner of Application Development and Customization is the Application Developer.

Note: *ITIL does not provide a detailed explanation of all aspects of Application Development. Rather, it highlights the most important activities and assists in identifying interfaces with other Service Management processes.*

A4. Answer option C is correct.

Baselines are important beginning points for highlighting improvement. They work as markers or starting points for future evaluation. Baselines are also used to set up an initial data point to decide whether a service or process needs to be improved. As a result, it is essential that baselines are documented, recognized, and accepted throughout the organization. They have to be established at each level, strategic goals and objectives, tactical process maturity, operational metrics, and KPIs. If a baseline is not initially created then the first measurement efforts will become the baseline.

Answer option A is incorrect. IT Architecture Management is used to define a blueprint for the future development of the technological landscape, taking into account the service strategy and newly available technologies. It is part of Service Design and the owner of IT Architecture Management is the IT Architect. A well-defined architecture blueprint is very important for IT organizations.

Answer option B is incorrect. Capability Maturity Model Integration (CMMI) was created by Software Engineering Institute (SEI). CMMI in software engineering and organizational development is a process improvement approach that provides organizations with the essential elements for effective process improvement. It can be used to guide process improvement across a project, a division, or an entire organization. CMMI can help integrate traditionally separate organizational functions, set process improvement goals and priorities, provide guidance for quality processes, and provide a point of reference for appraising current processes. CMMI is now the de facto standard for measuring the maturity of any process. Organizations can be assessed against the CMMI model using Standard CMMI Appraisal Method for Process Improvement (SCAMPI).

Answer option D is incorrect. Capabilities are types of assets, and organizations utilize them to construct value in the form of goods and services. They specify an organization's ability to control, coordinate, and deploy resources to produce value. They are usually experience-driven, knowledge-intensive, information-based, and firmly embedded within an organization's people, systems, processes, and technologies.

A5. Answer option B is correct.

Capability Maturity Model Integration (CMMI) was created by Software Engineering Institute (SEI). CMMI in software engineering and organizational development is a process improvement approach that provides organizations with the essential elements for effective process improvement. It can be used to guide process improvement across a project, a division, or an entire organization. CMMI can help integrate traditionally separate organizational functions, set process improvement goals and priorities, provide guidance for quality processes, and provide a point of reference for appraising current processes. CMMI is now the de facto standard for measuring the maturity of any process. Organizations can be assessed against the CMMI model using Standard CMMI Appraisal Method for Process Improvement (SCAMPI).

Answer option A is incorrect. COBIT stands for Control Objectives for Information and Related Technology. COBIT is a set of best practices (framework) for information technology (IT) management created by the Information Systems Audit and Control Association (ISACA), and the IT Governance Institute (ITGI) in 1996. COBIT provides managers, auditors, and IT users with a set of generally accepted measures, indicators, processes, and best practices to assist them in maximizing the benefits derived through the use of information technology and developing appropriate IT governance and control in a company.

Answer option C is incorrect. Service Portfolio represents a complete list of the services managed by a service provider; some of these services are visible to the customers, while others are not. It contains present contractual commitments, new service development, and ongoing service improvement plans initiated by Continual Service Improvement. It also includes third-party services, which are an integral part of service offerings to customers. Service Portfolio is divided into three phases, which are as follows:

• Service Pipeline

• Service Catalogue

• Retired Services

Answer option D is incorrect. Six Sigma is a business management strategy, initially implemented by Motorola. As of 2009 it enjoys widespread application in many sectors of industry, although its application is not without controversy.

Six Sigma seeks to improve the quality of process outputs by identifying and removing the causes of defects and variability in manufacturing and business processes. It uses a set of quality management methods, including statistical methods, and creates a special infrastructure of people within the organization ("Black Belts", "Green Belts", etc.) who are experts in these methods. Each Six Sigma project carried out within an organization follows a defined sequence of steps and has quantified financial targets (cost reduction or profit increase). The often used Six Sigma symbol is as follows:

Chapter 5 - Processes

Overview

The purpose of this unit is to help the candidate understand how the Service Management processes contribute to the Service Lifecycle, to explain the high level objectives, scope, basic concepts, activities and challenges for five of the core processes, and to state the objectives and some of the basic concepts for thirteen of the remaining processes including how they relate to each other. The list of activities to be included from each process is the minimum required and should not be taken as an exhaustive list. Specifically, candidates must be able to:

Service Strategy

State the objectives and basic concepts for:

- Demand Management

  The following list must be covered:

  - Challenges in managing demand for Services

  - Activity-based Demand Management (Patterns of business activity (PBAs)

  - Business activity patterns and user profiles

- Financial Management

  - Business case

Service Design

Explain the high level objectives, basic concepts, process activities and relationships for:

- Service Level Management (SLM)

  The following list must be covered:

  - Service-based SLA

  - Multi-level SLAs

  - Service level requirements (SLRs)

- SLAM chart

- Service review

- Service improvement plan (SIP)

State the objectives and basic concepts for:

Service Catalogue Management

Availability Management

- Service availability

- Component availability

- Reliability

- Maintainability

- Serviceability

Information Security Management (ISM)

- Security framework

- Information security policy

- Information security management system (ISMS)

Supplier Management

- Supplier Contract Database (SCD)

Capacity Management

- Capacity plan

- Business capacity management

- Service capacity management

- Component capacity management

IT Service Continuity Management

- Business Continuity Plans

- Business Continuity Management

- Business Impact Analysis

- Risk Analysis

Service Transition

Explain the high level objectives, basic concepts, process activities and relationships for:

- Change Management

  - Types of change request

  - Change process models and workflows

  - Standard change

  - Remediation Planning

  - Change Advisory Board / Emergency Change Advisory Board

- Service Asset and Configuration Management (SACM), to include:

  - The Configuration Model

  - Configuration items

  - Configuration Management System (CMS)

  - Definitive Media Library

  - Configuration baseline

State the objectives and basic concepts for:

- Release and Deployment Management

- Knowledge Management

- DIKW & SKMS

Service Operation

Explain the high level objectives, basic concepts, process activities and relationships for:

- Incident Management

- Problem Management

State the objectives and basic concepts for:

- Event Management

- Request Fulfilments

- Access Management

The recommended study period for this unit is minimum 10.0 hours.

Key Points

Service Strategy (State the objectives and basic concepts for)

Service Strategy is the center and origin point of the ITIL Service Lifecycle. It provides guidance on how to design, develop, and implement service management not only as an organizational capability but also as a strategic asset. Service Strategy provides guidance on clarification and prioritization of service provider investments in services. More generally, Service Strategy focuses on helping IT organizations improve and develop over the long term. In both cases, Service Strategy relies largely upon a market-driven approach.

- Service Strategy is useful in the framework of Service Design, Service Transition, Service Operation, and Continual Service Improvement. Service Strategy ensures that organizations are in a position to deal with the costs and risks associated with their Service Portfolios. Service Strategy is set up for operational effectiveness as well as for distinctive performance. Decisions made with respect to Service Strategy have broad consequences including those with delayed effect.

- IT Financial Management is the discipline of ensuring that the IT infrastructure is obtained at the most effective price (which does not necessarily mean cheapest) and calculating the cost of providing IT services so that an organization can understand the costs of its IT services. Costs are divided into costing units: Equipment; Software; Organization (staff, overtime; accommodation; transfer costs (costs of 3rd party service providers). These costs are divided into Direct and Indirect costs and may be Capital or Ongoing. These costs may then be recovered from the customer of the service.

- Service Portfolio Management is used to decide on a strategy to serve customers, and to develop the service provider's offerings and capabilities. It is part of Service Strategy. The Owner of Service Portfolio Management Process is the Service Portfolio Manager. Managing services as a portfolio is a new concept in ITIL V3. ITIL V3 introduces strategic thinking about how the Service Portfolio should be developed in the future. The following are the Sub-Processes of Service Portfolio Management:

- Strategic Service Assessment

- Service Strategy Definition

- Service Portfolio Update

- Strategic Planning

The major cost types defined under Financial Management for IT Services contain Hardware, Software, Transfer, Accommodation, People, and External Services.

IT Financial Management is the discipline of ensuring that the IT infrastructure is obtained at the most effective price (which does not necessarily mean cheapest) and calculating the cost of providing IT services so that an organization can understand the costs of its IT services.

Business Planning Data is an important input for the Service Strategy and Service Design processes.

Service Strategy Definition is used to define the overall goals that the service provider should pursue in its development.

Service Design (Explain the high level objectives, basic concepts, process activities, and relationships)

Service Design provides good practice guidance on the design of IT services, processes, and other aspects of the service management effort. It covers design principles and methods for converting strategic objectives into portfolios of services and service assets. The scope of Service Design is not limited to new services. Significantly, design within ITIL is understood to encompass all elements relevant to technology service delivery, rather than focusing solely on design of the technology itself.

As such, Service Design addresses how a planned service solution interacts with the larger business and technical environments. Service management systems require supporting the service and processes, which interacts with the service, technology, and architecture required to support the service, and the supply chain required to support the planned service. Within ITIL, design work for an IT service is aggregated into a single Service Design Package (SDP). Service Design Packages

(SDP), along with other information about services, is managed within the Service Catalog.

- Service Level Management provides for continual identification, monitoring and review of the levels of IT services specified in the service level agreements (SLAs). It ensures that arrangements are in place with internal IT Support Providers and external suppliers in the form of Operational Level Agreements (OLAs) and Underpinning Contracts (UCs). The process involves assessing the impact of change upon service quality and SLAs. The Service Level Management process is in close relation with the operational processes to control their activities. The central role of Service Level Management makes it the natural place for metrics to be established and monitored against a benchmark.

    Note: Service Level Management is the primary interface with the customer (as opposed to the user, who is serviced by the Service Desk).

- Capacity Management is the discipline which ensures that IT infrastructure is supplied at the right time, in the right quantity, and at the right price. It also ensures that IT is used in the most proficient way. Capacity Management supports the optimum and cost effective provision of IT services by helping organizations match their IT resources to the business demands. The high-level activities are Application Sizing, Workload Management, Demand Management, Modeling, Capacity Planning, Resource Management, and Performance Management. Capacity management is made up of three sub processes:

    - Business Capacity Management (BCM)

    - Service Capacity Management (SCM)

    - Resource Capacity Management (RCM)

IT Service Continuity Management is the process by which plans are put in place and managed to ensure that IT Services can recover and continue should a serious incident occur. It is not just about reactive measures, but also about proactive measures - reducing the risk of a disaster in the first instance. Continuity Management is very important in the sense that many organizations will not do business with IT service providers if contingency planning is not practiced within the service provider's organization.

Continuity Management is regarded as the recovery of the IT infrastructure used to deliver IT Services, but many businesses these days practice the much further reaching process of Business Continuity Planning (BCP), to ensure that the whole end-to-end business process can continue should a serious incident occur.

Availability Management allows organizations to sustain the IT service availability to support the business at a justifiable cost. The high-level activities are Realize Availability Requirements, Compile Availability Plan, Monitor Availability, and Monitor Maintenance Obligations. Availability is usually calculated based on a model involving the Availability Ratio and techniques such as Fault Tree Analysis.

Availability Management is the ability of an IT component to perform at an agreed level over a period of time.

Reliability: How reliable is the service? Ability of an IT component to perform at an agreed level at described conditions.

Maintainability: The ability of an IT component to remain in, or be restored to an operational state.

Serviceability: The ability of an external supplier to maintain the availability of component or function under a third party contract.

Resilience: A measure of freedom from operational failure and a method of keeping services reliable. One popular method of resilience is redundancy.

Security: A service may have associated data. Security refers to the confidentiality, integrity, and availability of that data. Availability gives us the clear overview of the end to end availability of the system.

Pop Quiz

Q1: Which Service Design process makes the most use of data supplied by Demand Management?

Ans: Capacity Management

- Security Management describes the structured fitting of information security in the management organization. ITIL Security Management is based on the code of practice for information security management also known as ISO/IEC 17799.

A basic concept of the Security Management is the information security. The primary goal of information security is to guarantee safety of information. Safety is to be protected against risks. Security is the means to be safe against risks. When protecting information, it is the value of the information that has to be protected. These values are stipulated by the confidentiality, integrity and availability. Inferred aspects are privacy, anonymity and verifiability.

The current move towards ISO/IEC 27001 may require some revision to the ITIL Security Management best practices which are often claimed to be rich in content for physical security, but weak in areas such as software/application security and logical security in the ICT infrastructure.

The Service Level Manager is responsible for negotiating Service Level Agreements and ensuring that these are met. He makes sure that all IT Service Management processes, Operational Level Agreements, and Underpinning Contracts are appropriate for the agreed service level targets. The Service Level Manager also monitors and reports on service levels.

- Supplier Management is used to ensure that all contracts with suppliers support the needs of the business, and that all suppliers meet their contractual commitments. It is part of the Service Design. The owner of Supplier Management is the Supplier Manager. In ITIL V3, Supplier Management is part of the Service Design process to allow for a better integration into the Service Lifecycle. The sub-processes of Supplier Management are as follows:

  - Providing the Supplier Management Framework

  - Evaluation of New Suppliers and Contracts

  - Establishing New Suppliers and Contracts

  - Processing of Standard Orders

  - Supplier and Contract Review

  - Contract Renewal or Termination

- Service Catalogue Management is used to ensure that a Service Catalogue is produced and maintained, containing accurate information on all operational services and those being prepared to be run operationally. It provides vital information for all other Service Management processes: Service details, current status, and the services' interdependencies. It is part of Service Design and the owner of Service Catalogue Management is the Service Catalogue Manager.

- Service Catalogue Management was added as a new process in ITIL V3. In ITIL V2, the Service Level Management process mentioned the concept of a Service Catalogue.

- Risk Management is used to identify, assess, and control risks. It includes analyzing the value of assets to the business, identifying threats to those assets, and evaluating how vulnerable each asset is to those threats. Risk Management is part of Service Design and the owner of the Risk Management is the Risk Manager.

- Risks are addressed within several processes in ITIL V3; however, there is no dedicated Risk Management process. ITIL V3 calls for "coordinated risk assessment exercises", so at IT Process Maps we decided to assign clear responsibilities for managing risks.

- Compliance Management is used to ensure that IT services, processes and systems comply with enterprise policies, and legal requirements. It is part of Service Design and the owner of Compliance Management is the Compliance Manager. Compliance issues are addressed within several processes in ITIL V2 and ITIL V3; however, there is no dedicated Compliance Management process. Compliance is an increasingly important topic for IT organizations.

- IT Architecture Management is used to define a blueprint for the future development of the technological landscape, taking into account the service strategy and newly available technologies. It is part of Service Design and the owner of IT Architecture Management is the IT Architect. A well-defined architecture blueprint is very important for IT organizations.

- Component Capacity Management is used to manage, control and predict the performance, utilization and capacity of IT resources and individual IT components.

- A Capacity Plan is used to manage the resources required to deliver IT services. The plan contains scenarios for different predictions of business demand, and cost options to deliver the agreed service level targets.

- ITSCM Support sub-process is used to make sure that all members of IT staff with responsibilities for fighting disasters are aware of their exact duties.

- A Recovery Plan is created mainly by Availability and IT Service Continuity Management.

- The Business Continuity Strategy is prepared by the business and serves as a starting point for producing the IT Service Continuity Strategy.

- Resource Capacity Management is also known as Component Capacity Management. It is used to manage, control, and predict the performance, utilization, and capacity of IT resources and individual IT components.

- Supplier Management is used to ensure that all contracts with suppliers support the needs of the business, and that all suppliers meet their contractual commitments. It is part of the Service Design.

- Business Capacity Management, Service Capacity Management, and Resource Capacity Management are sub-process of the Capacity Management process.

- Service Design provides good practice guidance on the design of IT services, processes, and other aspects of the service management effort.

- Capacity Management is the discipline which ensures that IT infrastructure is supplied at the right time, in the right quantity, and at the right price. It also ensures that IT is used in the most proficient way.

- Service Level Management provides for continual identification, monitoring and review of the levels of IT services specified in the service level agreements (SLAs).

- The Capacity Management process is responsible for determining the hardware requirements in order to support an application.

- Capacity Management is the discipline which ensures that IT infrastructure is supplied at the right time, in the right quantity, and at the right price.

- Capacity Management is the discipline which ensures that IT infrastructure is supplied at the right time, in the right quantity, and at the right price.

Service Transition (Explain the high level objectives, basic concepts, process activities and relationships for)

Service Transition relates to the delivery of services required by the business into live/operational use, and often encompasses the "project" side of IT rather than Business As Usual (BAU). It provides guidance for the development and improvement of capabilities for transitioning new and changed services into operations. Service Transition provides assistance on how the necessities of Service strategy determined in Service design, thus the necessities are effectively understood in Service operation while controlling the risks of failure and disruption.

- Service Transition provides assistance on managing the complication related to changes in services and service management processes, preventing undesired consequences while allowing for improvement. Assistance is provided on transferring the control of services between customers and service providers.

- Change Management is used to ensure that standardized methods and procedures are used for efficient handling of all changes. A change is "an event that results in a new status of one or more configuration items

150

(CI's)" approved by management, cost effective, enhances business process changes (fixes) - with a minimum risk to IT infrastructure. The main aims of Change Management are as follows:

- Minimal disruption of services

- Reduction in back-out activities

- Economic utilization of resources involved in the change

- Release Management is used for platform-independent and automated distribution of software and hardware, including license controls across the entire IT infrastructure. Proper software and hardware control ensures the availability of licensed, tested, and version-certified software and hardware, which functions as intended when introduced into existing infrastructure. Quality control during the development and implementation of new hardware and software is also the responsibility of Release Management. This guarantees that all software meets the demands of the business processes. The goals of Release Management are as follows:

- Plan the rollout of software.

- Design and implement procedures for the distribution and installation of changes to IT systems.

- Effectively communicate and manage expectations of the customer during the planning and rollout of new releases.

- Control the distribution and installation of changes to IT systems.

The focus of release management is the protection of the live environment and its services through the use of formal procedures and checks.

Service Validation and Testing is used to ensure that deployed releases and the resulting services meet customer expectations, and to verify that IT operations are able to support the new service. It is part of Service Transition and the owner of Service Validation and Testing is the Test Manager. Service Validation and Testing is a new process in ITIL V3. It includes details on the various testing stages during Service Transition and descriptions of the corresponding testing approaches. The sub-processes of Service Validation and Testing are as follows:

- Test Model Definition

- Service Design Validation

- Release Component Acquisition

- Release Test

- Service Acceptance Testing

Application Development and Customization is used to make available applications and systems which provide the required functionality for IT services. It includes the development and maintenance of custom applications as well as the customization of products from software vendors. It is part of Service Transition and the owner of Application Development and Customization is the Application Developer.

> **Note:** *ITIL does not provide a detailed explanation of all aspects of Application Development. Rather, it highlights the most important activities and assists in identifying interfaces with other Service Management processes.*

Knowledge Management is used to gather, analyze, store, and share knowledge and information within an organization. The primary purpose of Knowledge Management is to improve efficiency by reducing the need to rediscover knowledge. It is part of Service Transition and the owner of Knowledge Management is the Knowledge Manager. ITIL V3, however, defines Knowledge Management as the one central process responsible for providing knowledge to all other IT Service Management processes.

> **Note:** *Knowledge Management is dealt with in many other Service Management processes. The Knowledge Management process itself ensures that all information used within Service Management, stored in the Service Knowledge Management System, is consistent and readily available.*

Service Asset and Configuration Management is used to maintain information about Configuration Items (CI) required to deliver an IT service, including their relationships. It is part of Service Transition and the owner of Service Asset and Configuration Management is the Configuration Manager. Activities and process objectives of the Service Asset and Configuration Management process are broadly identical in ITIL V3 and V2. ITIL V3 introduces the "Configuration Management System (CMS)" as a logical data model, encompassing several Configuration Management Databases (CMDB). The sub-processes of Service Asset and Configuration Management are as follows:

- Configuration Management Support

- Configuration Verification and Audit

Release Management is used for platform-independent and automated distribution of software and hardware, including license controls across the entire IT infrastructure.

The Change Manager authorizes and documents all changes in the IT Infrastructure and its components (Configuration Items) in order to maintain a minimum amount of interruptive effects upon the running operation.

Service Asset and Configuration Management is responsible for controlling, recording, and reporting on versions, attributes, and relationships relating to components of the IT infrastructure.

Service Operation (Explain the high level objectives, basic concepts, process activities, and relationships for)

Service Operation is the best practice for achieving the delivery of agreed levels of services both to end-users and the customers (where "customers" refer to those individuals who pay for the service and negotiate the SLAs). Service Operation is the part of the lifecycle where the services and value are actually directly delivered. Also, the monitoring of problems and balance between service reliability and cost, etc. are considered.

Strategic objectives are eventually recognized through Service Operation, thus making it a critical capability. Assistance is provided on ways to sustain steadiness in service operations, allowing for changes in design, scale, scope and service levels. Organizations are provided with detailed process course of action, methods, and tools for use in two major control perspectives, which are as follows:

- Reactive

- Proactive.

Incident Management is used to restore normal service operation as quickly as possible and minimize the adverse effects on either the business or the user, at a cost-effective price, thus ensuring that the best possible levels of service quality and availability are maintained. 'Normal service operation' is defined here as service operation within Service Level Agreement (SLA) limits. The Activities of Incident Management are as follows:

- Incident detection and recording

- Classification and initial support

- Investigation and diagnosis

- Resolution and recovery

- Incident closure

- Incident ownership, monitoring, tracking, and communication

Problem Management is used to resolve the root cause of incidents, and thus to minimize the adverse impact of incidents and problems on business that are caused by errors within the IT infrastructure, and to prevent recurrence of incidents related to these errors. A problem is an unknown underlying cause of one or more incidents, and a known error is a problem that is successfully diagnosed and for which either a work-around or a permanent resolution has been identified. The CCTA defines problems and known errors as follows:

"A problem is a condition often identified as a result of multiple Incidents that exhibit common symptoms. Problems can also be identified from a single significant Incident, indicative of a single error, for which the cause is unknown, but for which the impact is significant."

"A known error is a condition identified by successful diagnosis of the root cause of a problem, and the subsequent development of a Work-around."

Problem management is different from Incident Management. The principal purpose of Problem Management is to find and resolve the root cause of a problem and prevention of incidents; the purpose of Incident Management is to return the service to normal level as soon as possible, with smallest possible business impact.

Request Fulfillment is added as a new process to ITIL V3 with the aim to have a dedicated process dealing with Service Requests. This was motivated by a clear distinction in ITIL V3 between Incidents (Service Interruptions) and Service Requests (standard requests from users, e.g. password resets). In ITIL V2, Service Requests were fulfilled by the Incident Management process. There are no sub-processes specified for Request Fulfillment according to ITIL V3.

- Event Management is used to filter and categorize Events and to decide on appropriate actions. It is one of the main activities of Service Operations. It is part of Service Operation and the owner of Event Management is the Operations Manager. Essentially, the activities and process objectives of the Event Management process are identical in ITIL V3 and V2 (Event Management is part of ICT Infrastructure Management in ITIL V2). Interfaces between Event Management and the other ITIL processes are adjusted in order to reflect the new ITIL V3 process structure. The sub-processes of Event Management are as follows:

  - Maintenance of Event Monitoring Mechanisms and Rules

  - Event Filtering and Categorization

  - Event Correlation and Response Selection

  - Event Review and Closure

Access Management is used to grant authorized users the right to use a service, while preventing access to non-authorized users. The Access

Management process essentially executes policies defined in IT Security Management. It is sometimes also referred to as Rights Management or Identity Management. It is part of Service Operation and the owner of Access Management is the Access Manager. Access Management is added as a new process to ITIL V3. The sub-processes of Access Management are as follows:

- Maintain Catalogue of User Roles and Access Profiles

- Manage User Access Requests

IT Facilities Management is used to manage the physical environment where the IT infrastructure is located. It includes all aspects of managing the physical environment, for example power and cooling, building access management, and environmental monitoring. It is part of Service Operation and the owner of IT Facilities Management is the IT Facilities Manager.

Fast tracking is a technique that allows activities to be done in parallel that would normally be done in sequence.

Event Management is used to filter and categorize Events and to decide on appropriate actions. It is one of the main activities of Service Operations.

Request Fulfillment is used to fulfill Service Requests, which in most cases are minor (standard) Changes (e.g. requests to change a password) or requests for information. It is part of Service Operation and the owner of Request Fulfillment is Incident Manager.

The functions within Service Operation perform the following types of communication:

- Communication involving Data Centre shifts

- Communication associated to changes

- Performance reporting

- Scheduled operational communication

Request Fulfillment is used to fulfill Service Requests, which in most cases are minor (standard) Changes (e.g. requests to change a password) or requests for information.

The Access Management process essentially executes policies defined in IT Security Management. It is sometimes also referred to as Rights Management or Identity Management.

Key Terms

- **Service Strategy** is the center and origin point of the ITIL Service Lifecycle.

- **Service Design** provides good practice guidance on the design of IT services, processes, and other aspects of the service management effort.

- **Service Level Management** provides for continual identification, monitoring and review of the levels of IT services specified in the service level agreements (SLAs).

- **Capacity Management** is the discipline which ensures that IT infrastructure is supplied at the right time, in the right quantity, and at the right price.

- The **Service Level Manager** is responsible for negotiating Service Level Agreements and ensuring that these are met.

- **Service Transition** relates to the delivery of services required by the business into live/operational use, and often encompasses the "project" side of IT rather than Business As Usual (BAU).

- **Application Development** and Customization is used to make available applications and systems which provide the required functionality for IT services.

- **Knowledge Management** is used to gather, analyze, store, and share knowledge and information within an organization.

- **Service Operation** is the best practice for achieving the delivery of agreed levels of services both to end-users and the customers (where "customers" refer to those individuals who pay for the service and negotiate the SLAs).

- **Access Management** is used to grant authorized users the right to use a service, while preventing access to non-authorized users.

Test Your Knowledge

Q1.   Financial Management for IT Services defines which of the following major cost types?

Each correct answer represents a complete solution. Choose all that apply.

A.   Hardware

B.   Software

C.   Accommodation

D.   People

E.   Customer service

F.   CRM

Q2.   Which of the following sub-processes of Capacity Management is used to manage, control, and predict the performance, utilization and capacity of IT resources and individual IT components?

A.   Capacity Management Reporting

B.   Component Capacity Management

C.   Business Capacity Management

D.   Service Capacity Management

Q3.   Which of the following is created mainly by Availability and IT Service Continuity Management?

A.   Recovery Plan

B.   IT Service Continuity Report

C.   Test Protocol

D.   IT Service Continuity Strategy

Q4.   In which of the following is defining the processes required to operate a new service?

A.   Service Transition: Plan and prepare for deployment

B.   Service Design: Design the processes

C.   Service Operation: IT Operations Management

D.   Service Strategy: Develop the offerings

Q5.   An analysis has been done regarding the expansion of the customer information database. The result specifies that the disk capacity must be increased to contain the projected growth of the database in the near future. Which process is accountable for sharing this information on time to ensure that the available disk space is adequate?

A.   Capacity Management

B.   ICT Infrastructure Management

C.   Security Management

D.   Change Management

Answer Explanation

A1.   Answer options A, B, C, and D are correct.

The major cost types defined under Financial Management for IT Services contain Hardware, Software, Transfer, Accommodation, People, and External Services. IT Financial Management is the discipline of ensuring that the IT infrastructure is obtained at the most effective price (which does not necessarily mean cheapest) and calculating the cost of providing IT services so that an organization can understand the costs of its IT services. Costs are divided into costing units: Equipment; Software; Organization (staff, overtime; accommodation; transfer costs (costs of 3rd party service providers). These costs are divided into Direct and Indirect costs and may be Capital or Ongoing. These costs may then be recovered from the customer of the service.

Answer option E is incorrect. All major costs may then be recovered from the customer taking the service.

Answer option F is incorrect. Customer Relationship Management (CRM) consists of the processes a company uses to track and organize its contacts with its current and prospective customers. CRM software is used to support these processes; information about customers and customer interactions can be entered, stored and accessed by employees in different company departments. Typical CRM goals are to improve services provided to customers, and to use customer contact information for targeted marketing.

A2.   Answer option B is correct.

Component Capacity Management is used to manage, control and predict the performance, utilization and capacity of IT resources and individual IT components.

Answer option A is incorrect. Capacity Management Reporting is used to provide other Service Management processes and IT Management with information related to service and resource utilization and performance.

Answer option C is incorrect. Business Capacity Management is used to translate business needs and plans into capacity and performance requirements for services and IT infrastructure. It also ensures that future capacity and performance needs can be fulfilled.

Answer option D is incorrect. Service Capacity Management is used to manage, control, and predict the performance and capacity of operational services. This includes initiating proactive and reactive action to ensure that the performances and capacities of services meet their agreed targets.

A3.   Answer option A is correct.

A Recovery Plan is created mainly by Availability and IT Service Continuity Management. The plans contain detailed instructions for returning services to a working state.

Answer option B is incorrect. The IT Service Continuity Report is created at regular intervals and provides other Service Management processes and IT Management with information related to disaster prevention.

Answer option C is incorrect. A Test Protocol is a protocol of the preparation, progress, and evaluation of a test, created for example during the various tests carried out by Availability, IT Service Continuity, or IT Security Management.

Answer option D is incorrect. The IT Service Continuity Strategy contains an outline of the approach to ensure the continuity of services in the case of disaster events. It includes a list of Vital Business Functions and applied risk reduction or recovery options. The IT Service Continuity Strategy should be based on a Business Continuity Strategy.

A4.   Answer option B is correct.

Service Design provides good practice guidance on the design of IT services, processes, and other aspects of the service management effort. It covers design principles and methods for converting strategic objectives into portfolios of services and service assets. The scope of Service Design is not limited to new services. Significantly, design within ITIL is understood to encompass all elements relevant to technology service delivery, rather than focusing solely on design of the technology itself.

As such, Service Design addresses how a planned service solution interacts with the larger business and technical environments. Service management systems require supporting the service and processes, which interacts with the service, technology, and architecture required to support the service, and the supply chain required to support the planned service. Within ITIL, design work for an IT service is aggregated into a single Service Design Package (SDP). Service Design Packages (SDP), along with other information about services, is managed within the Service Catalog.

Answer option A is incorrect. Service Transition relates to the delivery of services required by the business into live/operational use, and often encompasses the "project" side of IT rather than

Business As Usual (BAU). It provides guidance for the development and improvement of capabilities for transitioning new and changed services into operations. Service Transition provides assistance on how the necessities of Service strategy determined in Service design, thus the necessities are effectively understood in Service operation while controlling the risks of failure and disruption.

Service Transition provides assistance on managing the complication related to changes in services and service management processes, preventing undesired consequences while allowing for improvement. Assistance is provided on transferring the control of services between customers and service providers.

Answer option C is incorrect. Service Operation is the best practice for achieving the delivery of agreed levels of services both to end-users and the customers (where "customers" refer to those individuals who pay for the service and negotiate the SLAs). Service Operation is the part of the lifecycle where the services and value are actually directly delivered. Also, the monitoring of problems and balance between service reliability and cost, etc. are considered.

Strategic objectives are eventually recognized through Service Operation, thus making it a critical capability. Assistance is provided on ways to sustain steadiness in service operations, allowing for changes in design, scale, scope and service levels. Organizations are provided with detailed process course of action, methods, and tools for use in two major control perspectives, which are as follows:

1. Reactive

2. Proactive.

Answer option D is incorrect. Service Strategy is the center and origin point of the ITIL Service Lifecycle. It provides guidance on how to design, develop, and implement service management not only as an organizational capability but also as a strategic asset. Service Strategy provides guidance on clarification and prioritization of service provider investments in services. More generally, Service Strategy focuses on helping IT organizations improve and develop over the long term. In both cases, Service Strategy relies largely upon a market-driven approach.

Service Strategy is useful in the framework of Service Design, Service Transition, Service Operation, and Continual Service Improvement. Service Strategy ensures that organizations are in a position to deal with the costs and risks associated with their Service Portfolios. Service Strategy is set up for operational effectiveness as well as for distinctive performance. Decisions made with respect to Service

Strategy have broad consequences including those with delayed effect.

A5. Answer option A is correct.

The Capacity Management process is accountable for sharing this information on time to ensure that the available disk space is adequate. Capacity Management is the discipline which ensures that IT infrastructure is supplied at the right time, in the right quantity, and at the right price. It also ensures that IT is used in the most proficient way. Capacity Management supports the optimum and cost effective provision of IT services by helping organizations match their IT resources to the business demands. The high-level activities are Application Sizing, Workload Management, Demand Management, Modeling, Capacity Planning, Resource Management, and Performance Management. Capacity management is made up of three sub processes:

1. Business Capacity Management (BCM)

2. Service Capacity Management (SCM)

3. Resource Capacity Management (RCM)

Answer option B is incorrect. ICT Infrastructure Management processes recommend best practice for requirements analysis, planning, design, deployment, and ongoing operations management and technical support of an ICT Infrastructure. ("ICT" is an acronym for "Information and Communication Technology".)

The Infrastructure Management processes describe those processes within ITIL that directly relate to the ICT equipment and software that is involved in providing ICT services to customers. The services are as follows:

- ICT Design and Planning

- ICT Deployment

- ICT Operations

- ICT Technical Support

These disciplines are less well understood than those of Service Management, and therefore often some of their content is believed to be covered 'by implication' in Service Management disciplines.

Answer option C is incorrect. Security Management describes the structured fitting of information security in the management organization. ITIL Security Management is based on the code of practice for information security management also known as ISO/IEC 17799.

Answer option D is incorrect. Change Management is used to ensure that standardized methods and procedures are used for efficient handling of all changes. A change is "an event that results in a new status of one or more configuration items (CI's)" approved by management, cost effective, enhances business process changes (fixes) - with a minimum risk to IT infrastructure. The main aims of Change Management are as follows:

- Minimal disruption of services
- Reduction in back-out activities
- Economic utilization of resources involved in the change

Chapter 6 - Functions

Overview

The purpose of this unit is to help the candidate to explain the role, objectives and organizational structures of the Service Desk function, and to state the role, objectives and overlap of three other functions. Specifically, candidates must be able to:

- Explain the role, objectives and organizational structures for

  - The Service Desk function

- State the role, objectives and organizational overlap of:

  - The Technical Management function

  - The Application Management function

  - The IT Operations Management function (IT Operations Control and Facilities Management)

The recommended study period for this unit is minimum 1.0 hours.

Key Points

Explain the role, objectives, and organizational structures for the Service Desk function

There are three types of Service Desk structure, which are as follows:

- **Local Service Desk:** It is used to meet local business needs. It is practical only until multiple locations requiring support services are involved.

- **Central Service Desk:** It is used for organizations having multiple locations. It reduces operational costs and improves usage of available resources.

- **Virtual Service Desk:** It is used for organizations having multi-country locations. It can be situated and accessed from anywhere in the world due to advances in network performance and telecommunications, reducing operational costs and improving usage of available resources.

The primary functions of the Service Desk are as follows:

- **Incident Control:** It performs life cycle management of all Service Requests.

- **Communication:** It keeps customers informed of progress and advises on workarounds.

Pop Quiz

Q1: Which statement is used to describe a Service Desk activity?

Ans: Function as the first point when the customer contact

Q2: Which ITIL process requires to be set up to improve unmanaged situation?

Ans: Service Desk

The names by which the Service Desk function is known are as follows:

- **Call Center:** Its main emphasis is on professionally handling large call volumes of telephone-based transactions.

- **Help Desk:** It manages, co-ordinates, and resolve incidents as quickly as possible.

- **Service Desk:** It not only handles incidents, problems and questions but also provides an interface for other activities, such as change requests, maintenance contracts, software licenses, service level management, configuration management, availability management, Financial Management, and IT Services Continuity Management.

Service Desk is a primary IT capability called for in IT Service Management (ITSM) as defined by the Information Technology Infrastructure Library (ITIL). It is intended to provide a Single Point of Contact ("SPOC") to meet the communication needs of both Users and IT, and to satisfy both Customer and IT Provider objectives. ("User" refers to the actual user of the service, while "Customer" refers to the entity that is paying for service)

A Help Desk is an information and assistance resource that troubleshoots problems with computers or similar products. Corporations often provide help desk support to their customers via a toll-free number, Web site and/or email. There are also in-house help desks geared toward providing the same kind of help for employees only. Some schools offer classes in which they perform similar tasks as a help desk. In the Information Technology Infrastructure Library, within companies adhering to ISO/IEC 20000 or seeking to implement IT

Pop Quiz

Q1: Which activity does the Service Desk carry out?

Ans: Incident management, recording Incidents, and providing management information

Q2: Intermediate Recovery is primarily concerned with which of the following time periods?

Ans: 24 to 72 hours

Service Management best practice is a help desk that may offer a wider range of user centric services and be part of a larger Service Desk.

- The Service Level Manager relies on the other areas of the Service Delivery process to provide the necessary support, which ensures that the agreed services are provided in a cost effective, secure, and efficient manner.

- A Service Desk is a primary IT capability called for in IT Service Management (ITSM) as defined by the Information Technology Infrastructure Library (ITIL).

- There are three types of Service Desk structure: Local Service Desk, Central Service Desk, and Virtual Service Desk.

- The names by which the Service Desk function is known are Call Center, Help Desk, and Service Desk.

- ICT Infrastructure Management processes recommend best practice for requirements analysis, planning, design, deployment, and ongoing operations management and technical support of an ICT Infrastructure. ("ICT" is an acronym for "Information and Communication Technology"). The Infrastructure Management processes describe those processes within ITIL that directly relate to the ICT equipment and software that is involved in providing ICT services to customers. The services are as follows:

  - ICT Design and Planning

  - ICT Deployment

  - ICT Operations

- ICT Technical Support

These disciplines are less well understood than those of Service Management, and therefore often some of their content is believed to be covered 'by implication' in Service Management disciplines.

ICT Design and Planning provides a framework and approach for the Strategic and Technical Design and Planning of ICT infrastructures. It includes the necessary combination of Business (and overall IS) strategy, with technical design and architecture. ICT Design and Planning drives both the Procurement of new ICT solutions through the production of Statements of Requirement ("SOR") and Invitations to Tender ("ITT") and is responsible for the initiation and management of ICT Program for strategic business change. Key Outputs from Design and Planning are as follows:

- ICT Strategies, Policies, and Plans

- The ICT Overall Architecture & Management Architecture

- Feasibility Studies, ITTs, and SORs

- Business Cases

Software Asset Management (SAM) is the practice of integrating people, processes and technology to allow software licenses and usage to be systematically tracked, evaluated, and managed. The goal of SAM is to reduce IT expenditures, human resource overhead and risks inherent in owning and managing software assets. SAM practices include the following:

- Maintaining software license compliance

- Tracking inventory and software asset use

Maintaining standard policies and procedures surrounding definition, deployment, configuration, use, and retirement of software assets and the Definitive Software Library.

Pop Quiz

Q1: Who will offer staff to monitor events in a Network Operations Center?

Ans: IT Operations Management

Q2: Functions are BEST described as?

Ans: Self-Contained units of organizations

SAM represents the software component of IT asset management. This includes hardware asset management, because effective hardware inventory controls are critical to efforts to control software. This means overseeing software and hardware that comprise an organization's computers and network.

Application Management set encompasses a set of best practices proposed to improve the overall quality of IT software development and guides how business applications are developed, managed, improved, and when necessary, mark finish. It particularly gives attention to gathering and defining requirements that meet business objectives. ITIL takes a traditional approach and adds Operate and Optimize to the standard Software Development Lifecycle.

ICT Operations Management provides the day-to-day technical supervision of the ICT infrastructure.

ICT Design and Planning provides a framework and approach for the Strategic and Technical Design and Planning of ICT infrastructures.

To a business, customers, and users are the entry point to the process model. They get involved in service support through the following:

- Asking for changes

- Needing communication and updates

- Having difficulties and queries

- Real process delivery

Key Terms

- **Service Desk** is a primary IT capability called for in IT Service Management (ITSM) as defined by the Information Technology Infrastructure Library (ITIL).

- A **Help Desk** is an information and assistance resource that troubleshoots problems with computers or similar products.

- **Service Management** best practice is a help desk that may offer a wider range of user centric services and be part of a larger Service Desk.

- There are three types of **Service Desk** structure: Local Service Desk, Central Service Desk, and Virtual Service Desk.

- **ICT Infrastructure Management** processes recommend best practice for requirements analysis, planning, design, deployment and ongoing operations management and technical support of an ICT Infrastructure.

- **ICT Design and Planning** provides a framework and approach for the Strategic and Technical Design and Planning of ICT infrastructures.

- **Software Asset Management** (SAM) is the practice of integrating people, processes and technology to allow software licenses and usage to be systematically tracked, evaluated, and managed.

- To a business, customers, and users are the entry point to the **process model**.

Test Your Knowledge

Q1. Service Level Management provides for continual identification, monitoring, and review of the levels of IT services specified in the service level agreements (SLAs). What are the responsibilities of Service Level Management?

Each correct answer represents a part of the solution. Choose all that apply.

A.   Ensuring that the agreed IT services are delivered

B.   Liaising with Availability Management

C.   Ensuring the primary functions of the Service Desk

D.   Producing and maintaining a Service Catalog

E.   Ensuring that appropriate IT Service Continuity plans have been made

Q2. Incident Management (IcM) refers to the activities of an organization to identify, analyze, and correct hazards. Who is responsible for tracking and monitoring an incident?

A.   Call center

B.   Problem Management

C.   Service Desk

D.   Service Level Manager

Q3. Consider the following key outputs:

1. ICT Strategies, Policies, and Plans

2. The ICT Overall Architecture & Management Architecture

3. Feasibility Studies, ITTs, and SORs

4. Business Cases

Which of the following produces these outputs?

A.   ICT Design and Planning

B.   Process management

C.   ICT Deployment Management

D.   ICT Infrastructure Management

Q4. To a business, customers, and users are the entry point to the process model. How do they get involved in service support?

1. Asking for changes

2. Needing communication and updates

3. Having difficulties and queries

4. Real process delivery

5. Planning to implement service management

A. 1, 2, and 3 only

B. 1, 2, 3, and 4 only

C. 1, 3, and 5 only

D. 2, 3, and 5 only

E. 3 and 4 only

Q5. ITIL gives a detailed description of a number of important IT practices with comprehensive checklists, tasks and procedures that any IT organization can tailor to its needs. Which of the following roles or functions is responsible for monitoring activities and events in the IT Infrastructure?

A. Incident Management

B. ICT Technical Support

C. ICT Operations Management

D. IT Service Management

Answer Explanation

A1.   Answer options A, B, D, and E are correct.

The responsibilities of Service Level Management are as follows:

Ensuring that the agreed IT services are delivered when and where they are supposed to be.

Liaising with Availability Management, Capacity Management, Incident Management and Problem Management to ensure that the required levels and quality of service are achieved within the resources agreed with the Financial Management.

Producing and maintaining a Service Catalog (a list of standard IT service options and agreements made available to customers).

Ensuring that appropriate IT Service Continuity plans have been made to support the business and its continuity requirements.

The Service Level Manager relies on other areas of the Service Delivery process to provide the necessary support which ensures that the agreed services are provided in a cost effective, secure and efficient manner.

Answer option C is incorrect. This is not the responsibilities of Service Level Management. The primary functions of the Service Desk are as follows:

Incident Control: It performs life cycle management of all Service Requests.

Communication: It keeps customers informed of progress and advises on workarounds.

A2.   Answer option C is correct.

Service Desk is a primary IT capability called for in IT Service Management (ITSM) as defined by the Information Technology Infrastructure Library (ITIL). It is intended to provide a Single Point of Contact ("SPOC") to meet the communication needs of both Users and IT, and to satisfy both Customer and IT Provider objectives. ("User" refers to the actual user of the service, while "Customer" refers to the entity that is paying for service).

A Service Desk not only handles incidents, problems, and questions but also provides an interface for other activities, such as change requests, maintenance contracts, software licenses, service level management, configuration management, availability management, Financial Management, and IT Services Continuity Management.

Answer option A is incorrect. A Call center is a centralized office used for the purpose of receiving and transmitting a large volume of requests by telephone. A call centre is operated by a company to administer incoming product support or information inquiries from consumers. Outgoing calls for telemarketing, clientele, product services, and debt collection are also made. In addition to a call centre, collective handling of letters, faxes, live chat, and e-mails at one location is known as a contact centre.

Answer option B is incorrect. Problem Management is used to resolve the root cause of incidents, and thus to minimize the adverse impact of incidents and problems on business that are caused by errors within the IT infrastructure, and to prevent recurrence of incidents related to these errors. A problem is an unknown underlying cause of one or more incidents, and a known error is a problem that is successfully diagnosed and for which either a work-around or a permanent resolution has been identified. The CCTA defines problems and known errors as follows:

"A problem is a condition often identified as a result of multiple Incidents that exhibit common symptoms. Problems can also be identified from a single significant Incident, indicative of a single error, for which the cause is unknown, but for which the impact is significant."

"A known error is a condition identified by successful diagnosis of the root cause of a problem, and the subsequent development of a Work-around."

Problem management is different from Incident Management. The principal purpose of Problem Management is to find and resolve the root cause of a problem and prevention of incidents; the purpose of Incident Management is to return the service to normal level as soon as possible, with smallest possible business impact.

Answer option D is incorrect. The Service Level Manager relies on other areas of the Service Delivery process to provide the necessary support which ensures that the agreed services are provided in a cost effective, secure, and efficient manner.

A3.   Answer option A is correct.

ICT Design and Planning provides a framework and approach for the Strategic and Technical Design and Planning of ICT infrastructures. It includes the necessary combination of Business (and overall IS) strategy, with technical design and architecture. ICT Design and Planning drives both the Procurement of new ICT solutions through the production of Statements of Requirement ("SOR") and Invitations to Tender ("ITT") and is responsible for the initiation and management of ICT Program for strategic business change. Key Outputs from Design and Planning are as follows:

ICT Strategies, Policies, and Plans

The ICT Overall Architecture & Management Architecture

Feasibility Studies, ITTs, and SORs

Business Cases

Answer option B is incorrect. Process management is the ensemble of activities of planning and monitoring the performance of a process. Especially in the sense of business process, often confused with reengineering. Process Management is the application of knowledge, skills, tools, techniques and systems to define, visualize, measure, control, report, and improve processes with the goal to meet customer requirements profitably. Some people are of view that it is different from Program Management in the sense that Program Management is concerned with managing a group of inter-dependent projects. However, from another view point, Process Management includes Program Management.

ISO 9001 promotes the process approach to managing an organization.

...promotes the adoption of a process approach when developing, implementing and improving the effectiveness of a quality management system, to enhance customer satisfaction by meeting customer requirements. Source: clause 0.2 of ISO 9001:2000

Answer option C is incorrect. ICT Deployment provides a framework for the successful management of design, build, test, and roll-out (deploy) projects within an overall ICT program. It includes many project management disciplines in common with PRINCE2, but has a broader focus to include the necessary integration of Release Management and both functional and non functional testing.

Answer option D is incorrect. ICT Infrastructure Management processes recommend best practice for requirements analysis, planning, design, deployment and ongoing operations management and technical support of an ICT Infrastructure. ("ICT" is an acronym for "Information and Communication Technology".)

The Infrastructure Management processes describe those processes within ITIL that directly relate to the ICT equipment and software that is involved in providing ICT services to customers. The services are as follows:

ICT Design and Planning

ICT Deployment

ICT Operations

ICT Technical Support

These disciplines are less well understood than those of Service Management, and therefore often some of their content is believed to be covered 'by implication' in Service Management disciplines.

A4.   Answer option B is correct.

Service Support is one of the two disciplines that comprise ITIL Service Management. It is focused on users of the ICT services and is primarily concerned with ensuring that they have access to the appropriate services to support the business functions. To a business, customers, and users are the entry point to the process model. They get involved in service support by:

Asking for changes

Needing communication, updates

Having difficulties, queries

Real process delivery

The service desk is the single contact point for customers' problems. If there is a direct solution, it tries to resolve the problem. If not, it creates an incident. Incidents initiate a chain of processes: Incident Management, Problem Management, Change Management, Release Management and Configuration Management. This chain of processes is tracked using the Configuration Management Database (CMDB), which records each process, and creates output documents for traceability (Quality Management).

Answer options A, C, D, and E are incorrect. All the mentioned points except *Planning to implement service management* get involved in service support.

A5.   Answer option C is correct.

ICT Operations Management provides the day-to-day technical supervision of the ICT infrastructure. Often confused with the role of Incident Management from Service Support, Operations is more technical and is concerned not solely with Incidents reported by users, but with Events generated by or recorded by the Infrastructure.

ICT Operations may often work closely alongside Incident Management and the Service Desk, which are not-necessarily technical, to provide an 'Operations Bridge'. Operations should primarily work from documented processes and procedures and should be concerned with a number of specific sub-processes, such as: Output Management, Job Scheduling, Backup and Restore, Network Monitoring/Management, System Monitoring/Management, Database Monitoring/Management, and Storage Monitoring/Management. Operations are responsible for the following:

- A stable, secure ICT infrastructure

- A current, up to date Operational Documentation Library ("ODL")

- A log of all operational Events

- Maintenance of operational monitoring and management tools

- Operational Scripts

- Operational Procedures

Answer option A is incorrect. Incident Management is used to restore normal service operation as quickly as possible and minimize the adverse effects on either the business or the user, at a cost-effective price, thus ensuring that the best possible levels of service quality and availability are maintained. 'Normal service operation' is defined here as service operation within Service Level Agreement (SLA) limits. The Activities of Incident Management are as follows:

- Incident detection and recording

- Classification and initial support

- Investigation and diagnosis

- Resolution and recovery

- Incident closure

- Incident ownership, monitoring, tracking, and communication

Answer option B is incorrect. ICT Technical Support is the specialist technical function for infrastructure within ICT. Primarily as a support to other processes, both in Infrastructure Management and Service Management, Technical Support provides a number of specialist functions, which are as follows:

Research and Evaluation

Market Intelligence (particularly for Design and Planning and Capacity Management)

Proof of Concept and Pilot engineering

Specialist technical expertise (particularly for Operations and Problem Management)

Creation of documentation (perhaps for the Operational Documentation Library or Known Error Database)

Answer option D is incorrect. IT Service Management (ITSM) is a discipline for managing Information Technology (IT) systems, philosophically centered on the customer's perspective of IT's contribution to the business. ITSM stands in deliberate contrast to technology-centered approaches to IT management and business interaction. The following represents a characteristic statement from the ITSM literature:

Providers of IT services can no longer afford to focus on technology and their internal organization, they now have to consider the quality of the services they provide and focus on the relationship with customers.

ITSM is process-focused and in this sense have ties and common interests with process improvement movement (e.g., TQM, Six Sigma, Business Process Management, and CMMI) frameworks and methodologies. The discipline is not concerned with the details of how to use a particular vendor's product, or necessarily with the technical details of the systems under management. Instead, it focuses upon providing a framework to structure IT-related activities and the interactions of IT technical personnel with business customers and users.

Chapter 7 - Roles

Overview

The purpose of this unit is to help the candidate to account for and to be aware of the responsibilities of some of the key roles in Service Management. Specifically, candidates must be able to:

Account for the role and the responsibilities of the following:

- Process owner

- Service owner

Recognize the RACI model and explain its role in determining organizational structure.

The recommended study period for this unit is minimum 30 minutes.

Key Points

Account for the role and the responsibilities of the Process and Service owners

The Service Owner is responsible for a specific service, such as Infrastructure, Application, or Professional Service within an organization despite of where the underpinning technology components, processes, or professional capabilities are located. However, in order to ensure that a service is managed with a business focus, the definition of a single point of responsibility is absolutely necessary to give the level of attention and focus required for its delivery. Service ownership is as critical to service management as establishing ownership for processes which cross multiple vertical silos or departments.

- Service Owner is responsible for continuous improvement and the management of change affecting the services under their heed. The Service Owner is a prime stakeholder in all of the IT processes, which enable or support it.

- The Process Owner executes the crucial role of process champion, design lead, supporter, instructor, and protector. The Process Owner should be a senior level manager with credibility, influence, and authority across the various areas impacted by the activities of the process. The Process Owner must have the ability to influence and make sure compliance to the policies and procedures put in place across the cultural and departmental silos of the IT organization.

- The role of the Process Owner must be defined in the initial planning phase of any ITIL project. This role is responsible for the overall quality of the process and oversees the management of, and organizational compliance to, the process flows, procedures, data models, policies, and technologies associated with the IT business process.

Pop Quiz

Q1: What is the responsibility of a Process Owner?

Ans: Monitoring and improving the process

Q2: Which role is responsible for a particular service within an organization?

Ans: The Service Owner

- The Process Manager is responsible for planning and coordinating all Process Management activities. He supports all parties involved in managing and improving processes, in particular the Process Owners. This role will also coordinate all Changes to processes, thereby making sure that all processes cooperate in a seamless way.

- 1st Level Support is used to register and organize received Incidents, and carry out an urgent effort in order to restore a failed IT Service as quickly as possible. If no ad-hoc solution can be achieved, 1st Level Support will transport the Incident to expert Technical Support Groups, which is 2nd Level Support. 1st Level Support also processes Service Requests and keeps users up to date about their Incidents' status at approved intervals.

- 2nd Level Support is used to take over Incidents, which cannot be solved straight away with the means of 1st Level Support. If required, it will request external support, e.g. from software or hardware manufacturers. 2nd Level Support intends to restore a failed IT Service as quickly as possible. If no solution can be found, the 2nd Level Support transports the Incident to Problem Management.

- In Service Operation 3rd Level Support is normally located at hardware or software manufacturers. Its services are requested by 2nd Level Support if necessary for solving an Incident. 3rd Level Support intends to restore a failed IT Service as quickly as possible.

- Key Performance Indicators (KPIs) are a measure of performance. Such measures are commonly used to help an organization define and evaluate how successful it is, typically in terms of making progress towards its long term organizational goals. KPIs can be specified by answering the question, *"What is really important for different stakeholders?"* KPIs may be monitored using Business Intelligence techniques to assess the present state of the business and to assist in prescribing a course of action. The act of monitoring KPIs in real-time is known as Business Activity Monitoring (BAM).

- The KPIs differ depending on the nature of the organization and the organization's strategy. They help to evaluate the progress of an organization towards its vision and long term goals, especially toward difficult to quantify knowledge based goals.

- The IT Security Manager is responsible for ensuring the confidentiality, integrity, and availability of an organization's assets, information, data, and IT services.

- The Process Owner executes the crucial role of process champion, design lead, supporter, instructor, and protector.

- The Service Owner is responsible for a specific service such as Infrastructure, Application, or Professional Service within an organization despite of where the underpinning technology components, processes, or professional capabilities are located.

- The Configuration Manager maintains a logical model, containing the components of the IT infrastructure (CIs) and their associations.

- The CAB group usually consists of representatives from all areas within the IT Service Provider, the Business, and Third Parties such as Suppliers.

  1st Level Support is used to register and organize received Incidents and carry out an urgent effort in order to restore a failed IT Service as quickly as possible.

  The Incident Manager is responsible for the effective implementation of the process (Incident Management) and carries out the respective reporting method.

  The IT Operator is the staff who performs the day-to-day operational activities.

  The Service Owner is responsible for a specific service such as Infrastructure, Application, or Professional Service within an organization despite of where the underpinning technology components, processes, or professional capabilities are located.

  The Process Owner is responsible for defining Key Performance Indicators (KPIs).

Recognize the RACI model and explain its role in determining organizational structure

The sponsor is responsible to sign off on the closure documents of a project.

RACIO (CAIRO) is an expanded version, based on the standard RACI, with one additional participation type.

Out of the Loop (or Omitted): Designating individuals or groups who are specifically not part of the task. Specifying that a resource does not participate can be as beneficial to a task's completion as specifying those who do participate.

- A Responsibility Assignment Matrix (RAM), (also known as RACI matrix or Linear Responsibility Chart (LRC)), describes the participation by various roles in completing tasks or deliverables for a project or business process.

- A Responsibility Assignment Matrix (RAM), (also known as RACI matrix or Linear Responsibility Chart (LRC)), describes the participation by various roles in completing tasks or deliverables for a project or business process. It is especially useful in clarifying roles and responsibilities in cross-functional/departmental projects and processes.

- The matrix is typically created with a vertical axis (left-hand column) of tasks (e.g., from a work breakdown structure WBS) or deliverables (e.g., from a product breakdown structure PBS), and a horizontal axis (top row) of roles (e.g., from an organizational chart).

- There is a distinction between a role and individually identified people: a role is a descriptor of an associated set of tasks; may be performed by many people; and one person can perform many roles. For example, an organization may have 10 people who can perform the role of a project manager, although traditionally each project only has one project manager at any one time; and a person who is able to perform the role of a project manager may also be able to perform the role of a business analyst and tester.

- The responsibility assignment matrix is commonly known as a RACI matrix. RACI is an acronym derived from the four key responsibilities most typically used as follows:

Responsible:

Those who do the work to achieve the task. There is typically one role with a participation type of Responsible, although others can be delegated to assist in the work required (see also RASCI below for separately identifying those who participate in a supporting role).

Accountable (also Approver or final Approving authority):

Those who are ultimately accountable for the correct and thorough completion of the deliverable or task, and the one to whom Responsible is accountable. In other words, an Accountable must sign off (Approve) on work that Responsible provides. There must be only one Accountable specified for each task or deliverable.

Pop Quiz

Q1: What does RACI stand for?

Ans: Responsible Accountable Consulted Informed

Q2: Which version of the RACI is used by Project Management Institute (PMI)?

Ans: RSI

Consulted:

Those whose opinions are sought; and with whom there is a two-way communication.

Informed:

Those who are kept up-to-date on progress, often only on completion of the task or deliverable; and with whom there is just one-way communication.

Very often the role that is Accountable for a task or deliverable may also be Responsible for completing it (indicated on the matrix by the task or deliverable having a role Accountable for it, but no role Responsible for its completion, i.e. it is implied). Outside of this exception, it is generally recommended that each role in the project or process for each task receive, at most, just one of the participation types. Where more than one participation type is shown, this generally implies that participation has not yet been fully resolved, which can impede the value of this technique in clarifying the participation of each role on each task.

Alternatives

There are a number of alternatives to the RACI participation types:

RASCI (RASIC):

This is an expanded version, based on the standard RACI, breaking the Responsible participation into:

- **Responsible:** Those who are responsible for the task, ensuring that it is done as per the Approver.

- **Support:** Resources allocated to Responsible. Unlike Consulted, who may provide input to the task, Support will assist in completing the task.

- RACI-VS (VARISC)

- This is an expanded version, based on the standard RACI, with two additional participation types:

- **Verifier:** Those who check whether the product meets the acceptance criteria set forth in the product description.

- **Signatory:** Those who approve the Verify decision and authorize the product hand-off. It seems to make sense that the Signatory should be the party with the Accountable for its successor.

RACIO (CAIRO)

This is an expanded version, based on the standard RACI, with one additional participation type.

Out of the Loop (or Omitted): Designating individuals or groups who are specifically not part of the task. Specifying that a resource does not participate can be as beneficial to a task's completion as specifying those who do participate.

DACI

Another version that has been used to centralize decision making, and clarify who can re-open discussions.

Driver: A single Driver of overall project like the person steering a car.

Approver: One or more Approvers who make most project decisions are responsible if it fails.

Contributors: They are the worker-bees who are responsible for deliverables; and with whom there is a two-way communication.

Informed: Those who are impacted by the project and are provided status and informed of decisions; and with whom there is one-way communication.

> ## Pop Quiz
>
> Q1: Which version of RACI centralizes decision making and clarifies who can re-open discussions?
>
> *Ans: DACI*
>
> Q2: Which is NOT a typical type of metrics?
>
> *Ans: Baseline metrics*

RSI

A version used by the Project Management Institute:

Responsible: These people are the doers of the work. They must complete the task or objective or make the decision. Several people can be jointly responsible.

Sponsor: This person is the owner of the work. He or she must sign off or approve when the task, objective or decision is complete. This person must make sure that responsibilities are assigned in the matrix for all related activities. There is only one person accountable, which means that the buck stops there.

Informed: These people need to be kept in the picture. They need updates on progress or decision, but they do not need to be formally consulted, nor do they contribute directly to the task or decision.

PARIS

Primary: The role mainly responsible to complete a task.

Assigned: One or more additional roles that are assigned to support the primary role.

Review required: Those who should be consulted once work has been completed, e.g. checking for compliance with standards, etc.

Input required: Those who should be consulted as work is prepared, i.e. the driving input.

Signature required: Those who need to signed off on work, and are therefore the approver or accountable role.

Variations

There are also a number of variations to the meaning of RACI participation types, which are as follows:

RACI (alternative scheme)

There is an alternative coding, less widely published but used by some practitioners and process mapping software, which modifies the application of the R and A codes of the original scheme. The overall methodology remains the same but this alternative avoids potential confusion of the terms Accountable and Responsible understood by management professionals but not always so clearly differentiated by others:

Responsible: Those responsible for the performance of the task. There should be exactly one person with this assignment for each task.

Assists: Those who assist completion of the task.

Consulted: Those whose opinions are sought; and with whom there is a two-way communication.

Informed: Those who are kept up-to-date on progress; and with whom there is one-way communication.

RACI (decisions)

This alternative is focused only on documenting who has the authority to make which decisions. May be suitable for use within a small work group.

Recommends: Responsible to Recommend an answer to the decision.

Approves: Authorized to Approve an answer to the decision.

Consulted: Those whose opinions are sought; and with whom there is a two-way communication.

Informed: Those who are informed after the decision is made; and with whom there is one-way communication.

Pop Quiz

Q1: The RACI model is used to _____.

Ans: Define roles and responsibilities

Key Terms

- The **Service Owner** is responsible for a specific service, such as Infrastructure, Application, or Professional Service within an organization despite of where the underpinning technology components, processes, or professional capabilities are located.

- The **Process Owner** executes the crucial role of process champion, design lead, supporter, instructor, and protector.

- The **Process Manager** is responsible for planning and coordinating all Process Management activities.

- **1st Level Support** is used to register and organize received Incidents, and carry out an urgent effort in order to restore a failed IT Service as quickly as possible.

- **2nd Level Support** is used to take over Incidents, which cannot be solved straight away with the means of 1st Level Support.

- **Key Performance Indicators** (KPIs) are a measure of performance.

- The **sponsor** is responsible to sign off on the closure documents of a project.

- **RACIO** (CAIRO) is an expanded version, based on the standard RACI, with one additional participation type.

- The responsibility assignment matrix is commonly known as a **RACI matrix**.

Test Your Knowledge

Q1. Which of the following roles is used to ensure that the confidentiality, integrity, and availability of the services are maintained to the levels approved on the Service Level Agreement (SLA)?

 A. The Change Manager

 B. The IT Security Manager

 C. The Service Level Manager

 D. The Configuration Manager

Q2. Which of the following roles is responsible for a specific service within an organization?

 A. Service Level Manager

 B. Service Owner

 C. Continual Service Improvement Manager

 D. Process Manager

Q3. Which of the following roles in Service Transition is made up of representatives from all areas within the IT Service Provider, the Business, and Third Parties?

 A. The Emergency Change Advisory Board

 B. The Change Advisory Board

 C. The Application Developer

 D. The Change Manager

Q4. Which of the following is responsible to sign off on the closure documents of a project?

 A. Project Manager

 B. Project team members

 C. Sponsor

 D. End user

Q5. Which of the following versions of RACI includes Out of the Loop participation type?

A.   RACIO

B.   RASCI

C.   RACI-VS

D.   RSI

Answer Explanation

A1.   Answer option B is correct.

The IT Security Manager is responsible for ensuring the confidentiality, integrity, and availability of an organization's assets, information, data, and IT services. He is usually involved in an organizational approach to Security Management, which has a wider scope than the IT service provider, and includes handling of paper, building access, phone calls, etc for the entire organization.

Answer option A is incorrect. The Change Manager authorizes and documents all changes in the IT Infrastructure and its components (Configuration Items), in order to maintain a minimum amount of interruptive effects upon the running operation. In the case of further-reaching changes, he involves the Change Advisory Board (CAB).

Answer option C is incorrect. The Service Level Manager is responsible for negotiating Service Level Agreements and ensuring that these are met. He makes sure that all IT Service Management processes, Operational Level Agreements, and Underpinning Contracts are appropriate for the agreed service level targets. The Service Level Manager also monitors and reports on service levels.

Answer option D is incorrect. The Configuration Manager is responsible for maintaining information about Configuration Items (CI) required to deliver IT services. To this end he maintains a logical model, containing the components of the IT infrastructure (CIs) and their associations.

A2.   Answer option B is correct.

The Service Owner is responsible for a specific service, such as Infrastructure, Application, or Professional Service within an organization despite of where the underpinning technology components, processes, or professional capabilities are located. However, in order to ensure that a service is managed with a business focus, the definition of a single point of responsibility is absolutely necessary to give the level of attention and focus required for its delivery. Service ownership is as critical to service management as establishing ownership for processes which cross multiple vertical silos or departments.

Service Owner is responsible for continuous improvement and the management of change affecting the services under their heed. The Service Owner is a prime stakeholder in all of the IT processes, which enable or support it.

Answer option A is incorrect. The Service Level Manager is responsible for negotiating Service Level Agreements and ensuring that these are met. He makes sure that all IT Service Management processes, Operational Level Agreements, and Underpinning Contracts are appropriate for the agreed service level targets. The Service Level Manager also monitors and reports on service levels.

Answer option C is incorrect. The Continual Service Improvement (CSI) Manager is responsible for managing improvements to IT Service Management processes and IT services. He will continually measure the performance of the service provider and design improvements to processes, services and infrastructure in order to increase efficiency, effectiveness, and cost effectiveness.

Answer option D is incorrect. The Process Manager is responsible for planning and coordinating all Process Management activities. He supports all parties involved in managing and improving processes, in particular the Process Owners. This role will also coordinate all Changes to processes, thereby making sure that all processes cooperate in a seamless way.

A3. Answer option B is correct.

The Change Advisory Board (CAB) is a group of people that advises the Change Manager in the Assessment, prioritization, and scheduling of Changes. The CAB group usually consists of representatives from all areas within the IT Service Provider, the Business, and Third Parties such as Suppliers.

Answer option A is incorrect. The Emergency Change Advisory Board (ECAB) is a sub-set of the Change Advisory Board who makes decisions about high impact Emergency Changes. Membership of the ECAB may be decided at the time a meeting is called, and depends on the nature of the Emergency Change.

Answer option C is incorrect. The Application Developer is responsible for making available applications and systems which provide the required functionality for IT services. The Application Developer is also responsible for the development and maintenance of custom applications as well as the customization of products from software vendors.

Answer option D is incorrect. The Change Manager authorizes and documents all changes in the IT Infrastructure and its components (Configuration Items), in order to maintain a minimum amount of interruptive effects upon the running operation. In the case of further-reaching changes, he involves the Change Advisory Board (CAB).

A4.   Answer option C is correct.

The sponsor is responsible to sign off on the closure documents of a project.

Project closure is a final process group or stage of a project. This stage includes the formal acceptance of the project and the ending thereof. Administrative activities include the archiving of the files and documenting lessons learned.

Answer option A is incorrect. Project manager is the person responsible for managing the work associated with the project. Project manager creates documents, provides supporting documentation that illustrates that all deliverables have been successfully completed.

Answer option B is incorrect. Project team members are the experts who perform the work associated with the project.

Answer option D is incorrect. End user is the person who directly uses the product produced by the project. He has nothing to do with the closure of a project.

A5.   Answer option A is correct.

RACIO (CAIRO) is an expanded version, based on the standard RACI, with one additional participation type.

Out of the Loop (or Omitted): Designating individuals or groups who are specifically not part of the task. Specifying that a resource does not participate can be as beneficial to a task's completion as specifying those who do participate.

Answer option B is incorrect. RASCI (RASIC) is an expanded version, based on the standard RACI, breaking the Responsible participation into:

Responsible: Those who are responsible for the task, ensuring that it is done as per the Approver.

Support: Resources allocated to Responsible. Unlike Consulted, who may provide input to the task, Support will assist in completing the task.

Answer option C is incorrect. RACI-VS (VARISC) is an expanded version, based on the standard RACI, with two additional participation types:

Verifier: Those who check whether the product meets the acceptance criteria set forth in the product description.

Signatory: Those who approve the Verify decision and authorize the product hand-off. It seems to make sense that the Signatory should be the party with the Accountable for its successor.

Answer option D is incorrect. RSI is a version used by the Project Management Institute:

- Responsible: These people are the doers of the work. They must complete the task or objective or make the decision. Several people can be jointly responsible.

- Sponsor: This person is the owner of the work. He or she must sign off or approve when the task, objective or decision is complete. This person must make sure that responsibilities are assigned in the matrix for all related activities. There is only one person accountable, which means that the buck stops there.

- Informed: These people need to be kept in the picture. They need updates on progress or decision, but they do not need to be formally consulted, nor do they contribute directly to the task or decision.

Chapter 8 - Technology and Architecture

Overview

The purpose of this unit is to help the candidate to understand how Service Automation assists with integrating Service Management processes.

It is recommended that this unit is covered as part of the training in the other units.

Key Points

Understand how Service Automation assists with Integrating Service Management processes

ITIL introduces the concept of 'bounded rationality' in its discussion of the role of automation in IT.

Service Management. 'Bounded rationality' refers to the limits which constrain humans' ability to entertain more than a few factors at a time when seeking to make decisions in complex situations.

In the most fundamental sense, automation and technology play an important role in IT Service Management by helping human decision makers effectively confront vastly more complex scenarios than they might otherwise be able to. Some examples include:

- Use of automation to identify patterns and trends in large data sets, such as event logs, incident logs, etc.

- Use of automation to help guarantee consistency during design efforts.

- Use of automation to accurately record high volumes of detailed data, e.g. incident logs.

- Use of automation to avoid arbitrary assignment of priority to incidents, problems, changes, etc.

- Use of automation to respond to events in real time.

ITIL urges the point that all phases of the Service Lifecycle can be supported very effectively using technology and automation.

Automation Tips

ITIL offers some discussion of how automation can best be used to support processes. It's most essential recommendations include:

- Process definition should precede attempts to purchase or apply technology to processes

- Processes should be simplified prior to automating them

- Information Systems Discussed Within ITIL

ITIL describes a number of information systems which represent the application of technology/automation to the IT Service Management effort. The most important of these include:

- Service Knowledge Management System (SKMS)

- Service Portfolio/Catalog

- Availability Management Information System (AMIS)

- Configuration Management System/Configuration Management Database (CMS/CMDB)

- Capacity Database (CDB) or Capacity Management Information System (CMIS)

- Known Error Database (KEDB)

- Security Management Information System (SMIS)

Planning To Implement Service Management is ITIL discipline that attempts to provide practitioners with a framework for the alignment of business needs and IT provision requirements. The processes and approaches incorporated within the guidelines suggest the development of a Continuous Service Improvement Program (CSIP) as the basis for implementing other ITIL disciplines as projects within a controlled program of work. Planning To Implement Service Management is mainly focused on the Service Management processes, but is also generically applicable to other ITIL disciplines, which are as follows:

- Create vision

- Analyze organization

- Set goals

- Implement IT service management

IT Service Management (ITSM) is a discipline for managing Information Technology (IT) systems, philosophically centered on the customer's perspective of IT's contribution to the business. ITSM stands in

194

deliberate contrast to technology-centered approaches to IT management and business interaction. The following represents a characteristic statement from the ITSM literature:

Providers of IT services can no longer afford to focus on technology and their internal organization, they now have to consider the quality of the services they provide and focus on the relationship with customers.

ITSM is process-focused and in this sense have ties and common interests with process improvement movement (e.g., TQM, Six Sigma, Business Process Management, and CMMI) frameworks and methodologies. The discipline is not concerned with the details of how to use a particular vendor's product, or necessarily with the technical details of the systems under management. Instead, it focuses upon providing a framework to structure IT-related activities and the interactions of IT technical personnel with business customers and users.

Pop Quiz

Q1: Which group sanctions changes that have to be installed quicker than the normal process?

Ans: Emergency CAB (ECAB)

Q2: What is the basis of the ITIL approach to Service Management?

Ans: Interrelated activities

Project management is the discipline of planning, organizing, and managing resources to bring about the successful completion of specific project goals and objectives. It is often closely related to and sometimes conflated with program management.

A project is a temporary endeavor, having a defined beginning and end, undertaken to meet particular goals and objectives, usually to bring about beneficial change or added value. In practice, the management of these two systems is often found to be quite different, and as such requires the development of distinct technical skills and the adoption of separate management.

The primary challenge of project management is to achieve all of the project goals and objectives while honoring the preconceived project constraints. Typical constraints are scope, time, and budget. The secondary and more ambitious challenge is to optimize the allocation and integration of inputs necessary to meet pre-defined objectives.

These are the correct grouping of concepts and ITIL processes:

- CMDB AND Configuration Management

- DSL AND Release Management

- MTBF AND Availability Management

- SLA AND Service Level Management

Key Terms

- **IT Service Management** (ITSM) is a discipline for managing Information Technology (IT) systems, philosophically centered on the customer's perspective of IT's contribution to the business.

- **Project management** is the discipline of planning, organizing, and managing resources to bring about the successful completion of specific project goals and objectives.

Test Your Knowledge

Q1.   Which is the correct grouping of concepts and ITIL processes?

Concepts:

    1. CMDB

    2. DSL

    3. MTBF

    4. SLA

Processes:

    a. Availability Management

    b. Configuration Management

    c. Service Level Management

    d. Release Management

  A.   1-c, 2-a, 3-d, 4-b

  B.   1-d, 2-c, 3-b, 4-a

  C.   1-b, 2-d, 3-a, 4-c

  D.   1-a, 2-b, 3-c, 4-d

Q2.   Which of the following management techniques is based on a philosophy of continuous improvement of processes?

  A.   Six Sigma

  B.   Kaizen

  C.   Ishikawa

  D.   Rule of seven

Q3.   Release Management is used for platform-independent and automated distribution of software and hardware, including license controls across the entire IT infrastructure. Which of the following is NOT a type of Release unit?

  A.   Delta Release

  B.   Full Release

C.   Packaged Release

D.   Surviving Change Release

Q4.   Release Management is used for platform-independent and automated distribution of software and hardware, including license controls across the entire IT infrastructure. Which levels are related to releasing hardware or software into an IT infrastructure?

Each correct answer represents a complete solution. Choose all that apply.

A.   Major

B.   Minor

C.   Emergency

D.   Delta

E.   Package

Q5.   You are the project manager of the ATZ project. The project is finished and is delayed due to some unfortunate circumstances. As the delay cost has adversely affected your organization, you add the information to the lesson learned document. In which of the following activities in future projects will the information not help?

A.   Cost estimating

B.   Resource allocation

C.   Activity scheduling

D.   Product verification

Answer Explanation

A1.   Answer option C is correct.

These are the correct grouping of concepts and ITIL processes:

1. CMDB AND Configuration Management

2. DSL AND Release Management

3. MTBF AND Availability Management

4. SLA AND Service Level Management

Configuration Management (CM) is an Information Technology Infrastructure Library (ITIL) IT Service Management (ITSM) process. It tracks all of the individual Configuration Items (CI) in an IT system, which may be as simple as a single server, or as complex as the entire IT department. In large organizations a configuration manager may be appointed to oversee and manage the CM process.

Release Management is used for platform-independent and automated distribution of software and hardware, including license controls across the entire IT infrastructure. Proper software and hardware control ensures the availability of licensed, tested, and version-certified software and hardware, which functions as intended when introduced into existing infrastructure. Quality control during the development and implementation of new hardware and software is also the responsibility of Release Management. This guarantees that all software meets the demands of the business processes. The goals of Release Management are as follows:

*   Plan the rollout of software

*   Design and implement procedures for the distribution and installation of changes to IT systems

*   Effectively communicate and manage expectations of the customer during the planning and rollout of new releases

*   Control the distribution and installation of changes to IT systems

The focus of release management is the protection of the live environment and its services through the use of formal procedures and checks.

Availability Management allows organizations to sustain the IT service availability to support the business at a justifiable cost. The high-level activities are Realize Availability Requirements, Compile Availability Plan, Monitor Availability, and Monitor Maintenance

Obligations. Availability is usually calculated based on a model involving the Availability Ratio and techniques, such as Fault Tree Analysis.

Availability Management is the ability of an IT component to perform at an agreed level over a period of time.

Reliability: How reliable is the service? Ability of an IT component to perform at an agreed level at described conditions.

Maintainability: The ability of an IT component to remain in, or be restored to an operational state.

Serviceability: The ability of an external supplier to maintain the availability of component or function under a third party contract.

Resilience: A measure of freedom from operational failure and a method of keeping services reliable. One popular method of resilience is redundancy.

Security: A service may have associated data. Security refers to the confidentiality, integrity, and availability of that data. Availability gives us the clear overview of the end to end availability of the system.

Service Level Management provides for continual identification, monitoring and review of the levels of IT services specified in the service level agreements (SLAs). It ensures that arrangements are in place with internal IT Support Providers and external suppliers in the form of Operational Level Agreements (OLAs) and Underpinning Contracts (UCs). The process involves assessing the impact of change upon service quality and SLAs. The Service Level Management process is in close relation with the operational processes to control their activities. The central role of Service Level Management makes it the natural place for metrics to be established and monitored against a benchmark.

Note: *Service Level Management is the primary interface with the customer (as opposed to the user, who is serviced by the Service Desk).*

Answer options A, B, and D are incorrect. These are incorrect grouping of concepts and ITIL processes.

A2. Answer option B is correct.

Kaizen (kai-change, zen-good) is a Japanese philosophy for improving processes continuously. Kaizen is a daily activity, the purpose of which goes beyond simple productivity improvement. It is also a process that, when done correctly, humanizes the workplace, eliminates overly hard work, and teaches people how to perform experiments on their work using the scientific method and how to learn to spot and eliminate waste in business processes. The philosophy can be defined as bringing back the thought process into the automated production environment dominated by repetitive tasks that traditionally required little mental participation from the employees. While kaizen usually delivers small improvements, the culture of continual aligned small improvements and standardization yields large results in the form of compound productivity improvement.

Answer option A is incorrect. Six Sigma is a quality improvement program to reduce the number of defects in a process.

Answer option C is incorrect. In project management, Ishikawa refers to Ishikawa diagram. The Ishikawa diagram (or fishbone diagram or also cause-and-effect diagram) are diagrams, that shows the causes of a certain event. A common use of the Ishikawa diagram is to identify potential factors causing an overall effect. It helps identify causal factors and contributing causes.

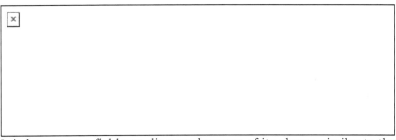

It is known as a fishbone diagram because of its shape, similar to the side view of a fish skeleton. It is considered as a basic tool of quality management.

Answer option D is incorrect. In a control chart, whenever there are seven measurements, all on one side of the mean, it is called the rule of seven and is an assignable cause. It represents a trend that can be analyzed.

A3.   Answer option D is correct.

There is no such Release unit as Surviving Change Release. However, in Surviving Change, the IT infrastructure changes can impact the manner in which business is conducted or the continuity of business operations. It is important that business managers take notice of these changes and ensure that steps are taken to safeguard the business from adverse side effects.

Answer options A, B, and C are incorrect. The different types of Release units are as follows:

Delta Release: It is a release of only that part of software which has been changed. For example, security patches.

Full Release: It means the entire software program is deployed. For example, a new version of an existing application.

Packaged Release: It is a combination of many changes. For example, an operating system image which also contains specific applications.

A4.   Answer options A, B, and C are correct.

The release management levels are as follows:

Major release: It typically introduces new capabilities/functions. A major release might accumulate all the changes from preceding minor releases. Major releases advance the version number by a full increment. For example, from version 7.70 to version 8.

Minor release: It integrates a number of fixes for known problems into the baseline, or trusted state, of an item. A minor release typically increments the version number at the first decimal place. For example, version 7.10 will change to version 7.20.

Emergency release: It is a quick fix to repair unpredicted problems or short-term measures to prevent the disruption of important services. An emergency release increments the version number at the second decimal place. For example, from 7.1 to 7.11.

Answer option D is incorrect. A Delta release is also known as partial release. It contains the elements of a hardware or software Configuration Item (CI) that have changed or are new since the previous Full/Delta release. The changes are added to the existing version of the CI. In delta release, it is not always possible to analyze how changes will influence the rest of the live environment.

Answer option E is incorrect. A package release moves the changes to different Configuration Item (CI) into a single release. A package release might contain changes to hardware and software CI and can contain delta and full releases. A package release reduces disturbance in the IT environment.

A5.   Answer option D is correct.

As a project is unique and is created for producing a unique product, the product verification will not be affected by the information added to the lesson learned document.

Answer options A, B, and C are incorrect. Cost estimating, resource allocation, and activity scheduling will be the activities where the information can be effectively used.

Section C
Full length Practice Test

Full Length Practice Test Questions

Q1. Processes provide transformation towards a goal. They make use of feedback for self-reinforcing and self-counteractive action to function as closed-loop systems. Which of the following are the characteristics of processes?

1. Processes are measurable

2. Processes have specific results

3. Processes have customers

4. Processes respond to specific events

Each correct answer represents a complete solution. Choose all that apply.

A. 1 and 2

B. 3 and 4 only

C. 1, 2, and 3

D. 1, 2, 3, and 4

E. 2, 3, and 4 only

Q2. Julia is the project manager of the WR2 Project and she has completed the project deliverables. She wants to ensure that the project customers inspect the project work to gain their formal acceptance of what she and her project team have created. What process does Julia need to initiate?

A. Verify scope

B. Scope validation

C. Perform quality control

D. Project closure

Q3. Which of the following parts of the Service Lifecycle considers the business outcomes and value creation as its principles?

A. Service Design

B. Service Transition

C. Service Strategy

D. Continual Service Improvement

Q4. Which of the following is an annual financial plan that provides an estimate of projected expenditures of service management processes within the IT organization?

    A.   Invoice

    B.   IT Budget

    C.   Budget Request

    D.   Budget Allocation

Q5. What is the key output handed over to Service Transition within Service Design?

    A.   ITIL Small-Scale Implementation

    B.   Service Portfolio Management

    C.   Service Design Package

    D.   Business Perspective

Q6. Service Transition contains detailed descriptions of which of the following processes?

    A.   Change Management, Capacity Management, Event Management, and Service Request Management

    B.   Service Level Management, Service Portfolio Management, Service Asset and Configuration Management

    C.   Service Asset and Configuration Management, Release Management, and Request Fulfillment

    D.   Change Management, Service Asset and Configuration Management, Release and Deployment Management

Q7. Event Management, Problem Management, Access Management, and Request Fulfillment are part of which of the following stages of the Service Lifecycle?

    A.   Service Operation

    B.   Service Strategy

    C.   Continual Service Improvement

    D.   Service Transition

Q8. Which of the following processes is used to list "Understanding Pattern of Business Activity" (PBA) as a major role?

   A.   Service Desk

   B.   Demand Management

   C.   Request Fulfillment

   D.   Supplier Management

Q9. Which document refers to the steps that must be taken if there is a major gap in the projected delivery quality of a service and the actual delivery?

   A.   Service Improvement Plan

   B.   Service Quality Plan

   C.   Service Level Agreement

   D.   Business Service Catalogue

Q10. What are the elements of a service's business value from customers' perspective?

Each correct answer represents a complete solution. Choose all that apply.

   A.   Utility

   B.   Availability

   C.   Warranty

   D.   Configuration Item

Q11. In which of the following phases is the Service Portfolio divided?

Each correct answer represents a part of the solution. Choose all that apply.

   A.   Service pipeline

   B.   Service catalogue

   C.   Service audit

   D.   Retired Services

Q12. What is the name specified to the type of charging where no money is exchanged inter-departmentally mainly involving the IT Department & the customer?

   A.   Full Charging

   B.   Notional Charging

C.   No Charging

D.   Chargeback

Q13. You are the project manager for BBT project. You are in a process of risk identification. You call your concerned team members in the meeting room. You ask each of them to write down the risks, they think, the project faces. They are instructed to use Sticky-backed notes using one paper for each risk. You stick all such paper received up to a white board. You ask the team members to review all the risks posted on the board, rank them, and prioritize them. Which of the following techniques have you used to identify risks in the project?

A.   Brainstorming

B.   Delphi

C.   Nominal Group

D.   Assumptions Analysis

Q14. You work as a Project Manager for uCertify Inc. You are working on a project. A risk that has been identified and analyzed in the project planning processes is now coming into fruition. Who should respond to the risk with the preplanned risk response?

A.   You

B.   Project sponsor

C.   Risk owner

D.   Subject matter expert

Q15. In which of the following documents will you see an outline of actual service achievements against targets?

A.   Service Level Agreement (SLA)

B.   Underpinning Contract (UC)

C.   SLA Monitoring Chart (SLAM)

D.   Operational Level Agreement (OLA)

Q16. The Business has submitted requirements for a new ERP system. Which authority is responsible for documenting the Service Level Requirements (SLRs) with the Business delegate?

A.   Service Level Management

B.   Service Level Manager

C.   Project Management

D.   Service Owner

Q17. Which of the following roles is responsible for review and risk analysis of all contracts on a regular basis?

A.   The Service Catalogue Manager

B.   The Supplier Manager

C.   The Configuration Manager

D.   The IT Service Continuity Manager

Q18. Match the Availability Measurements with their correct definition:

MEASUREMENTS:

1. MTTR

2. MTBF

3. MTBSI

4. MTTF

DEFINITIONS:

a. The predicted elapsed time between inherent failures of a system during operation.

b. The elapsed time between the occurrence of one system or service failure and the next.

c. The average elapsed time from the occurrence of an incident to the repair of the failed component.

d. The average time taken to repair a Configuration Item or IT Service after a failure.

A.   1d, 2a, 3c, 4b

B.   1d, 2a, 3b, 4c

C.   1a, 2b, 3d, 4c

D.   1a, 2b, 3c, 4d

Q19. Which of the following is the central repository of the IT organization's data, information, and knowledge?

A. Service Knowledge Management System

B. Compliance Management

C. Supplier and Contract Database

D. Knowledge Management

Q20. Which of the following activities are helped by recording relationships between Configuration Items (CIs)?

1. Assessing the impact and cause of Incidents and Problems

2. Assessing the impact of proposed Changes

3. Planning and designing a Change to an existing service

4. Planning a technology refresh or software upgrade

Each correct answer represents a complete solution. Choose two.

A. 1, 3 and 4 only

B. 1 and 2

C. 1, 2, 3, and 4

D. 1, 2, and 4 only

Q21. You need to write off a set percentage of an IT asset every year. Which of the following methods will you use to accomplish this?

A. Straight Line

B. Declining Balance

C. Reducing Balance

D. Composite Depreciation

Q22. What will be the status of the problem if its root cause has been successfully diagnosed?

A. Incident

B. Work-around

C. Known Error

D. Request for Change

Q23. Which of the following activities in the Problem Management process is responsible for generating Requests for Change (RFCs)?

A.   Error Control

B.   Problem Management Process

C.   Problem Control Process

D.   Business Transaction Management

Q24. Which of the following roles in Service Strategy is used to decide on a strategy to serve customers in co-operation with the IT Steering Group?

A.   The Financial Manager

B.   The Service Portfolio Manager

C.   The Service Level Manager

D.   The IT Steering Group

Q25. Which of the following roles in Service Design is responsible for designing infrastructure components and systems required to provide a service, and also includes the specification of technologies and products as a basis for their procurement and customization?

A.   The Application Analysts and Architects

B.   The Risk Manager

C.   The Capacity Manager

D.   Technical Analysts/Architects

Q26. Which of the following roles in Service Design defines a blueprint for the future development of the technological landscape?

A.   The IT Architect

B.   The Application Analysts and Architects

C.   The Supplier Manager

D.   Technical Analysts/Architects

Q27. Which of the following are commonly used terms when discussing service improvement outcomes?

1.   Improvements

2.   Benefits

3.   Return On Investment (ROI)

4.   Value On Investment(VOI)

5. Resources

A. 1, 2, and 4 only

B. 1, 2, 3, and 4 only

C. 2, 3, and 5 only

D. 2, 3, 4, and 5 only

E. 1, 2, 3, 4, and 5

Q28. Which of the following is the process of comparing the business processes and performance metrics including cost, cycle time, productivity, or quality?

A. Benchmarking

B. COBIT

C. Agreement

D. Service Improvement Plan

Q29. Which of the following is prepared by the business and serves as a starting point for producing the IT Service Continuity Strategy?

A. Disaster Invocation Guideline

B. Index of Disaster-Relevant Information

C. Business Continuity Strategy

D. Availability/ ITSCM/ Security Testing Schedule

Q30. Which of the following ITIL processes is responsible for determining the hardware requirements in order to support an application?

A. Software Asset Management

B. Change Management

C. Configuration Management

D. Capacity Management

Q31. Which of the following is the most constructive model to define an organizational structure?

A. RACI Model

B. Plan, Do, Check, Act (PDCA) Model

C. Service Model

D. Continual Service Improvement Model

Q32. You work as a Project Manager for uCertify Inc. You are working on a high-profile project. Your project team has team from all departments within the organization, and each team member has a number of activities to complete each week to contribute to the project. Management would like you to create a chart to show each project team member's work assignment using a simple legend. What type of chart is management asking you to create?

A.   Pareto chart

B.   Resource histogram chart

C.   RACI Chart

D.   Resource Breakdown Structure

Q33. You work as a Project Manager for uCertify Inc. You have been requested by the management to show graphical representation of roles and responsibilities of different project team members. Which of the following will you produce?

A.   RACI chart

B.   Pareto chart

C.   Resource histogram chart

D.   Organization chart

Q34. Who is responsible for defining Key Performance Indicators (KPIs)?

A.   The Process Owner

B.   The Service Level Manager

C.   The Service Owner

D.   The Process Manager

Q35. Which of the following roles in Service Operation is responsible for the effective implementation of the process and carries out the respective reporting method?

A.   The Major Incident Team

B.   The Problem Manager

C.   The Service Request Fulfillment Group

D.   The Incident Manager

Q36. Which of the following levels in Service Operation is used to register and organize received Incidents and carry out an urgent effort in order to restore a failed IT Service as quickly as possible?

A.   2nd Level Support

B.   0 Level Support

C.   1st Level Support

D.   3rd Level Support

Q37.   Which of the following roles in Service Transition is used to maintain a logical model, containing the components of the IT infrastructure (CIs) and their associations?

A.   The Test Manager

B.   The Release Manager

C.   The Knowledge Manager

D.   The Configuration Manager

Q38.   Who is responsible for ensuring that the Request Fulfillment process is being performed according to the agreed and documented process?

A.   Service Owner

B.   Customer

C.   Process Owner

D.   Service Operation

Q39.   What are the names by which the Service Desk function is known?

Each correct answer represents a complete solution. Choose all that apply.

A.   Call Center

B.   Service Request

C.   Help Desk

D.   Service Desk

Q40.   uCertify.com plans on implementing a new Network Operating System (NOS). However, before the actual implementation is carried out, the approach for achieving the implementation is conversed. Under whose management should this conversation be held?

A.   The Change Manager

B.   The Service Level Manager

C.   The Process Manager

D.   The Continual Service Improvement Manager

Answer Explanation

A1.   Answer options A, C, and D are correct.

The characteristics of processes are as follows:

Processes are measurable: They are performance driven. Managers are required to measure cost, quality, and other variables whereas practitioners are concerned with duration and productivity.

Processes have specific results: The reason processes exist is to deliver a specific result. The result has to be independently identifiable and countable.

Processes have customers: Every process delivers its prime results to a customer or stakeholder.

Processes respond to specific events: While a process can be iterative, it should be traceable to a definite trigger.

Answer options B and E are incorrect. All the mentioned points are characteristics of processes.

A2.   Answer option A is correct.

Scope verification is the process of obtaining stakeholder's formal acceptance of the project deliverables. Verify scope is a process of formalizing acceptance of the completed project deliverables. It is an inspection-driven process the stakeholders will complete to inspect the project scope deliverables. It is typically performed at the end of the phase and at the end of the project.

Answer option B is incorrect. Scope validation is not a valid project management term.

Answer option C is incorrect. The perform quality control process precedes scope verification and is done without the project customers.

Answer option D is incorrect. Project closure is the closure of the project and the project contracts.

A3.   Answer option C is correct.

Service Strategy considers the business outcomes and value creation as its principles. Service Strategy is the center and origin point of the ITIL Service Lifecycle. It provides guidance on how to design, develop, and implement service management not only as an organizational capability but also as a strategic asset. Service Strategy provides guidance on clarification and prioritization of service provider investments in services. More generally, Service Strategy focuses on helping IT organizations improve and develop over the long term. In both cases, Service Strategy relies largely upon a market-driven approach.

Service Strategy is useful in the framework of Service Design, Service Transition, Service Operation, and Continual Service Improvement. Service Strategy ensures that organizations are in a position to deal with the costs and risks associated with their Service Portfolios. Service Strategy is set up for operational effectiveness as well as for distinctive performance. Decisions made with respect to Service Strategy have broad consequences including those with delayed effect.

Answer option A is incorrect. Service Design provides good practice guidance on the design of IT services, processes, and other aspects of the service management effort. It covers design principles and methods for converting strategic objectives into portfolios of services and service assets. The scope of Service Design is not limited to new services. Significantly, design within ITIL is understood to encompass all elements relevant to technology service delivery, rather than focusing solely on design of the technology itself.

As such, Service Design addresses how a planned service solution interacts with the larger business and technical environments. Service management systems require supporting the service and processes, which interacts with the service, technology, and architecture required to support the service, and the supply chain required to support the planned service. Within ITIL, design work for an IT service is aggregated into a single Service Design Package (SDP). Service Design Packages (SDP), along with other information about services, is managed within the Service Catalog.

Answer option B is incorrect. Service Transition relates to the delivery of services required by the business into live/operational use, and often encompasses the "project" side of IT rather than Business As Usual (BAU). It provides guidance for the development and improvement of capabilities for transitioning new and changed services into operations. Service Transition provides assistance on how the necessities of Service strategy determined in Service design, thus the necessities are effectively understood in Service operation while controlling the risks of failure and disruption.

Service Transition provides assistance on managing the complication related to changes in services and service management processes, preventing undesired consequences while allowing for improvement. Assistance is provided on transferring the control of services between customers and service providers.

Answer option D is incorrect. Continual Service Improvement (CSI) align and realign IT Services to changing business needs by identifying and implementing improvements to the IT services that support the Business Processes. The perspective of CSI on improvement is the business perspective of service quality, even though CSI aims to improve process effectiveness, efficiency and cost effectiveness of the IT processes through the whole lifecycle. To manage improvement, CSI should clearly define what should be controlled and measured.

Assistance is provided for linking improvement efforts and outcomes with Service Strategy, Design, and Transition. A closed-loop feedback system, based on the Plan-Do-Check-Act (PDCA) model specified in ISO/IEC 20000, is established and capable of receiving inputs for change from any planning perspective. CSI needs to be treated just like any other service practice. There needs to be upfront planning, training and awareness, ongoing scheduling, roles created, ownership assigned, and activities identified to be successful. CSI must be planned and scheduled as process with defined activities, inputs, outputs, roles and reporting.

A4. Answer option B is correct.

The IT Budget is an annual financial plan that provides an estimate of projected expenditures and allocates financial resources to a variety of service management processes and organizational units within the IT organization.

Answer option A is incorrect. An Invoice is the delivery of a service or product.

Answer option C is incorrect. A Budget Request is issued from any of the Service Management processes at the same time when compiling a Request for Change. An approved Budget Request means that the necessary financial resources for implementing a Change are approved by Financial Management.

Answer option D is incorrect. A Budget Allocation is performed by the Financial Manager to implement a Change. Budget Allocations are issued in response to Budget Requests originating from any Service Management process in combination with Requests for Change.

A5. Answer option C is correct.

The key output handed over to Service Transition is Service Design Package (SDP). Service Design provides good practice guidance on the design of IT services, processes, and other aspects of the service management effort. It covers design principles and methods for converting strategic objectives into portfolios of services and service assets. The scope of Service Design is not limited to new services.

Significantly, design within ITIL is understood to encompass all elements relevant to technology service delivery, rather than focusing solely on design of the technology itself.

As such, Service Design addresses how a planned service solution interacts with the larger business and technical environments. Service management systems require supporting the service and processes, which interacts with the service, technology, and architecture required to support the service, and the supply chain required to support the planned service. Within ITIL, design work for an IT service is aggregated into a single Service Design Package (SDP). Service Design Packages (SDP), along with other information about services, is managed within the Service Catalog.

Answer option A is incorrect. ITIL Small-Scale Implementation provides an approach to ITIL framework implementation for smaller IT units or departments. It is primarily an auxiliary work that covers many of the same best practice guidelines as Planning To Implement Service Management, Service Support, and Service Delivery but provides additional guidance on the combination of roles and responsibilities, and avoiding conflict between ITIL priorities.

Answer option B is incorrect. Service Portfolio Management is the process responsible for the assembly of an initial Service Design Package (SDP) for each service and its maintenance through the service life cycle. This also involves cooperating with the Continual Service Improvement Process. The SDP may be altered and extended by other Service Management processes.

Answer option D is incorrect. The Business Perspective is the name given to the collection of best practices that is suggested to address some of the issues often encountered in understanding and improving IT service provision, as a part of the entire business requirement for high IS quality management.

A6.   Answer option D is correct.

Service Transition contains the detailed description of the Service Asset and Configuration Management, Transition Planning and Support, Release and deployment Management, Change Management, Knowledge Management, as well as the key roles of staff engaged in Service Transition. Service Transition relates to the delivery of services required by the business into live/operational use, and often encompasses the "project" side of IT rather than Business As Usual (BAU). It provides guidance for the development and improvement of capabilities for transitioning new and changed services into operations. Service Transition provides assistance on how the necessities of Service strategy determined in Service design, thus the necessities are effectively understood in Service operation while controlling the risks of failure and disruption.

Service Transition provides assistance on managing the complication related to changes in services and service management processes, preventing undesired consequences while allowing for improvement. Assistance is provided on transferring the control of services between customers and service providers.

Answer options A, B, and C are incorrect. Service Transition does not contain detailed description of the Capacity Management, Event Management, Service Request Management, Service Level Management, Service Portfolio Management, and Request Fulfillment.

A7.   Answer option A is correct.

Event management, Incident management, Problem management, Request fulfillment, Access Management, and Service desk are part of Service Operation stage of the Service Lifecycle. The functions include technical management, application management, operations management, and Service Desk as well as, responsibilities for staff engaged in Service Operation.

Service Operation is the best practice for achieving the delivery of agreed levels of services both to end-users and the customers (where "customers" refer to those individuals who pay for the service and negotiate the SLAs). Service Operation is the part of the lifecycle where the services and value are actually directly delivered. Also, the monitoring of problems and balance between service reliability and cost, etc. are considered.

Strategic objectives are eventually recognized through Service Operation, thus making it a critical capability. Assistance is provided on ways to sustain steadiness in service operations, allowing for changes in design, scale, scope and service levels. Organizations are provided with detailed process course of action, methods, and tools for use in two major control perspectives, which are as follows:

- Reactive

- Proactive.

Answer option B is incorrect. Service Portfolio Management, Demand Management, and IT Financial Management are part of Service Strategy stage.

Answer option C is incorrect. Continual Service Improvement (CSI) align and realign IT Services to changing business needs by identifying and implementing improvements to the IT services that support the Business Processes. The perspective of CSI on improvement is the business perspective of service quality, even though CSI aims to improve process effectiveness, efficiency and cost effectiveness of the IT processes through the whole lifecycle. To manage improvement, CSI should clearly define what should be controlled and measured.

Assistance is provided for linking improvement efforts and outcomes with Service Strategy, Design, and Transition. A closed-loop feedback system, based on the Plan-Do-Check-Act (PDCA) model specified in ISO/IEC 20000, is established and capable of receiving inputs for change from any planning perspective. CSI needs to be treated just like any other service practice. There needs to be upfront planning, training and awareness, ongoing scheduling, roles created, ownership assigned, and activities identified to be successful. CSI must be planned and scheduled as process with defined activities, inputs, outputs, roles and reporting.

Answer option D is incorrect. Service Asset and Configuration Management, Transition Planning and Support, Release and Deployment Management, Change Management, and Knowledge Management are part of Service Transition stage, as well as the key roles of staff engaged in Service Transition.

A8.   Answer option B is correct.

Demand Management has two aspects that should be considered, which are as follows:

1. It concerns operational support activity

2. It relates to strategic intent

The Demand Management process is first and foremost concerned with understanding Patterns of Business Activity (PBA). Demand Management is about understanding where the demand is coming from.

Demand management is the art or science of controlling economic demand to avoid a recession. It refers to policies to control consumer demand for environmentally sensitive or harmful goods. Within manufacturing firms the term is used to describe the activities of demand forecasting, planning, and order fulfillment.

Answer option A is incorrect. Service Desk is a primary IT capability called for in IT Service Management (ITSM) as defined by the Information Technology Infrastructure Library (ITIL). It is intended to provide a Single Point of Contact ("SPOC") to meet the communication needs of both Users and IT, and to satisfy both Customer and IT Provider objectives. ("User" refers to the actual user of the service, while "Customer" refers to the entity that is paying for service)

Answer option C is incorrect. Request Fulfillment is added as a new process to ITIL V3 with the aim to have a dedicated process dealing with Service Requests. This was motivated by a clear distinction in ITIL V3 between Incidents (Service Interruptions) and Service Requests (standard requests from users, e.g. password resets). In ITIL V2, Service Requests were fulfilled by the Incident Management process. There are no sub-processes specified for Request Fulfillment according to ITIL V3.

Answer option D is incorrect. Supplier Management is used to ensure that all contracts with suppliers support the needs of the business, and that all suppliers meet their contractual commitments. It is part of the Service Design. The owner of Supplier Management is the Supplier Manager. In ITIL V3, Supplier Management is part of the Service Design process to allow for a better integration into the Service Lifecycle. The sub-processes of Supplier Management are as follows:

• Providing the Supplier Management Framework

• Evaluation of New Suppliers and Contracts

• Establishing New Suppliers and Contracts

• Processing of Standard Orders

• Supplier and Contract Review

• Contract Renewal or Termination

A9. Answer option A is correct.

The Service Improvement Plan (SIP) refers to the steps that must be taken if there is a major gap in the projected delivery quality of a service and the actual delivery. SIP is a model that belongs to the Service Level Management (SLM) process. SLM is mainly defined in the Service Design of ITIL v3, but like many processes in v3, SLM is also documented in other volumes. SIP is particularly documented in Continual Service Improvement (CSI). SIP is also referred to when capital budgeting is being discussed with reference to preference decisions.

Answer option B is incorrect. The Service Quality Plan contains all management information for the measurement of the IT Service quality upon the basis of Performance Indicators and the contribution by internal and external suppliers for the provision of IT Services.

Answer option C is incorrect. Service Level Agreement (SLA) is a part of a service contract where the level of service is formally defined. In practice, the term SLA is sometimes used to refer to the contracted delivery time (of the service) or performance.

Answer option D is incorrect. Business Service Catalogue includes details of all of the IT services delivered to customers. It also includes the IT services together with relationships to the business units and the business processes that rely on the IT services. Business Service Catalogue is the customers' perspective of the Service Catalogue.

A10. Answer options A and C are correct.

The two elements of a service's business value from customers' perspective are Utility and Warranty.

Utility	Warranty
It provides the functionality offered by a product or service as the customers' view it.	It promises that the product or service will meet the approved requirements.
It specifies what the customers get.	It specifies how it is delivered.
It provides fitness for purpose.	It provides fitness for use: Three characteristics of warranty are as follows: 1. It is provided in terms of the availability or capacity of services. 2. It ensures that customers' assets continue to get utility. 3. It looks after the security for value creating potential of the customers' assets.
It increases performance average.	It reduces performance variations.

Answer option B is incorrect. Availability is the most basic aspect of assuring value to customers. It gives surety to the customer that services will be available for use under agreed terms and conditions. The availability of a service is its most happily perceived attribute from a user's perspective. A service is available only if users can access it in an agreed approach. Perceptions and preferences vary by customer and by business context. Availability of a service is more delicate than a binary evaluation of available and unavailable. The time period for which the customer can wait to avail the service should be determined and factored into service design.

Answer option is incorrect. A Configuration item (CI) is an IT asset or a combination of IT assets that may depend and have relationships with other IT processes. A CI will have attributes which may be hierarchical and relationships that will be assigned by the configuration manager in the CM database.

A11. Answer options A, B, and D are correct.

The Service Portfolio is divided into three phases, which are as follows:

- Service pipeline
- Service catalogue
- Retired services

The service pipeline is one of the three phases of Service Portfolio. It is a future based concept that defines the strategic future direction for the service provider. It is the concept that defines the variety of services that are currently under development in Service Portfolio. The pipeline is an excellent indicator on the overall strength of the service provider, as it shows the services that are under development for customers or markets.

A service catalog is a list of services that an organization provides, often to its employees or customers. Each service within the catalog typically includes the following:

- A description of the service
- Timeframes or Service Level Agreement (SLA) for fulfilling the service
- Who is entitled to request/view the service
- Costs (if any)
- How to fulfill the service

Retired services are not available for use by present customers. However, if the customers give a strong business case, the service providers can restore the phased out service. Although these services are fully terminated, information and data added while services were under operation are stored in the knowledge base of the company. Retiring the services is a normal event in a service lifecycle.

Answer option C is incorrect. There is no such phase as service audit in which the Service Portfolio is divided.

A12.   Answer option B is correct.

Notional Charging is used to show to the business how they will be charged in a real life situation. It is a good way of getting the customer use to the idea for full or partial charging at a later date. Notional Charging may show the detail of what would be charged if full charging were in place without transactions actually being applied to the financial ledgers (Notional Charging). Notional Charging may also be used as a way of piloting Full Charging.

Answer option A is incorrect. Charging need not necessarily mean money changing hands. This is known as Full Charging.

Answer option C is incorrect. Charging may take the form of information passed to management on the cost of provision of IT services. This is known as No Charging.

Answer option D is incorrect. A chargeback is the return of funds to a consumer, forcibly initiated by the consumer's issuing bank. Specifically, it is the reversal of a prior outbound transfer of funds from a consumer's bank account or line of credit.

A13.   Answer options A and D are correct.

The Business Case is a justification for an important item of expenditure. It includes information about cost, benefits, options, issues, risks, and potential problems. It is a decision support and planning tool that projects the expected outcome of a business action. It uses qualitative terms. A typically business case structure is as follows:

- Introduction: It provides business objectives address.

- Methods and assumptions: It specifies the boundaries of the business case.

- Business impacts: It provides financial and non-financial business case results.

- Risks and contingencies

- Recommendations: It specifies specific actions.

226

Answer options B, C, and E are incorrect. All the given points are part of a typically business case structure.

A14. Answer option C is correct.

In this instance, you are using the nominal group technique to identify risks involved in the project. The nominal group technique (NGT) is a structured process to gather information from a group. It requires participants to be together in the same room. Each participant jots down risks in the project on piece of papers. Each piece of paper lists only one risk. These risks are posted on a board and analyzed by the participants. It is then ranked and prioritized in writing.

Answer option A is incorrect. Brainstorming involves subject matter experts, team members, risk management team members to participate for risk identification. In a room, they are asked to identify possible risk events. After a long session of discussion, risk events are identified.

Answer option B is incorrect. Delphi is lot a like brainstorming; only the people in the meeting don't know each other.

Answer option D is incorrect. Assumption analysis is a matter of identifying and documenting the assumptions made regarding the project and then using them as a jumping-off point to further identify risks.

A15. Answer option C is correct.

The risk owner is the individual on the project team that is closest to the risk event. The risk owner can be an individual or an organization responsible for implementing risk responses or contingency plan. The risk owner should be empowered with the ability to respond to the risk as it was planned.

Answer option A is incorrect. You are the project manager and likely won't be the risk owner as well.

Answer option B is incorrect. The project sponsor authorizes the project but does not participate in the execution of the project.

Answer option D is incorrect. While a subject matter expert may be the risk owner on some occasions, he won't be the risk owner on every occasion.

A16. Answer option C is correct.

SLA Monitoring Chart (SLAM) is used to see an outline of actual service achievements against targets. It monitors existing agreements. It is usually used to monitor the following:

- Quality of service

- All other contract aspects

- Agreement for end of service

Answer option A is incorrect. Service Level Agreement (frequently abbreviated as SLA) is a part of a service contract where the level of service is formally defined. In practice, the term SLA is sometimes used to refer to the contracted delivery time (of the service) or performance.

Answer option B is incorrect. Underpinning Contract (UC) is a contract between an IT service provider and a third party. In another way, it is an agreement between the IT organization and an external provider about the delivery of one or more services. The third party provides services that support the delivery of a service to a customer. The Underpinning Contract defines targets and responsibilities that are required to meet agreed Service Level targets in an SLA.

Answer option D is incorrect. An Operational Level Agreement (OLA) defines the interdependent relationships among the internal support groups of an organization working to support a Service Level Agreement. The agreement describes the responsibilities of each internal support group toward other support groups, including the process and timeframe for delivery of their services. The objective of the OLA is to present a clear, concise, and measurable description of the service provider's internal support relationships. OLA is sometimes expanded to other phrases but they all have the same meaning:

- Organizational Level Agreement

- Operating Level Agreement

- Operations Level Agreement

A17.   Answer option A is correct.

The Service Level Management will work with the Business delegate (Business Owner) to document the Service Level Requirements. Service Level Management provides for continual identification, monitoring and review of the levels of IT services specified in the service level agreements (SLAs). It ensures that arrangements are in place with internal IT Support Providers and external suppliers in the form of Operational Level Agreements (OLAs) and Underpinning Contracts (UCs). The process involves assessing the impact of change upon service quality and SLAs. The Service Level Management process is in close relation with the operational processes to control their activities. The central role of Service Level Management makes it the natural place for metrics to be established and monitored against a benchmark.

Note: *Service Level Management is the primary interface with the customer (as opposed to the user, who is serviced by the Service Desk).*

Answer option B is incorrect. The Service Level Manager is responsible for negotiating Service Level Agreements and ensuring that these are met. He makes sure that all IT Service Management processes, Operational Level Agreements, and Underpinning Contracts are appropriate for the agreed service level targets. The Service Level Manager also monitors and reports on service levels.

Answer option C is incorrect. Project management is the discipline of planning, organizing, and managing resources to bring about the successful completion of specific project goals and objectives. It is often closely related to and sometimes conflated with program management.

A project is a temporary endeavor, having a defined beginning and end, undertaken to meet particular goals and objectives, usually to bring about beneficial change or added value. In practice, the management of these two systems is often found to be quite different, and as such requires the development of distinct technical skills and the adoption of separate management.

The primary challenge of project management is to achieve all of the project goals and objectives while honoring the preconceived project constraints. Typical constraints are scope, time, and budget. The secondary and more ambitious challenge is to optimize the allocation and integration of inputs necessary to meet pre-defined objectives.

Answer option D is incorrect. The Service Owner is responsible for a specific service such as Infrastructure, Application, or Professional Service within an organization despite of where the underpinning technology components, processes, or professional capabilities are located. However, in order to ensure that a service is managed with a business focus, the definition of a single point of responsibility is absolutely necessary to give the level of attention and focus required for its delivery. Service ownership is as critical to service management as establishing ownership for processes which cross multiple vertical silos or departments.

Service Owner is responsible for continuous improvement and the management of change affecting the services under their heed. The

Service Owner is a prime stakeholder in all of the IT processes, which enable or support it.

A18. Answer option B is correct.

The Supplier Manager role is responsible for review and risk analysis of all contracts on a regular basis. The Supplier Manager is responsible for ensuring that value for money is obtained from all suppliers. He makes sure that contracts with suppliers support the needs of the business, and that all suppliers meet their contractual commitments.

Answer option A is incorrect. The Service Catalogue Manager is responsible for maintaining the Service Catalogue, ensuring that all information within the Service Catalogue is accurate and up to date.

Answer option C is incorrect. The Configuration Manager is responsible for maintaining information about Configuration Items that are required to deliver IT services. He also maintains a logical model, containing the components of the IT infrastructure (CIs) and their associations.

Answer option D is incorrect. The IT Service Continuity Manager is responsible for managing risks that could seriously impact IT services. He ensures that the IT service provider can provide minimum agreed service levels in cases of disaster, by reducing the risk to an acceptable level and planning for the recovery of IT services.

A19. Answer option B is correct.

The Availability Measurements are matched as follows:

1. MTTR = Mean Time To Repair (MTTR) is the average time taken to repair a Configuration Item or IT Service after a failure. It represents the average time required to repair a failed component or device. Expressed mathematically, it is the total corrective maintenance time divided by the total number of corrective maintenance actions during a given period of time. It generally does not include lead time for parts not readily available or other Administrative or Logistic Downtime (ALDT).

   MTTR is often part of a maintenance contract, where a system whose MTTR is 24 hours is generally more valuable than for one of 7 days if mean time between failures is equal, because its Operational Availability is higher. MTTR is every now and then incorrectly used to mean Mean Time to Restore Service.

2. MTBF = Mean Time Between Failures (MTBF) is the predicted elapsed time between inherent failures of a system during

operation. MTBF can be calculated as the arithmetic mean time between failures of a system. MTBF is typically part of a model that assumes the failed system is immediately repaired, as a part of a renewal process. This is in contrast to the Mean Time To Failure (MTTF), which measures average time between failure with the modeling assumption that the failed system is not repaired.

3. MTBSI = Mean Time Between Service Incidents (MTBSI) is a metric used to measure and report reliability. MTBSI is the mean time starting from when a system or IT service fails, until it next fails. MTBSI is equivalent to MTBF + MTRS. Mean Time Between Service Incidents (MTBSI) is used in Service Design of ITIL.

4. MTTF = Mean Time To Failure (MTTF) is an approximate of the average, or mean time until a component's first failure, or disruption in the operation of the product, process, procedure, or design takes place. MTTF presumes that the product CANNOT be repaired and the product CANNOT continue any of its regular operations.

In many designs and components, MTTF is especially near to the MTBF, which is a bit longer than MTTF. This is due to the fact that MTBF adds the repair time of the designs or components. MTBF is the average time between failures to include the average repair time, or MTTR.

Answer options A, C, and D are incorrect. These are incorrect matches of the Availability Measurements.

A20. Answer option A is correct.

The Service Knowledge Management System is the central repository of the IT organization's data, information and knowledge. It extends the concept of the infrastructure-focused Configuration Management System to include further information on services, capabilities, and initiatives.

Answer option B is incorrect. Compliance Management is used to ensure that IT services, processes and systems comply with enterprise policies, and legal requirements. It is part of Service Design and the owner of Compliance Management is the Compliance Manager. Compliance issues are addressed within several processes in ITIL V2 and ITIL V3; however, there is no dedicated Compliance Management process. Compliance is an increasingly important topic for IT organizations.

Answer option C is incorrect. Supplier and Contract Database (SCD) is a database or structured document used to manage supplier contracts throughout their lifecycle. The SCD contains key attributes of all contracts and suppliers, and should be part of the Service Knowledge Management System.

Answer option D is incorrect. Knowledge Management is used to gather, analyze, store, and share knowledge and information within an organization. The primary purpose of Knowledge Management is to improve efficiency by reducing the need to rediscover knowledge. It is part of Service Transition and the owner of Knowledge Management is the Knowledge Manager. ITIL V3, however, defines Knowledge Management as the one central process responsible for providing knowledge to all other IT Service Management processes.

Note: Knowledge Management is dealt with in many other Service Management processes. The Knowledge Management process itself ensures that all information used within Service Management, stored in the Service Knowledge Management System, is consistent and readily available.

A21.   Answer options B and C are correct.

A Configuration item (CI) is an IT asset or a combination of IT assets that may depend and have relationships with other IT processes. A CI will have attributes which may be hierarchical and relationships that will be assigned by the configuration manager in the CM database. The term Configuration Item (CI) refers to the fundamental structural unit of a configuration management system. Examples of CIs include individual requirements documents, software, models, plans, and people. Configuration Management systems oversee the life of the CIs through a combination of process and tools. The objective of these systems is to avoid the introduction of errors related to lack of testing or incompatibilities with other CIs.

CIs role in Configuration Management

From the perspective of the implementer of a change, the configuration item is the "what" of the change. Altering a specific baseline version of a configuration item creates a new version of the same configuration item, itself a baseline. In examining the effect of a change, first ask:

1.   What configuration items are affected?

2.   How have the configuration items been affected?

A release (itself a versioned entity) may consist of several configuration items. The set of changes to each configuration item will appear in the release notes, and the notes may contain specific headings for each configuration item.

As well as participating in the implementation of a change and in the management of a change, the listing and definition of each configuration item may act as a common vocabulary across all groups connected to the product. It should be defined at a level such that an individual involved with product marketing and an individual at the coal face of implementation can agree to a common definition when they use the name of the configuration item. Selection and identification of configuration items for a particular project can be seen as the first step in developing an overall architecture from the top down.

Answer options A and D are incorrect. All the mentioned activities are helped by recording relationships between Configuration Items (CIs).

A22. Answer option C is correct.

In order to write off a set percentage of an IT Asset each and every year, you will use the Reducing Balance method to accomplish this. The Reducing Balance method of depreciation uses a set percentage for the asset value reduction every year. This method is an alternative to the commonly used Straight Line method. The Reducing Balance method is often used for tax purposes, but less often in published accounts. Rather than charging a fixed amount every year, a fixed percentage of the remaining value of the asset is charged every year.

Answer option A is incorrect. The Straight Line method is the simplest and most often used technique. In this method, the company estimates the salvage value of the asset at the end of the period during which it will be used to generate revenues and will expense a portion of original cost in equal increments over that period. The salvage value is an estimate of the value of the asset at the time it will be sold or disposed of; it may be zero or even negative. Salvage value is also known as scrap value or residual value.

Answer option B is incorrect. The Declining Balance method provides for a higher depreciation charge in the first year of an asset's life and gradually decreasing charges in subsequent years. This may be a more realistic reflection of an asset's actual expected benefit from the use of the asset: many assets are most useful when they are new. One popular accelerated method is the declining-balance method. Under this method the Book Value is multiplied by a fixed rate.

Annual Depreciation = Depreciation Rate * Book Value at Beginning of Year

Answer option D is incorrect. The Composite Depreciation method is applied to a collection of assets that are not similar, and have different service lives. For example, computers and printers are not similar, but both are part of the office equipment. Depreciation on all assets is determined by using the straight-line-depreciation method.

A23.   Answer option C is correct.

A known error is a condition recognized by successful diagnosis of the root cause of a problem, and the subsequent development of a Work-around.

Incidents may match with existing 'Known Problems' (without a known root cause) or 'Known Errors' (with a root cause) under the control of Problem Management and registered in the Known Error Database (KeDB). Where existing work-arounds have been developed, it is suggested that accessing these will allow the Service Desk to provide a quick first-line fix. Where an incident is not the result of a Known Problem or Known Error, it may either be an isolated or individual occurrence or may (once the initial issue has been addressed) require that Problem Management becomes involved, possibly resulting in a new problem record being raised.

Answer option A is incorrect. An incident is any event which is not part of the standard operation of a service and which causes, or may cause, an interruption to, or a reduction in, the quality of service. The stated ITIL objective is to restore normal operations as quickly as possible with the least possible impact on either the business or the user, at a cost-effective price.

ISO 20000 defines an incident as:

Any event which is not part of the standard operation of a service and which causes or may cause an interruption to, or a reduction in, the quality of that service.

Incidents can be classified into three primary categories, which are as follows:

1. Software

2. Hardware

3. Service requests

Note that service requests are not always regarded as an incident, but rather a request for change. However, the handling of failures and the handling of service requests are similar, and therefore, are included in the definition and scope of the process of incident management.

Answer options B and D are incorrect. Incidents are the result of failures or errors in the IT infrastructure. The cause of Incidents may be apparent and the cause may be addressed without the need for further investigation, resulting in a repair, a Work-around or a request for change (RFC) to remove the error.

Where an incident is considered to be serious in nature, or multiple occurrences of similar incidents are observed, a problem record might be created as a result. The management of a problem varies from the process of managing an incident and is typically performed by different staff and therefore is controlled by the Problem Management process. When a problem has been properly identified and a work-around is known, the problem becomes a 'known problem'. When its 'root cause' has been identified, it becomes a 'known error'. Finally, a request for change (RFC) may be raised to modify the system by resolving the known error. This process is covered by the Change Management process.

A request for new additional service is not regarded as an incident, but as a Request for Service (RFS).

A24.   Answer option A is correct.

The Error Control Process is an iterative process to diagnose known errors until they are eliminated by the successful implementation of a change under the control of the Change Management process.

Answer option B is incorrect. The Problem Management Process is intended to reduce the number and severity of incidents and problems of the business, and report it in documentation to be available for the first-line and second line of the help desk. The proactive process identifies and resolves problems before incidents occur. These activities are as follows:

Trend analysis

Targeting support action

These two provides information to the organization.

Answer option C is incorrect. The Problem Control Process aims to handle problems in an efficient way. Problem control identifies the root cause of incidents and reports it to the service desk. Other activities are as follows:

- Problem identification and recording

- Problem classification

- Problem investigation and diagnosis

The standard technique for identifying the root cause of a problem is to use an Ishikawa diagram, also referred to as a cause-and-effect diagram, tree diagram, or fishbone diagram. A brainstorming session, in which group members offer product improvement ideas, typically results in an Ishikawa diagram. For problem-solving, the goal is to find causes and effects of the problem.

Answer option D is incorrect. Business Transaction Management (BTM) is an approach to managing IT from a business transaction perspective. BTM aims to guarantee service quality for users conducting business transactions while simultaneously optimizing the IT applications and infrastructure across which those transactions execute. At the heart of BTM lies the ability to capture and to track all transactions, across all IT tiers, automatically and continuously.

BTM is ideally suited to managing performance and availability problems because it clearly identifies exactly where transactions are held up. But for IT, problem management is just the tip of the iceberg. BTM also enables proactive problem prevention as well as the generation of business service intelligence for optimization of resource provisioning and virtualization.

A25.   Answer option B is correct.

The Service Portfolio Manager decides on a strategy to serve customers in co-operation with the IT Steering Group, and develops the service provider's offerings and capabilities.

Answer option A is incorrect. The Financial Manager is responsible for managing an IT service provider's budgeting, accounting, and charging requirements.

Answer option C is incorrect. The Service Level Manager is responsible for negotiating Service Level Agreements and ensuring that these are met. He makes sure that all IT Service Management processes, Operational Level Agreements, and Underpinning Contracts are appropriate for the agreed service level targets. The Service Level Manager also monitors and reports on service levels.

Answer option D is incorrect. The IT Steering Group (ISG) is a formal group that is accountable for ensuring that the Business and the IT Service provider strategies and plans are very much associated with each other. It takes in senior representatives from the Business and the IT Service provider. IT Steering Group (ISG) sets the direction and strategy for IT Services. It includes members of senior management from business and IT. It reviews the business and IT strategies in order to make sure that they are aligned. It also sets priorities of service development programs/ projects.

A26.   Answer option D is correct.

Technical Analysts/Architects is a term that refers to any staff member in Technical Management who performs the activities, excluding the daily operational actions. The Technical Analyst/Architect is responsible for designing infrastructure components and systems required to provide a service. This includes the specification of technologies and products as a basis for their procurement and customization. The roles of Technical Analysts/Architects are as follows:

Working with Application Management and other areas in Technical Management to decide the utmost level of system requirements necessary to meet the requirements within budget and technology constraints.

Working with users, sponsors, Application Management, and all other stakeholders to decide their developing needs.

Performing cost-benefit analyses to decide the appropriate means to meet the declared requirements.

Developing Operational Models that will ensure optimal use of resources and the appropriate level of performance.

Ensuring the consistent performance of the infrastructure to deliver the required level of service to the business.

Defining all tasks required to manage the infrastructure and ensuring that these tasks are performed appropriately.

Input into the design of configuration data required to administer and track the application effectively.

Answer option A is incorrect. The Application Analysts and Architects are responsible for matching requirements to application specifications. They are responsible for designing applications required to provide a service. They include the specification of technologies, application architectures, and data structures as a basis for application development or customization. The specific activities are as follows:

Working with users, sponsors, and all other stakeholders to decide the developing needs.

Performing cost-benefit analyses to decide the means to meet up the declared requirement.

Input into the design of configuration data required to handle and track the application effectively.

Developing Operational Models that will make sure optimal use of resources and the appropriate level of performance.

Ensuring that applications are designed to be efficiently managed given the organization's technology architecture, available skills, and tools.

Developing and maintaining standards for application sizing, performance, modeling, etc.

Generating a set of acceptance test requirements, mutually with the designers, test engineers, and the users.

Working with Technical Management to decide the utmost level of system requirements necessary to meet up the business requirements within financial plan and technology constraints.

Answer option B is incorrect. The Risk Manager is responsible for identifying, assessing, and controlling risks. This includes analyzing the value of assets to the business, identifying threats to those assets, and evaluating how vulnerable each asset is to those threats.

Answer option C is incorrect. The Capacity Manager is responsible for ensuring that services and infrastructure are competent to deliver the agreed capacity and performance targets in a cost effective and timely manner. He considers all resources required to deliver the service, and plans for short, medium, and long term business requirements.

A27.   Answer option A is correct.

The IT Architect defines a blueprint for the future development of the technological landscape, taking into account the service strategy and newly available technologies.

Answer option B is incorrect. The Application Analysts and Architects are responsible for matching requirements to application specifications. They are responsible for designing applications required to provide a service. They include the specification of technologies, application architectures, and data structures as a basis for application development or customization. The specific activities are as follows:

- Working with users, sponsors, and all other stakeholders to decide the developing needs.

- Performing cost-benefit analyses to decide the means to meet up the declared requirement.

- Input into the design of configuration data required to handle and track the application effectively.

- Developing Operational Models that will make sure optimal use of resources and the appropriate level of performance.

- Ensuring that applications are designed to be efficiently managed given the organization's technology architecture, available skills, and tools.

- Developing and maintaining standards for application sizing, performance, modeling, etc.

- Generating a set of acceptance test requirements, mutually with the designers, test engineers, and the users.

- Working with Technical Management to decide the utmost level of system requirements necessary to meet up the business requirements within financial plan and technology constraints.

Answer option C is incorrect. The Supplier Manager is responsible for ensuring that value for money is obtained from all suppliers. He makes sure that contracts with suppliers support the needs of the business, and that all suppliers meet their contractual commitments.

Answer option D is incorrect. Technical Analysts/Architects is a term that refers to any staff member in Technical Management who performs the activities, excluding the daily operational actions. The Technical Analyst/Architect is responsible for designing infrastructure components and systems required to provide a service. This includes the specification of technologies and products as a basis for their procurement and customization. The roles of Technical Analysts/Architects are as follows:

- Working with Application Management and other areas in Technical Management to decide the utmost level of system requirements necessary to meet the requirements within budget and technology constraints.

- Working with users, sponsors, Application Management, and all other stakeholders to decide their developing needs.

- Performing cost-benefit analyses to decide the appropriate means to meet the declared requirements.

- Developing Operational Models that will ensure optimal use of resources and the appropriate level of performance.

- Ensuring the consistent performance of the infrastructure to deliver the required level of service to the business.

- Defining all tasks required to manage the infrastructure and ensuring that these tasks are performed appropriately.

- Input into the design of configuration data required to administer and track the application effectively.

A28.   Answer option B is correct.

There are four commonly used terms when discussing service improvement outcomes, which are as follows:

Improvements: It is the outcome that is once compared to the earlier state, which shows a computable increase in a desirable metric or decrease in an undesirable metric.

- Benefits: It is the profit achieved through realization of improvements.

- Return On Investment (ROI): It is the difference between the benefit achieved and the amount spent to achieve that benefit, it is expressed as a percentage.

- Value On Investment (VOI): It is the extra value produced by establishment of benefits that include long-term outcomes. ROI is a sub-component of VOI.

Answer option A is incorrect. Return On Investment (ROI) is also a commonly used term when discussing service improvement outcomes.

Answer options C, D, and E are incorrect. Resources are types of assets and they are direct inputs for production. Organizations use them to create value in the form of goods and services. Management, organization, people, and knowledge are used to transform resources. It is comparatively easy to obtain resources compared to capabilities.

A29.   Answer option A is correct.

Benchmarking is also recognized as Best Practice Benchmarking or Process Benchmarking. It is a process used in management and mostly useful for strategic management. It is the process of comparing the business processes and performance metrics including cost, cycle time, productivity, or quality to another that is widely considered to be an industry standard benchmark or best practice. It allows organizations to develop plans on how to implement best practice with the aim of increasing some aspect of performance.

Benchmarking might be a one-time event, although it is frequently treated as a continual process in which organizations continually seek out to challenge their practices. It allows organizations to develop plans on how to make improvements or adapt specific best practices, usually with the aim of increasing some aspect of performance.

Answer option B is incorrect. COBIT stands for Control Objectives for Information and Related Technology. COBIT is a set of best practices (framework) for information technology (IT) management created by the Information Systems Audit and Control Association (ISACA), and the IT Governance Institute (ITGI) in 1996. COBIT provides managers, auditors, and IT users with a set of generally accepted measures, indicators, processes, and best practices to assist them in maximizing the benefits derived through the use of information technology and developing appropriate IT governance and control in a company.

Answer option C is incorrect. An agreement is a meeting of minds between two or more legally competent parties, about their relative duties and rights regarding current or future performance. When people feel or think the same way about something, they agree. Sometimes it is important to write down or make a promise to what has been agreed upon. This is called an agreement. Agreements are common in law and business. For example, when a person takes a loan or hires someone to work, an agreement is usually signed so everyone understands what must be done and in what time it must be done.

Answer option D is incorrect. The Service Improvement Plan (SIP) is a formal plan to implement improvements to services and IT processes. The SIP is used to manage and log improvement initiatives triggered by Continual Service Improvement. Generally, improvement initiatives are either of the following:

- Internal initiatives pursued by the service provider on his own behalf, for example to improve processes or make better use of resources.

- Initiatives which require the customer's cooperation, for example if some of the agreed service levels are found to be no longer adequate.

A30. Answer option C is correct.

The Business Continuity Strategy is an outline of the approach to ensure the continuity of Vital Business Functions in the case of disaster events. The Business Continuity Strategy is prepared by the business and serves as a starting point for producing the IT Service Continuity Strategy.

Answer option A is incorrect. Disaster Invocation Guideline is a document produced by IT Service Continuity Management with detailed instructions on when and how to invoke the procedure for fighting a disaster. Most importantly, the guideline defines the first step to be taken by the Service Desk after learning that a disaster has occurred.

Answer option B is incorrect. Index of Disaster-Relevant Information is a catalogue of all information that is relevant in the event of disasters. This document is maintained and circulated by IT Service Continuity Management to all members of IT staff with responsibilities for fighting disasters.

Answer option D is incorrect. Availability/ ITSCM/ Security Testing Schedule is a schedule for the regular testing of all availability, continuity, and security mechanisms jointly maintained by Availability, IT Service Continuity, and IT Security Management.

A31. Answer option D is correct.

The Capacity Management process is responsible for determining the hardware requirements in order to support an application. Capacity Management is the discipline which ensures that IT infrastructure is supplied at the right time, in the right quantity, and at the right price. It also ensures that IT is used in the most proficient way. Capacity Management supports the optimum and cost effective provision of IT services by helping organizations match their IT resources to the business demands. The high-level activities are Application Sizing, Workload Management, Demand Management, Modeling, Capacity Planning, Resource Management, and Performance Management. Capacity management is made up of three sub processes:

1. Business Capacity Management (BCM)

2. Service Capacity Management (SCM)

3. Resource Capacity Management (RCM)

Answer option A is incorrect. Software Asset Management (SAM) is the practice of integrating people, processes and technology to allow software licenses and usage to be systematically tracked, evaluated, and managed. The goal of SAM is to reduce IT expenditures, human resource overhead and risks inherent in owning and managing software assets. SAM practices include the following:

- Maintaining software license compliance

- Tracking inventory and software asset use

Maintaining standard policies and procedures surrounding definition, deployment, configuration, use, and retirement of software assets and the Definitive Software Library.

SAM represents the software component of IT asset management. This includes hardware asset management, because effective hardware inventory controls are critical to efforts to control software. This means overseeing software and hardware that comprise an organization's computers and network.

Answer option B is incorrect. Change Management is used to ensure that standardized methods and procedures are used for efficient handling of all changes. A change is "an event that results in a new status of one or more configuration items (CI's)" approved by management, cost effective, enhances business process changes (fixes) - with a minimum risk to IT infrastructure. The main aims of Change Management are as follows:

- Minimal disruption of services

- Reduction in back-out activities

- Economic utilization of resources involved in the change

Answer option C is incorrect. Configuration Management (CM) is an Information Technology Infrastructure Library (ITIL) IT Service Management (ITSM) process. It tracks all of the individual Configuration Items (CI) in an IT system, which may be as simple as a single server, or as complex as the entire IT department. In large organizations a configuration manager may be appointed to oversee and manage the CM process.

A32. Answer option C is correct.

Management is asking you to create a RACI chart. A RACI chart uses the legend of responsible, accountable, consult, and inform to map each team member to the work that needs to be done. Responsibility, Accountability, Consult, and Inform (RACI) chart is a type of responsibility assignment matrix (RAM). RACI is important to ensure clear divisions of roles and expectations when the team consists of internal and external resources.

Answer option A is incorrect as a Pareto chart is a quality control chart to show categories of failure.

Answer option B is incorrect as resource histogram shows utilization of project team members, not what their assignments are.

Answer option D is incorrect as a Resource Breakdown Structure shows the assignment of project team members according to the Work Breakdown Structure.

A33.   Answer option A is correct.

Responsibility, Accountability, Consult, and Inform (RACI) chart is a type of responsibility assignment matrix (RAM). RACI is important to ensure clear divisions of roles and expectations when the team consists of internal and external resources.

Answer option B is incorrect. A Pareto chart is a special type of bar chart where the values being plotted are arranged in descending order. The graph is accompanied by a line graph, which shows the cumulative totals of each category, left to right. The chart is named after Vilfredo Pareto, and its use in quality assurance was popularized by Joseph M. Juran and Kaoru Ishikawa.

Answer option C is incorrect. Resource histogram shows utilization of project team members, not what their assignments are.

Answer option D is incorrect. An organizational chart (often called organization chart or org chart) is a diagram that shows the structure of an organization and the relationships and relative ranks of its parts and positions/jobs. Organization chart is a method for depicting interrelationships among a group of persons working together toward a common objective.

A34.   Answer option A is correct.

The Process Owner is responsible for defining Key Performance Indicators (KPIs). The Process Owner executes the crucial role of process champion, design lead, supporter, instructor, and protector. The Process Owner should be a senior level manager with credibility, influence, and authority across the various areas impacted by the activities of the process. The Process Owner must have the ability to influence and make sure compliance to the policies and procedures put in place across the cultural and departmental silos of the IT organization.

The role of the Process Owner must be defined in the initial planning phase of any ITIL project. This role is responsible for the overall quality of the process and oversees the management of, and organizational compliance to, the process flows, procedures, data models, policies, and technologies associated with the IT business process.

Answer option B is incorrect. The Service Level Manager is responsible for negotiating Service Level Agreements and ensuring that these are met. He makes sure that all IT Service Management processes, Operational Level Agreements, and Underpinning Contracts are appropriate for the agreed service level targets. The Service Level Manager also monitors and reports on service levels.

Answer option C is incorrect. The Service Owner is responsible for a specific service such as Infrastructure, Application, or Professional Service within an organization despite of where the underpinning technology components, processes, or professional capabilities are located. However, in order to ensure that a service is managed with a business focus, the definition of a single point of responsibility is absolutely necessary to give the level of attention and focus required for its delivery. Service ownership is as critical to service management as establishing ownership for processes which cross multiple vertical silos or departments.

Service Owner is responsible for continuous improvement and the management of change affecting the services under their heed. The Service Owner is a prime stakeholder in all of the IT processes, which enable or support it.

Answer option D is incorrect. The Process Manager is responsible for planning and coordinating all Process Management activities. He supports all parties involved in managing and improving processes, in particular the Process Owners. This role will also coordinate all Changes to processes, thereby making sure that all processes cooperate in a seamless way.

A35. Answer option D is correct.

The Incident Manager is responsible for the effective implementation of the process (Incident Management) and carries out the respective reporting method. He represents the first stage of growth for Incidents, should these not be resolvable within the agreed Service Levels.

Answer option A is incorrect. The Major Incident Team is a dynamically established team of IT managers and technical experts, under the leadership of the Incident Manager. The team is formulated to concentrate on the resolution of a Major Incident.

Answer option B is incorrect. The Problem Manager is responsible for managing the lifecycle of all Problems. The primary objectives of the Problem Manager are to prevent Incidents from happening, and to curtail the impact of Incidents that cannot be prohibited. For this purpose, he maintains information about Known Errors and Workarounds.

Answer option C is incorrect. The Service Request Fulfillment Group (SRFG) specializes on the fulfillment of definite types of Service

Requests. Typically, 1st Level Support will process simpler requests, while others are forwarded to the specialized Fulfillment Groups.

A36.   Answer option C is correct.

1st Level Support is used to register and organize received Incidents, and carry out an urgent effort in order to restore a failed IT Service as quickly as possible. If no ad-hoc solution can be achieved, 1st Level Support will transport the Incident to expert Technical Support Groups, which is 2nd Level Support. 1st Level Support also processes Service Requests and keeps users up to date about their Incidents' status at approved intervals.

Answer option A is incorrect. 2nd Level Support is used to take over Incidents, which cannot be solved straight away with the means of 1st Level Support. If required, it will request external support, e.g. from software or hardware manufacturers. 2nd Level Support intends to restore a failed IT Service as quickly as possible. If no solution can be found, the 2nd Level Support transports the Incident to Problem Management.

Answer option B is incorrect. There is no such level as 0 Level Support in Service Operation.

Answer option D is incorrect. In Service Operation 3rd Level Support is normally located at hardware or software manufacturers. Its services are requested by 2nd Level Support if necessary for solving an Incident. 3rd Level Support intends to restore a failed IT Service as quickly as possible.

A37.   Answer option D is correct.

The Configuration Manager is responsible for maintaining information about Configuration Items that are required to deliver IT services. He also maintains a logical model, containing the components of the IT infrastructure (CIs) and their associations.

Answer option A is incorrect. The Test Manager ensures that deployed Releases and the resulting services meet customer expectations, and verifies that IT operations are able to support the new service.

Answer option B is incorrect. The Release Manager is responsible for planning, scheduling and controlling the movement of Releases to test and live environments. The primary objective of the Release Manager is to ensure that the integrity of the live environment is protected and that the correct components are released.

Answer option C is incorrect. The Knowledge Manager ensures that the IT organization is able to gather, analyze, store and share knowledge and information. The primary goal of the Knowledge Manager is to improve efficiency by reducing the need to rediscover knowledge.

A38.   Answer option C is correct.

The Process Owner executes the crucial role of process champion, design lead, supporter, instructor, and protector. The Process Owner should be a senior level manager with credibility, influence, and authority across the various areas impacted by the activities of the process. The Process Owner must have the ability to influence and make sure compliance to the policies and procedures put in place across the cultural and departmental silos of the IT organization.

The role of the Process Owner must be defined in the initial planning phase of any ITIL project. This role is responsible for the overall quality of the process and oversees the management of, and organizational compliance to, the process flows, procedures, data models, policies, and technologies associated with the IT business process.

Answer option A is incorrect. The Service Owner is responsible for a specific service such as Infrastructure, Application, or Professional Service within an organization despite of where the underpinning technology components, processes, or professional capabilities are located. However, in order to ensure that a service is managed with a business focus, the definition of a single point of responsibility is absolutely necessary to give the level of attention and focus required for its delivery. Service ownership is as critical to service management as establishing ownership for processes which cross multiple vertical silos or departments.

Service Owner is responsible for continuous improvement and the management of change affecting the services under their heed. The Service Owner is a prime stakeholder in all of the IT processes, which enable or support it.

Answer option B is incorrect. Customer, also client, buyer, or purchaser is usually used to refer to a current or potential buyer or user of products of an individual or organization, mostly called the supplier or seller. This is typically through purchasing or renting goods or services. However, in certain contexts the term customer also includes by extension anyone who uses or experiences the services of another. A customer may also be a viewer of the product or goods which are being sold. In this case, a customer can walk into a building intending to buy a product but are not satisfied with what he or she may find in the store, resulting in them leaving without a purchase.

Answer option D is incorrect. Service Operation is the best practice for achieving the delivery of agreed levels of services both to end-users and the customers (where "customers" refer to those individuals who pay for the service and negotiate the SLAs). Service Operation is the part of the lifecycle where the services and value are actually directly delivered. Also, the monitoring of problems and balance between service reliability and cost, etc. are considered.

Strategic objectives are eventually recognized through Service Operation, thus making it a critical capability. Assistance is provided on ways to sustain steadiness in service operations, allowing for changes in design, scale, scope and service levels. Organizations are provided with detailed process course of action, methods, and tools for use in two major control perspectives, which are as follows:

1. Reactive

2. Proactive.

A39.   Answer options A, C, and D are correct.

The names by which the Service Desk function is known are as follows:

Call Center: Its main emphasis is on professionally handling large call volumes of telephone-based transactions.

Help Desk: It manages, co-ordinates, and resolve incidents as quickly as possible.

Service Desk: It not only handles incidents, problems and questions but also provides an interface for other activities such as change requests, maintenance contracts, software licenses, service level management, configuration management, availability management, Financial Management, and IT Services Continuity Management.

Answer option B is incorrect. This is not a name by which the Service Desk function is known. A Service Request is a request from a user for information, advice, a standard change, or access to an IT service. For example, to reset a password, or to provide standard IT services for a new user. Service Requests are usually handled by a service desk or a request fulfillment group, and do not require an RFC to be submitted.

A40.   Answer option A is correct.

The Change Manager authorizes and documents all changes in the IT Infrastructure and its components (CIs) to maintain a least amount of interruptive effects after the running operation. The succession of the individual stages is planned and communicated to recognize any overlapping as early as possible. In the case of further-reaching changes, he involves the Change Advisory Board (CAB).

Answer option B is incorrect. The Service Level Manager is responsible for negotiating Service Level Agreements and ensuring that these are met. He makes sure that all IT Service Management processes, Operational Level Agreements, and Underpinning Contracts are appropriate for the agreed service level targets. The Service Level Manager also monitors and reports on service levels.

Answer option C is incorrect. The Process Manager is responsible for planning and coordinating all Process Management activities. He supports all parties involved in managing and improving processes, in particular the Process Owners. This role will also coordinate all Changes to processes, thereby making sure that all processes cooperate in a seamless way.

Answer option D is incorrect. The Continual Service Improvement (CSI) Manager is responsible for managing improvements to IT Service Management processes and IT services. He will continually measure the performance of the service provider and design improvements to processes, services and infrastructure in order to increase efficiency, effectiveness, and cost effectiveness.

Acronyms

ACD	Automatic Call Distribution
AM	Availability Management
AMIS	Availability Management Information System
ASP	Application Service Provider
BCM	Business Capacity Management
BCM	Business Continuity Management
BCP	Business Continuity Plan
BIA	Business Impact Analysis
BRM	Business Relationship Manager
BSI	British Standards Institution
BSM	Business Service Management
CAB	Change Advisory Board
CAB/EC	Change Advisory Board / Emergency Committee
CAPEX	Capital Expenditure
CCM	Component Capacity Management
CFIA	Component Failure Impact Analysis
CI	Configuration Item
CMDB	Configuration Management Database
CMIS	Capacity Management Information System
CMM	Capability Maturity Model
CMMI	Capability Maturity Model Integration
CMS	Configuration Management System
COTS	Commercial off the Shelf

CSF	Critical Success Factor
CSI	Continual Service Improvement
CSIP	Continual Service Improvement Programme
CSP	Core Service Package
CTI	Computer Telephony Integration
DIKW	Data-to-Information-to-Knowledge-to-Wisdom
eSCM-CL	eSourcing Capability Model for Client Organizations
eSCM-SP	eSourcing Capability Model for Service Providers
FMEA	Failure Modes and Effects Analysis
FTA	Fault Tree Analysis
IRR	Internal Rate of Return
ISG	IT Steering Group
ISM	Information Security Management
ISMS	Information Security Management System
ISO	International Organization for Standardization
ISP	Internet Service Provider
IT	Information Technology
ITSCM	IT Service Continuity Management
ITSM	IT Service Management
itSMF	IT Service Management Forum
IVR	Interactive Voice Response
KEDB	Known Error Database
KPI	Key Performance Indicator
LOS	Line of Service
MoR	Management of Risk

MTBF	Mean Time Between Failures
MTBSI	Mean Time Between Service Incidents
MTRS	Mean Time to Restore Service
MTTR	Mean Time to Repair
NPV	Net Present Value
OGC	Office of Government Commerce
OLA	Operational Level Agreement
OPEX	Operational Expenditure
OPSI	Office of Public Sector Information
PBA	Pattern of Business Activity
PFS	Prerequisite for Success
PIR	Post Implementation Review
PSA	Projected Service Availability
QA	Quality Assurance
QMS	Quality Management System
RCA	Root Cause Analysis
RFC	Request for Change
ROI	Return on Investment
RPO	Recovery Point Objective
RTO	Recovery Time Objective
SAC	Service Acceptance Criteria
SACM	Service Asset and Configuration Management
SCD	Supplier and Contract Database
SCM	Service Capacity Management
SFA	Service Failure Analysis

SIP	Service Improvement Plan
SKMS	Service Knowledge Management System
SLA	Service Level Agreement
SLM	Service Level Management
SLP	Service Level Package
SLR	Service Level Requirement
SMO	Service Maintenance Objective
SoC	Separation of Concerns
SOP	Standard Operating Procedures
SOR	Statement of requirements
SPI	Service Provider Interface
SPM	Service Portfolio Management
SPO	Service Provisioning Optimization
SPOF	Single Point of Failure
TCO	Total Cost of Ownership
TCU	Total Cost of Utilization
TO	Technical Observation
TOR	Terms of Reference
TQM	Total Quality Management
UC	Underpinning Contract
UP	User Profile
VBF	Vital Business Function
VOI	Value on Investment
WIP	Work in Progress

Glossary

Acceptance

Formal agreement that an IT Service, Process, Plan, or other Deliverable is complete, accurate, Reliable and meets its specified Requirements. Acceptance is usually preceded by Evaluation or Testing and is often required before proceeding to the next stage of a Project or Process.

Access Management

(Service Operation) The Process responsible for allowing Users to make use of IT Services, data, or other Assets. Access Management helps to protect the Confidentiality, Integrity and Availability of Assets by ensuring that only authorized Users are able to access or modify the Assets. Access Management is sometimes referred to as Rights Management or Identity Management.

Account Manager

(Service Strategy) A Role that is very similar to Business Relationship Manager, but includes more commercial aspects. Most commonly used when dealing with External Customers.

Accounting

(Service Strategy) The Process responsible for identifying actual Costs of delivering IT Services, comparing these with budgeted costs, and managing variance from the Budget.

Accredited

Officially authorised to carry out a Role. For example an Accredited body may be authorised to provide training or to conduct Audits.

Active Monitoring

(Service Operation) Monitoring of a Configuration Item or an IT Service that uses automated regular checks to discover the current status.

Activity

A set of actions designed to achieve a particular result. Activities are usually defined as part of Processes or Plans, and are documented in Procedures.

Agreed Service Time

(Service Design) A synonym for Service Hours, commonly used in formal calculations of Availability. See Downtime.

Agreement

A Document that describes a formal understanding between two or more parties. An Agreement is not legally binding, unless it forms part of a Contract. An agreement is a meeting of minds between two or more legally competent parties, about their relative duties and rights regarding current or future performance. When people feel or think the same way about something, they agree. Sometimes it is important to write down or make a promise to what has been agreed upon. This is called an agreement. Agreements are common in law and business. For example, when a person takes a loan or hires someone to work, an agreement is usually signed so everyone understands what must be done and in what time it must be done.

Alert

(Service Operation) A warning that a threshold has been reached, something has changed, or a Failure has occurred. Alerts are often created and managed by System Management tools and are managed by the Event Management Process.

Analytical Modelling

(Service Strategy) (Service Design) (Continual Service Improvement) A technique that uses mathematical Models to predict the behaviour of a Configuration Item or IT Service. Analytical Models are commonly used in Capacity Management and Availability Management.

Application

Software that provides Functions that are required by an IT Service. Each Application may be part of more than one IT Service. An Application runs on one or more Servers or Clients.

Application Development and Customization

Application Development and Customization is used to make available applications and systems which provide the required functionality for IT services. It includes the development and maintenance of custom applications as well as the customization of products from software vendors. It is part of Service Transition and the owner of Application Development and Customization is the Application Developer.

Application Management

(Service Design) (Service Operation) Application Management set encompasses a set of best practices proposed to improve the overall quality of IT software development and guides how business applications are developed, managed, improved, and when necessary, mark finish. It particularly gives attention to gathering and defining requirements that meet business objectives. ITIL takes a traditional approach and adds Operate and Optimize to the standard Software Development Lifecycle.

Application Portfolio

(Service Design) A database or structured Document used to manage Applications throughout their Lifecycle. The Application Portfolio contains key Attributes of all Applications. The Application Portfolio is sometimes implemented as part of the Service Portfolio, or as part of the Configuration Management System.

Application Service Provider (ASP)

(Service Design) An External Service Provider that provides IT Services using Applications running at the Service Provider's premises. Users access the Applications by network connections to the Service Provider.

Application Sizing

(Service Design) The Activity responsible for understanding the Resource Requirements needed to support a new Application, or a major Change to an existing Application. Application Sizing helps to ensure that the IT Service can meet its agreed Service Level Targets for Capacity and Performance.

Architecture

(Service Design) The structure of a System or IT Service, including the Relationships of Components to each other and to the environment they are in. Architecture also includes the Standards and Guidelines which guide the design and evolution of the System.

Assembly

(Service Transition) A Configuration Item that is made up from a number of other CIs. For example a Server CI may contain CIs for CPUs, Disks, Memory etc.; an IT Service CI may contain many Hardware, Software and other CIs.

Assessment

Inspection and analysis to check whether a Standard or set of Guidelines is being followed, that Records are accurate, or that Efficiency and Effectiveness targets are being met.

Access Management

Access Management is used to grant authorized users the right to use a service, while preventing access to non-authorized users. The Access Management process essentially executes policies defined in IT Security Management. It is sometimes also referred to as Rights Management or Identity Management. It is part of Service Operation and the owner of Access

Management is the Access Manager. Access Management is added as a new process to ITIL V3.

Asset

(Service Strategy) Any Resource or Capability. Assets of a Service Provider include anything that could contribute to the delivery of a Service. Assets can be one of the following types: Management, Organisation, Process, Knowledge, People, Information, Applications, Infrastructure, and Financial Capital.

Asset Management

(Service Transition) Asset Management is the Process responsible for tracking and reporting the value and ownership of financial Assets throughout their Lifecycle. Asset Management is part of an overall Service Asset and Configuration Management Process.

Asset Register

(Service Transition) A list of Assets, which includes their ownership and value. The Asset Register is maintained by Asset Management.

Attribute

(Service Transition) A piece of information about a Configuration Item. Examples are name, location, Version number, and Cost. Attributes of CIs are recorded in the Configuration Management Database (CMDB).

Audit

Formal inspection and verification to check whether a Standard or set of Guidelines is being followed, that Records are accurate, or that Efficiency and Effectiveness targets are being met. An Audit may be carried out by internal or external groups.

Authority Matrix

Synonym for RACI.

Automatic Call Distribution (ACD)

(Service Operation) Use of Information Technology to direct an incoming telephone call to the most appropriate person in the shortest possible time. ACD is sometimes called Automated Call Distribution.

Availability

(Service Design) Availability is the most basic aspect of assuring value to customers. It gives surety to the customer that services will be available for use under agreed terms and conditions. The availability of a service is its most happily perceived attribute from a user's perspective. A service is available only if users can access it in an agreed approach. Perceptions and preferences vary by customer and by business context. Availability of a service is more delicate than a binary evaluation of available and unavailable. The time period for which the customer can wait to avail the service should be determined and factored into service design.

Availability Management

(Service Design) Availability Management allows organizations to sustain the IT service availability to support the business at a justifiable cost. The high-level activities are Realize Availability Requirements, Compile Availability Plan, Monitor Availability, and Monitor Maintenance Obligations. Availability is usually calculated based on a model involving the Availability Ratio and techniques such as Fault Tree Analysis.

Availability Management Information System (AMIS)

(Service Design) A virtual repository of all Availability Management data, usually stored in multiple physical locations.

Availability Plan

(Service Design) A Plan to ensure that existing and future Availability Requirements for IT Services can be provided Cost Effectively.

Back-out

Synonym for Remediation.

Back-out plan

A back-out plan documents all actions to be taken to reinstate the service if the related Change or Release fails or partially fails. A back-out plan might offer a full or partial reversal. However, in extreme situations, a back-out plan might just call for the IT Service Continuity Plan to be called.

Backup

(Service Design) (Service Operation) Copying data to protect against loss of Integrity or Availability of the original.

Balanced Scorecard

(Continual Service Improvement) A management tool developed by Drs. Robert Kaplan (Harvard Business School) and David Norton. A Balanced Scorecard enables a Strategy to be broken down into Key Performance Indicators. Performance against the KPIs is used to demonstrate how well the Strategy is being achieved. A Balanced Scorecard has 4 major areas, each of which has a small number of KPIs. The same 4 areas are considered at different levels of detail throughout the Organisation.

Benefits

It is the profit achieved through realization of improvements.

Baselines

(Continual Service Improvement) Baselines are important beginning points for highlighting improvement. They work as markers or starting points for future evaluation. Baselines are also used to set up an initial data point to decide whether a service or process needs to be improved. As a result, it is essential that baselines are documented, recognized, and accepted throughout the organization. They have to be established at each level, strategic goals and objectives, tactical process maturity, operational metrics, and KPIs. If a baseline is not initially created then the first measurement efforts will become the baseline.

Benchmark

(Continual Service Improvement) The recorded state of something at a specific point in time. A Benchmark can be created for a Configuration, a Process, or any other set of data.

Benchmarking

(Continual Service Improvement) Benchmarking is also recognized as Best Practice Benchmarking or Process Benchmarking. It is a process used in management and mostly useful for strategic management. It is the process of comparing the business processes and performance metrics including cost, cycle time, productivity, or quality to another that is widely considered to be an industry standard benchmark or best practice. It allows organizations to develop plans on how to implement best practice with the aim of increasing some aspect of performance.

Best Practice

Proven Activities or Processes that have been successfully used by multiple Organisations. ITIL is an example of Best Practice.

Brainstorming

(Service Design) A technique that helps a team to generate ideas. Ideas are not reviewed during the Brainstorming session, but at a later stage. Brainstorming is often used by Problem Management to identify possible causes.

British Standards Institution (BSI)

The UK National Standards body, responsible for creating and maintaining British Standards. See http://www.bsi-global.com for more information.

Budget

A list of all the money an Organisation or Business Unit plans to receive, and plans to pay out, over a specified period of time.

Budgeting

The Activity of predicting and controlling the spending of money. Consists of a periodic negotiation cycle to set future Budgets (usually annual) and the day-to-day monitoring and adjusting of current Budgets.

Build

(Service Transition) The Activity of assembling a number of Configuration Items to create part of an IT Service. The term Build is also used to refer to a Release that is authorised for distribution. For example Server Build or laptop Build.

Build Environment

(Service Transition) A controlled Environment where Applications, IT Services and other Builds are assembled prior to being moved into a Test or Live Environment.

Business

(Service Strategy) An overall corporate entity or Organisation formed of a number of Business Units. In the context of ITSM, the term Business includes public sector and not-for-profit organisations, as well as companies. An IT Service Provider provides IT Services to a Customer within a Business. The IT Service Provider may be part of the same Business as their Customer (Internal Service Provider), or part of another Business (External Service Provider).

Business Capacity Management (BCM)

(Service Design) In the context of ITSM, Business Capacity Management is the Activity responsible for understanding future Business Requirements for use in the Capacity Plan.

Business Case

(Service Strategy) The Business Case is a justification for an important item of expenditure. It includes information about cost, benefits, options, issues, risks, and potential problems. It is a decision support and planning tool that projects the expected outcome of a business action. It uses qualitative terms.

Business Continuity Management (BCM)

(Service Design) The Business Process responsible for managing Risks that could seriously impact the Business. BCM safeguards the interests of key stakeholders, reputation, brand and value creating activities. The BCM Process involves reducing Risks to an acceptable level and planning for the recovery of Business Processes should a disruption to the Business occur. BCM sets the Objectives, Scope and Requirements for IT Service Continuity Management.

Business Continuity Plan (BCP)

(Service Design) A Plan defining the steps required to Restore Business Processes following a disruption. The Plan will also identify the triggers for Invocation, people to be involved, communications etc. IT Service Continuity Plans form a significant part of Business Continuity Plans.

Business Customer

(Service Strategy) A recipient of a product or a Service from the Business. For example if the Business is a car manufacturer then the Business Customer is someone who buys a car.

Business Impact Analysis (BIA)

(Service Strategy) BIA is the Activity in Business Continuity Management that identifies Vital Business Functions and their dependencies. These dependencies may include Suppliers, people, other Business Processes, IT Services etc.

BIA defines the recovery requirements for IT Services. These requirements include Recovery Time Objectives, Recovery Point Objectives and minimum Service Level Targets for each IT Service.

Business Objective

(Service Strategy) The Objective of a Business Process, or of the Business as a whole. Business Objectives support the Business Vision, provide guidance for the IT Strategy, and are often supported by IT Services.

Business Operations

(Service Strategy) The day-to-day execution, monitoring and management of Business Processes.

Business Perspective

(Continual Service Improvement) An understanding of the Service Provider and IT Services from the point of view of the Business, and an understanding of the Business from the point of view of the Service Provider.

Business Process

A Process that is owned and carried out by the Business. A Business Process contributes to the delivery of a product or Service to a Business Customer. For example, a retailer may have a purchasing Process which helps to deliver Services to their Business Customers. Many Business Processes rely on IT Services.

Business Relationship Management

(Service Strategy) The Process or Function responsible for maintaining a Relationship with the Business.

Business Relationship Manager (BRM)

(Service Strategy) A Role responsible for maintaining the Relationship with one or more Customers. This Role is often combined with the Service Level Manager Role.

Business Service

An IT Service that directly supports a Business Process, as opposed to an Infrastructure Service which is used internally by the IT Service Provider and is not usually visible to the Business.

The term Business Service is also used to mean a Service that is delivered to Business Customers by Business Units. For example delivery of financial services to Customers of a bank, or goods to the Customers of a retail store. Successful delivery of Business Services often depends on one or more IT Services.

Business Service Catalogue

Business Service Catalogue includes details of all of the IT services delivered to customers. It also includes the IT services together with relationships to the business units and the business processes that rely on the IT services. Business Service Catalogue is the customers' perspective of the Service Catalogue.

Business Service Management (BSM)

(Service Strategy) (Service Design) An approach to the management of IT Services that considers the Business Processes supported and the Business value provided.

This term also means the management of Business Services delivered to Business Customers.

Business Transaction Management

Business Transaction Management (BTM) is an approach to managing IT from a business transaction perspective. BTM aims to guarantee service quality for users conducting business transactions while simultaneously optimizing the IT applications and infrastructure across which those transactions execute. At the heart of BTM lies the ability to capture and to track all transactions, across all IT tiers, automatically and continuously.

BTM is ideally suited to managing performance and availability problems because it clearly identifies exactly where transactions are held up. But for IT, problem management is just the tip of the iceberg. BTM also enables proactive problem prevention as well as the generation of business service intelligence for optimization of resource provisioning and virtualization.

Business Unit

(Service Strategy) A segment of the Business which has its own Plans, Metrics, income and Costs. Each Business Unit owns Assets and uses these to create value for Customers in the form of goods and Services.

Call

(Service Operation) A telephone call to the Service Desk from a User. A Call could result in an Incident or a Service Request being logged.

Call Centre

(Service Operation) An Organisation or Business Unit which handles large numbers of incoming and outgoing telephone calls.

Call Type

(Service Operation) A Category that is used to distinguish incoming requests to a Service Desk. Common Call Types are Incident, Service Request and Complaint.

Capabilities

(Service Strategy) Capabilities are types of assets, and organizations utilize them to construct value in the form of goods and services. They specify an organization's ability to control, coordinate, and deploy resources to produce value. They are usually experience-driven, knowledge-intensive, information-based, and firmly embedded within an organization's people, systems, processes, and technologies.

Capability Maturity Model (CMM)

(Continual Service Improvement) The Capability Maturity Model for Software (also known as the CMM and SW-CMM) is a model used to identify Best Practices to help increase Process Maturity. CMM was developed at the Software Engineering Institute (SEI) of Carnegie Mellon University. In 2000, the SW-CMM was upgraded to CMMI® (Capability Maturity Model Integration). The SEI no longer maintains the SW-CMM model, its associated appraisal methods, or training materials.

Capability Maturity Model Integration (CMMI)

(Continual Service Improvement) Capability Maturity Model Integration (CMMI) was created by Software Engineering Institute (SEI). CMMI in software engineering and organizational development is a process improvement approach that provides organizations with the essential elements for effective process improvement. It can be used to guide process improvement across a project, a division, or an entire organization. CMMI can help integrate traditionally separate organizational functions, set process improvement goals and priorities, provide guidance for quality processes, and provide a point of reference for appraising current processes. CMMI is now the de facto standard for measuring the maturity of any process. Organizations can be assessed against the CMMI model using Standard CMMI Appraisal Method for Process Improvement (SCAMPI).

Capacity

(Service Design) The maximum Throughput that a Configuration Item or IT Service can deliver whilst meeting agreed Service Level Targets. For some types of CI, Capacity may be the size or volume, for example a disk drive.

Capacity Management (Service Design) The Process responsible for ensuring that the Capacity of IT Services and the IT Infrastructure is able to deliver agreed Service Level Targets in a Cost Effective and timely manner. Capacity Management considers all Resources required to deliver the IT Service, and plans for short, medium and long term Business Requirements.

Capacity Management

Capacity Management is the discipline which ensures that IT infrastructure is supplied at the right time, in the right quantity, and at the right price. It also ensures that IT is used in the most proficient way. Capacity Management supports the optimum and cost effective provision of IT services by helping organizations match their IT resources to the business demands. The high-level activities are Application Sizing, Workload Management, Demand Management, Modeling, Capacity Planning, Resource Management, and Performance Management.

Change Manager

The Change Manager authorizes and documents all changes in the IT Infrastructure and its components (CIs) to maintain a least amount of interruptive effects after the running operation. The succession of the individual stages is planned and communicated to recognize any overlapping as early as possible. In the case of further-reaching changes, he involves the Change Advisory Board (CAB).

Capacity Manager

The Capacity Manager is responsible for ensuring that services and infrastructure are competent to deliver the agreed capacity and performance targets in a cost effective and timely manner. He considers all resources required to deliver the service, and plans for short, medium, and long term business requirements.

Capacity Management Information System (CMIS)

(Service Design) A virtual repository of all Capacity Management data, usually stored in multiple physical locations.

Capacity Plan

(Service Design) A Capacity Plan is used to manage the Resources required to deliver IT Services. The Plan contains scenarios for different predictions of Business demand, and costed options to deliver the agreed Service Level Targets.

Capacity Planning

(Service Design) The Activity within Capacity Management responsible for creating a Capacity Plan.

Capital Expenditure (CAPEX)

(Service Strategy) The Cost of purchasing something that will become a financial Asset, for example computer equipment and buildings. The value of the Asset is Depreciated over multiple accounting periods.

Capital Item

(Service Strategy) An Asset that is of interest to Financial Management because it is above an agreed financial value.

Capitalization

(Service Strategy) Identifying major Cost as capital, even though no Asset is purchased. This is done to spread the impact of the Cost over multiple accounting periods. The most common example of this is software development, or purchase of a software license.

Category

A named group of things that have something in common. Categories are used to group similar things together. For example Cost Types are used to group similar types of Cost. Incident Categories are used to group similar types of Incident, CI Types are used to group similar types of Configuration Item.

Certification

Issuing a certificate to confirm Compliance to a Standard. Certification includes a formal Audit by an independent and Accredited body. The term Certification is also used to mean awarding a certificate to verify that a person has achieved a qualification.

Change

(Service Transition) The addition, modification or removal of anything that could have an effect on IT Services. The Scope should include all IT Services, Configuration Items, Processes, Documentation etc.

Change Advisory Board (CAB)

(Service Transition) The Change Advisory Board (CAB) is a group of people that advise the Change Manager in the assessment, prioritization, and scheduling of changes. This board is made up of representatives from all areas within AccessPlus who will be affected by the change, including third party suppliers as appropriate. This board is chaired by the Change Manager who is the only permanent CAB member.

A key part of managing changes in IT is to have a Change Advisory Board (CAB). A CAB offers multiple perspectives necessary to ensure proper decision making. The CAB is tasked with reviewing and prioritizing requested changes, monitoring the change process and providing managerial feedback.

Change Case

(Service Operation) A technique used to predict the impact of proposed Changes. Change Cases use specific scenarios to clarify the scope of proposed Changes and to help with Cost Benefit Analysis.

Change History

(Service Transition) Information about all changes made to a Configuration Item during its life. Change History consists of all those Change Records that apply to the CI.

Change Management

(Service Transition) The Process responsible for controlling the Lifecycle of all Changes. The primary objective of Change Management is to enable beneficial Changes to be made, with minimum disruption to IT Services.

Change Model

(Service Transition) A repeatable way of dealing with a particular Category of Change. A Change Model defines specific pre-defined steps that will be followed for a Change of this Category. Change Models may be very simple, with no requirement for approval (e.g. Password Reset) or may be very complex with many steps that require approval (e.g. major software Release).

Change Record

(Service Transition) A Record containing the details of a Change. Each Change Record documents the Lifecycle of a single Change. A Change Record is created for every Request for Change that is received, even those that are subsequently rejected. Change Records should reference the Configuration Items that are affected by the Change. Change Records are stored in the Configuration Management System.

Change Request

Synonym for Request for Change.

Change Schedule

(Service Transition) A Document that lists all approved Changes and their planned implementation dates. A Change Schedule is sometimes called a Forward Schedule of Change, even though it also contains information about Changes that have already been implemented.

Change Window

(Service Transition) A regular, agreed time when Changes or Releases may be implemented with minimal impact on Services. Change Windows are usually documented in SLAs.

Charging

(Service Strategy) Requiring payment for IT Services. Charging for IT Services is optional, and many Organisations choose to treat their IT Service Provider as a Cost Centre.

Chronological Analysis

(Service Operation) A technique used to help identify possible causes of Problems. All available data about the Problem is collected and sorted by date and time to provide a detailed timeline. This can make it possible to identify which Events may have been triggered by others.

Change Management

Change Management is used to ensure that standardized methods and procedures are used for efficient handling of all changes. A change is "an event that results in a new status of one or more configuration items (CI's)" approved by management, cost effective, enhances business process changes (fixes) - with a minimum risk to IT infrastructure.

CI Type

(Service Transition) A Category that is used to Classify CIs. The CI Type identifies the required Attributes and Relationships for a Configuration Record. Common CI Types include: hardware, Document, User etc.

Classification

The act of assigning a Category to something. Classification is used to ensure consistent management and reporting. CIs, Incidents, Problems, Changes etc. are usually classified.

Client

A generic term that means a Customer, the Business or a Business Customer. For example Client Manager may be used as a synonym for Account Manager.

Closed

(Service Operation) The final Status in the Lifecycle of an Incident, Problem, Change etc. When the Status is Closed, no further action is taken.

Closure

(Service Operation) The act of changing the Status of an Incident, Problem, Change etc. to Closed.

COBIT

(Continual Service Improvement) COBIT stands for Control Objectives for Information and Related Technology. COBIT is a set of best practices (framework) for information technology (IT) management created by the Information Systems Audit and Control Association (ISACA), and the IT Governance Institute (ITGI) in 1996. COBIT provides managers, auditors, and IT users with a set of generally accepted measures, indicators, processes, and best practices to assist them in maximizing the benefits derived through the use of information technology and developing appropriate IT governance and control in a company.

Call Center

Its main emphasis is on professionally handling large call volumes of telephone-based transactions.

Central Service Desk

It is used for organizations having multiple locations. It reduces operational costs and improves usage of available resources.

Code of Practice

A Guideline published by a public body or a Standards Organisation, such as ISO or BSI. Many Standards consist of a Code of Practice and a Specification. The Code of Practice describes recommended Best Practice.

Cold Standby

Synonym for Gradual Recovery.

Commercial off the Shelf (COTS)

(Service Design) Application software or Middleware that can be purchased from a Third Party.

Compliance

Ensuring that a Standard or set of Guidelines is followed, or that proper, consistent accounting or other practices are being employed.

Compliance Management

Compliance Management is used to ensure that IT services, processes and systems comply with enterprise policies, and legal requirements. It is part of Service Design and the owner of Compliance Management is the Compliance Manager. Compliance issues are addressed within several processes in ITIL V2 and ITIL V3; however, there is no dedicated Compliance Management process. Compliance is an increasingly important topic for IT organizations.

Component

A general term that is used to mean one part of something more complex. For example, a computer System may be a component of an IT Service, an Application may be a Component of a Release Unit. Components that need to be managed should be Configuration Items.

Component Capacity Management (CCM)

(Service Design) (Continual Service Improvement) The Process responsible for understanding the Capacity, Utilisation, and Performance of Configuration Items. Data is collected, recorded and analysed for use in the Capacity Plan.

Component CI

(Service Transition) A Configuration Item that is part of an Assembly. For example, a CPU or Memory CI may be part of a Server CI.

Component Failure Impact Analysis (CFIA)

(Service Design) A technique that helps to identify the impact of CI failure on IT Services. A matrix is created with IT Services on one edge and CIs on the other. This enables the identification of critical CIs (that could cause the failure of multiple IT Services) and of fragile IT Services (that have multiple Single Points of Failure).

Computer Telephony Integration (CTI)

(Service Operation) CTI is a general term covering any kind of integration between computers and telephone Systems. It is most commonly used to refer to Systems where an Application displays detailed screens relating to incoming or outgoing telephone calls.

Concurrency

A measure of the number of Users engaged in the same Operation at the same time.

Confidentiality

(Service Design) A security principle that requires that data should only be accessed by authorised people.

Configuration

(Service Transition) A generic term, used to describe a group of Configuration Items that work together to deliver an IT Service, or a recognizable part of an IT Service. Configuration is also used to describe the parameter settings for one or more CIs.

Configuration Baseline

(Service Transition) A Baseline of a Configuration that has been formally agreed and is managed through the Change Management process. A Configuration Baseline is used as a basis for future Builds, Releases and Changes.

Configuration Control

(Service Transition) The Activity responsible for ensuring that adding, modifying or removing a CI is properly managed, for example by submitting a Request for Change or Service Request.

Configuration Identification

(Service Transition) The Activity responsible for collecting information about Configuration Items and their Relationships, and loading this information into the CMDB. Configuration Identification is also responsible for labelling the CIs themselves, so that the corresponding Configuration Records can be found.

Configuration Item (CI)

(Service Transition) A Configuration item (CI) is an IT asset or a combination of IT assets that may depend and have relationships with other IT processes. A CI will have attributes which may be hierarchical and relationships that will be assigned by the configuration manager in the CM database.

Configuration Management

(Service Transition) Configuration Management (CM) is an Information Technology Infrastructure Library (ITIL) IT Service Management (ITSM) process. It tracks all of the individual Configuration Items (CI) in an IT system, which may be as simple as a single server, or as complex as the entire IT department. In large organizations a configuration manager may be appointed to oversee and manage the CM process.

Configuration Management Database (CMDB)

(Service Transition) Configuration Management Database is the fundamental component of the ITIL Configuration Management (CM). CMDB represents the authorized configuration of the significant components of the IT environment. It helps an organization understand the relationships between these components and track their configuration.

CMDB implementations often involve federation, the inclusion of data into the CMDB from other sources, such as Asset Management, in such a way that the source of the data retains control of the data. Federation is usually distinguished from ETL (extract, transform, and load) solutions in which data is copied into the CMDB.

Configuration Management System (CMS)

(Service Transition) A set of tools and databases that are used to manage an IT Service Provider's Configuration data. The CMS also includes information about Incidents, Problems, Known Errors, Changes and Releases; and may contain data about employees, Suppliers, locations, Business Units, Customers and Users. The CMS includes tools for collecting, storing, managing, updating, and presenting data about all Configuration Items and their Relationships. The CMS is maintained by Configuration Management and is used by all IT Service Management Processes.

Configuration Record

(Service Transition) A Record containing the details of a Configuration Item. Each Configuration Record documents the Lifecycle of a single CI. Configuration Records are stored in a Configuration Management Database.

Configuration Structure

(Service Transition) The hierarchy and other Relationships between all the Configuration Items that comprise a Configuration.

Continual Service Improvement (CSI)

(Continual Service Improvement) Continual Service Improvement (CSI) align and realign IT Services to changing business needs by identifying and implementing improvements to the IT services that support the Business Processes. The perspective of CSI on improvement is the business perspective of service quality, even though CSI aims to improve process effectiveness, efficiency and cost effectiveness of the IT processes through the whole lifecycle. To manage improvement, CSI should clearly define what should be controlled and measured.

Continual Service Improvement Manager

The Continual Service Improvement (CSI) Manager is responsible for managing improvements to IT Service Management processes and IT services. He will continually measure the performance of the service provider and design improvements to processes, services and infrastructure in order to increase efficiency, effectiveness, and cost effectiveness.

Continuous Availability

Service Design) An approach or design to achieve 100% Availability. A Continuously Available IT Service has no planned or unplanned Downtime.

Continuous Operation

(Service Design) An approach or design to eliminate planned Downtime of an IT Service. Note that individual Configuration Items may be down even though the IT Service is Available.

Contract

A legally binding Agreement between two or more parties.

Contract Portfolio

(Service Strategy) A database or structured Document used to manage Service Contracts or Agreements between an IT Service Provider and their Customers. Each IT Service delivered to a Customer should have a Contract or other Agreement which is listed in the Contract Portfolio.

Change

It is the addition, modification, or removal of CIs.

Control

A means of managing a Risk, ensuring that a Business Objective is achieved, or ensuring that a Process is followed. Example Controls include Policies, Procedures, Roles, RAID, door-locks etc. A control is sometimes called a Countermeasure or safeguard.

Control Objectives for Information and related Technology (COBIT)

See COBIT.

Control perspective

(Service Strategy) An approach to the management of IT Services, Processes, Functions, Assets etc. There can be several different Control Perspectives on the same IT Service, Process etc., allowing different individuals or teams to focus on what is important and relevant to their specific Role. Example Control Perspectives include Reactive and Proactive management within IT Operations, or a Lifecycle view for an Application Project team.

Control Processes

The ISO/IEC 20000 Process group that includes Change Management and Configuration Management.

Core Service

(Service Strategy) An IT Service that delivers basic Outcomes desired by one or more Customers.

Core Service Package (CSP)

(Service Strategy) A detailed description of a Core Service that may be shared by two or more Service Level Packages.

Cost

The amount of money spent on a specific Activity, IT Service, or Business Unit. Costs consist of real cost (money), notional cost such as people's time, and Depreciation.

Cost Benefit Analysis

An Activity that analyses and compares the Costs and the benefits involved in one or more alternative courses of action.

Cost Centre

(Service Strategy) A Business Unit or Project to which Costs are assigned. A Cost Centre does not charge for Services provided. An IT Service Provider can be run as a Cost Centre or a Profit Centre.

Cost Effectiveness

A measure of the balance between the Effectiveness and Cost of a Service, Process or activity, A Cost Effective Process is one which achieves its Objectives at minimum Cost.

Cost Element

(Service Strategy) The middle level of category to which Costs are assigned in Budgeting and Accounting. The highest level category is Cost Type. For example a Cost Type of "people" could have cost elements of payroll, staff benefits, expenses, training, overtime etc. Cost Elements can be further broken down to give Cost Units. For example the Cost Element "expenses" could include Cost Units of Hotels, Transport, Meals etc.

Cost Management

(Service Strategy) A general term that is used to refer to Budgeting and Accounting, sometimes used as a synonym for Financial Management

Cost Type

(Service Strategy) The highest level of category to which Costs are assigned in Budgeting and Accounting. For example hardware, software, people, accommodation, external and Transfer.

Cost Unit

(Service Strategy) The lowest level of category to which Costs are assigned, Cost Units are usually things that can be easily counted (e.g. staff numbers, software licences) or things easily measured (e.g. CPU usage, Electricity consumed). Cost Units are included within Cost Elements. For example a Cost Element of "expenses" could include Cost Units of Hotels, Transport, Meals etc.

Countermeasure

Can be used to refer to any type of Control. The term Countermeasure is most often used when referring to measures that increase Resilience, Fault Tolerance or Reliability of an IT Service.

Course Corrections

Changes made to a Plan or Activity that has already started, to ensure that it will meet its Objectives. Course corrections are made as a result of Monitoring progress.

CRAMM

A methodology and tool for analysing and managing Risks. CRAMM was developed by the UK Government, but is now privately owned.

Crisis Management

The Process responsible for managing the wider implications of Business Continuity. A Crisis Management team is responsible for Strategic issues such as managing media relations and shareholder confidence, and decides when to invoke Business Continuity Plans.

Critical Success Factor (CSF)

Something that must happen if a Process, Project, Plan, or IT Service is to succeed. KPIs are used to measure the achievement of each CSF. For example a CSF of "protect IT Services when making Changes" could be measured by KPIs such as "percentage reduction of unsuccessful Changes", "percentage reduction in Changes causing Incidents" etc.

CSI Monitoring

CSI Monitoring is used to verify whether improvement initiatives are proceeding according to plan, and to introduce corrective measures where necessary. It is part of Continual Service Improvement and the owner of CSI Monitoring is the CSI Manager.

Culture

A set of values that is shared by a group of people, including expectations about how people should behave, ideas, beliefs, and practices.

Customer

Someone who buys goods or Services. The Customer of an IT Service Provider is the person or group who defines and agrees the Service Level Targets. The term Customers is also sometimes informally used to mean Users, for example "this is a Customer focussed Organisation".

Customer Relationship Management

Customer Relationship Management (CRM) consists of the processes a company uses to track and organize its contacts with its current and prospective customers. CRM software is used to support these processes; information about customers and customer interactions can be entered, stored and accessed by employees in different company departments. Typical CRM goals are to improve services provided to customers, and to use customer contact information for targeted marketing.

Customer Portfolio

Service Strategy) A database or structured Document used to record all Customers of the IT Service Provider. The Customer Portfolio is the Business Relationship Manager's view of the Customers who receive Services from the IT Service Provider.

Dashboard

(Service Operation) A graphical representation of overall IT Service Performance and Availability. Dashboard images may be updated in real-time, and can also be included in management reports and web pages. Dashboards can be used to support Service Level Management, Event Management or Incident Diagnosis.

Data-to-Information-to-Knowledge-to-Wisdom (DIKW)

A way of understanding the relationships between data, information, knowledge, and wisdom. DIKW shows how each of these builds on the others.

Direct

It is used for monitoring and measuring to set path for activities in order to meet up targets. It is the most common reason for monitoring and measuring.

Definitive Media Library (DML)

(Service Transition) The Definitive Media Library (DML) is a secure library where software that has been properly reviewed and authorized is stored. Technically, Configuration Items (CIs) are what is stored in the DML after they meet up organizational standards. It is a single logical storage area even if there are multiple locations. All software in the DML is under the control of Change and Release Management and is recorded in the Configuration Management System.

Deliverable

Something that must be provided to meet a commitment in a Service Level Agreement or a Contract. Deliverable is also used in a more informal way to mean a planned output of any Process.

Demand Management

Activities that understand and influence Customer demand for Services and the provision of Capacity to meet these demands. At a Strategic level Demand Management can involve analysis of Patterns of Business Activity and User Profiles. At a Tactical level it can involve use of Differential Charging to encourage Customers to use IT Services at less busy times.

DIKW Hierarchy

The DIKW Hierarchy, also known variously as the "Wisdom Hierarchy", the "Knowledge Hierarchy", the "Information Hierarchy", or the "Knowledge Pyramid". It refers loosely to a class of models for representing purported structural and/or functional relationships between data, information, knowledge, and wisdom. Typically information is defined in terms of data, knowledge in terms of information, and wisdom in terms of knowledge.

Deming Cycle

Synonym for Plan Do Check Act.

Dependency

The direct or indirect reliance of one Process or Activity upon another.

Deployment

(Service Transition) The Activity responsible for movement of new or changed hardware, software, documentation, Process, etc to the Live Environment. Deployment is part of the Release and Deployment Management Process.

Delta Release

It is a release of only that part of software which has been changed. For example, security patches.

Definitive Software Library

The Definitive Software Library (DSL) is one or more locations in which the definitive and approved versions of all software Configuration Items (CIs) are securely stored. It may also contain associated CIs such as licenses and documentation. It is a single logical storage area even if there are multiple locations. All software in the DSL is under the control of Change and Release Management and recorded in the CMDB. Only software from the DSL is acceptable for use in a Release.

Depreciation

(Service Strategy) A measure of the reduction in value of an Asset over its life. This is based on wearing out, consumption or other reduction in the useful economic value.

Design

(Service Design) An Activity or Process that identifies Requirements and then defines a solution that is able to meet these Requirements.

Detection

(Service Operation) A stage in the Incident Lifecycle. Detection results in the Incident becoming known to the Service Provider. Detection can be automatic, or can be the result of a User logging an Incident.

Development

(Service Design) The Process responsible for creating or modifying an IT Service or Application. Also used to mean the Role or group that carries out Development work.

Development Environment

(Service Design) An Environment used to create or modify IT Services or Applications. Development Environments are not typically subjected to the same degree of control as Test Environments or Live Environments.

Diagnosis

(Service Operation) A stage in the Incident and Problem Lifecycles. The purpose of Diagnosis is to identify a Workaround for an Incident or the Root Cause of a Problem.

Diagnostic Script

(Service Operation) A structured set of questions used by Service Desk staff to ensure they ask the correct questions, and to help them Classify, Resolve and assign Incidents. Diagnostic Scripts may also be made available to Users to help them diagnose and resolve their own Incidents.

Differential Charging

A technique used to support Demand Management by charging different amounts for the same IT Service Function at different times.

Direct Cost

(Service Strategy) A cost of providing an IT Service which can be allocated in full to a specific Customer, Cost Centre, Project etc. For example cost of providing non-shared servers or software licenses.

Directory Service

(Service Operation) An Application that manages information about IT Infrastructure available on a network, and corresponding User access Rights.

Do Nothing

(Service Design) A Recovery Option. The Service Provider formally agrees with the Customer that Recovery of this IT Service will not be performed.

Document

Information in readable form. A Document may be paper or electronic. For example a Policy statement, Service Level Agreement, Incident Record, diagram of computer room layout.

Downtime

(Service Design) (Service Operation) The time when a Configuration Item or IT Service is not Available during its Agreed Service Time. The Availability of an IT Service is often calculated from Agreed Service Time and Downtime.

Driver

Something that influences Strategy, Objectives or Requirements. For example new legislation or the actions of competitors.

Early Life Support

(Service Transition) Support provided for a new or Changed IT Service for a period of time after it is Released. During Early Life Support the IT Service Provider may review the KPIs, Service Levels and Monitoring Thresholds, and provide additional Resources for Incident and Problem Management.

Economies of scale

(Service Strategy) The reduction in average Cost that is possible from increasing the usage of an IT Service or Asset.

Economies of scope

(Service Strategy) The reduction in Cost that is allocated to an IT Service by using an existing Asset for an additional purpose. For example delivering a new IT Service from existing IT Infrastructure.

Effectiveness

(Continual Service Improvement) A measure of whether the Objectives of a Process, Service or Activity have been achieved. An Effective Process or Activity is one that achieves its agreed Objectives.

Efficiency

(Continual Service Improvement) A measure of whether the right amount of resources have been used to deliver a Process, Service or Activity. An Efficient Process achieves its Objectives with the minimum amount of time, money, people or other resources.

Emergency Change

(Service Transition) A Change that must be introduced as soon as possible. For example to resolve a Major Incident or implement a Security patch. The Change Management Process will normally have a specific Procedure for handling Emergency Changes.

Emergency release

It is a quick fix to repair unpredicted problems or short-term measures to prevent the disruption of important services. An emergency release increments the version number at the second decimal place. For example, from 7.1 to 7.11.

Emergency Change Advisory Board (ECAB)

(Service Transition) A sub-set of the Change Advisory Board who make decisions about high impact Emergency Changes. Membership of the ECAB may be decided at the time a meeting is called, and depends on the nature of the Emergency Change.

Environment

(Service Transition) A subset of the IT Infrastructure that is used for a particular purpose. For Example: Live Environment, Test Environment, Build Environment. It is possible for multiple Environments to share a Configuration Item, for example Test and Live Environments may use different partitions on a single mainframe computer. Also used in the term Physical Environment to mean the accommodation, air conditioning, power system etc. Environment is also used as a generic term to mean the external conditions that influence or affect something.

Error

(Service Operation) A design flaw or malfunction that causes a Failure of one or more Configuration Items or IT Services. A mistake made by a person or a faulty Process that impacts a CI or IT Service is also an Error.

Escalation

(Service Operation) An Activity that obtains additional Resources when these are needed to meet Service Level Targets or Customer expectations. Escalation may be needed within any IT Service Management Process, but is most commonly associated with Incident Management, Problem Management and the management of Customer complaints. There are two types of Escalation, Functional Escalation and Hierarchic Escalation.

eSourcing Capability Model for Client Organizations (eSCM-CL)

(Service Strategy) A framework to help Organisations guide their analysis and decisions on Service Sourcing Models and Strategies. eSCM-CL was developed by Carnegie Mellon University.

eSourcing Capability Model for Service Providers (eSCM-SP)

(Service Strategy) A framework to help IT Service Providers develop their IT Service Management Capabilities from a Service Sourcing perspective. eSCM-SP was developed by Carnegie Mellon University.

Estimation

The use of experience to provide an approximate value for a Metric or Cost. Estimation is also used in Capacity and Availability Management as the cheapest and least accurate Modelling method.

Evaluation

(Service Transition) The Process responsible for assessing a new or Changed IT Service to ensure that Risks have been managed and to help determine whether to proceed with the Change.

Event

(Service Operation) A change of state which has significance for the management of a Configuration Item or IT Service.

The term Event is also used to mean an Alert or notification created by any IT Service, Configuration Item or Monitoring tool. Events typically require IT Operations personnel to take actions, and often lead to Incidents being logged.

Event Management

(Service Operation) Event Management is used to filter and categorize Events and to decide on appropriate actions. It is one of the main activities of Service Operations. It is part of Service Operation and the owner of Event Management is the Operations Manager. Essentially, the activities and process objectives of the Event Management process are identical in ITIL V3 and V2 (Event Management is part of ICT Infrastructure Management in ITIL V2). Interfaces between Event Management and the other ITIL processes are adjusted in order to reflect the new ITIL V3 process structure.

Exception Report

A Document containing details of one or more KPIs or other important targets that have exceeded defined Thresholds. Examples include SLA targets being missed or about to be missed, and a Performance Metric indicating a potential Capacity problem.

Expanded Incident Lifecycle

(Availability Management) Detailed stages in the Lifecycle of an Incident. The stages are Detection, Diagnosis, Repair, Recovery, Restoration. The Expanded Incident Lifecycle is used to help understand all contributions to the Impact of Incidents and to Plan how these could be controlled or reduced.

External Customer

A Customer who works for a different Business to the IT Service Provider.

External Metric

A Metric that is used to measure the delivery of IT Service to a Customer. External Metrics are usually defined in SLAs and reported to Customers.

External Service Provider

(Service Strategy) An IT Service Provider which is part of a different Organisation to their Customer. An IT Service Provider may have both Internal Customers and External Customers.

External Sourcing

Synonym for Outsourcing.

Facilities Management (Service Operation)

The Function responsible for managing the physical Environment where the IT Infrastructure is located. Facilities Management includes all aspects of managing the physical Environment, for example power and cooling, building Access Management, and environmental Monitoring.

Full Release

It means the entire software program is deployed. For example, a new version of an existing application.

Failure

(Service Operation) Loss of ability to Operate to Specification, or to deliver the required output. The term Failure may be used when referring to IT Services, Processes, Activities, Configuration Items etc. A Failure often causes an Incident.

Forward Schedule of Changes (FSC)

It is a schedule that contains details of all forthcoming Changes.

Failure Modes and Effects Analysis (FMEA)

An approach to assessing the potential Impact of Failures. FMEA involves analysing what would happen after Failure of each Configuration Item, all the way up to the effect on the Business. FMEA is often used in Information Security Management and in IT Service Continuity Planning.

Fast Recovery

(Service Design) A Recovery Option which is also known as Hot Standby. Provision is made to Recover the IT Service in a short period of time, typically less than 24 hours. Fast Recovery typically uses a dedicated Fixed Facility with computer Systems, and software configured ready to run the IT Services. Immediate Recovery may take up to 24 hours if there is a need to Restore data from Backups.

Fault

Synonym for Error.

Fault Tolerance

(Service Design) The ability of an IT Service or Configuration Item to continue to Operate correctly after Failure of a Component part.

Fault Tree Analysis (FTA)

(Service Design) (Continual Service Improvement) A technique that can be used to determine the chain of Events that leads to a Problem. Fault Tree Analysis represents a chain of Events using Boolean notation in a diagram.

Financial Management

(Service Strategy) The Function and Processes responsible for managing an IT Service Provider's Budgeting, Accounting and Charging Requirements.

First-line Support

(Service Operation) The first level in a hierarchy of Support Groups involved in the resolution of Incidents. Each level contains more specialist skills, or has more time or other Resources.

Fishbone Diagram

Synonym for Ishikawa Diagram.

Fit for Purpose

An informal term used to describe a Process, Configuration Item, IT Service etc. that is capable of meeting its Objectives or Service Levels. Being Fit for Purpose requires suitable Design, implementation, Control and maintenance.

Fixed Cost

(Service Strategy) A Cost that does not vary with IT Service usage. For example the cost of Server hardware.

Fixed Facility

(Service Design) A permanent building, available for use when needed by an IT Service Continuity Plan.

Follow the Sun

(Service Operation) A methodology for using Service Desks and Support Groups around the world to provide seamless 24 * 7 Service. Calls, Incidents, Problems and Service Requests are passed between groups in different time zones.

Forward Schedule of Change

Forward Schedule of Change (FSC) holds information of all the changes approved for implementation and their projected implementation dates. FSC should be approved by the customers, Service Level Management, Service Desk, and Availability Management. When FSC is approved, Service Desk should communicate to the user community using the most effective methods available.

The objective of FSC is to notify the recipients of the UPCOMING Changes. A simple form of FSC would be like RFC No, Change Summary, Planned date of implementation, and status of the RFC. FSC should be accessible to everyone inside the organization. FSC acts like the change calendar for external users. It allows the IT and business people to schedule their RFC accordingly.

Fulfilment

Performing Activities to meet a need or Requirement. For example by providing a new IT Service, or meeting a Service Request.

Function

Functions are units of organizations specialized to execute specific types of work and also accountable for specific outcomes. They are independent with capabilities and resources required for their performance and outcomes. Capabilities contain work methods internal to the functions. Functions have their own body of knowledge. They provide structure and stability to organizations and provide a way of structuring organizations to apply the specialization standard. Functions define roles and the related authority and responsibility for a specific performance and outcomes. Functions have a tendency to optimize their work methods locally to focus on assigned outcomes.

Functional Escalation

(Service Operation) Transferring an Incident, Problem or Change to a technical team with a higher level of expertise to assist in an Escalation.

Gap Analysis

(Continual Service Improvement) An Activity which compares two sets of data and identifies the differences. Gap Analysis is commonly used to compare a set of Requirements with actual delivery.

Good practices

Good practices are commodities, usually accepted, confirmed, and effective ways of doing things, which were earlier considered best practices of pioneering organizations.

Governance

Ensuring that Policies and Strategy are actually implemented, and that required Processes are correctly followed. Governance includes defining Roles and responsibilities, measuring and reporting, and taking actions to resolve any issues identified.

Gradual Recovery

(Service Design) A Recovery Option which is also known as Cold Standby. Provision is made to Recover the IT Service in a period of time greater than 72 hours. Gradual Recovery typically uses a Portable or Fixed Facility that has environmental support and network cabling, but no computer Systems. The hardware and software are installed as part of the IT Service Continuity Plan.

Guideline

A Document describing Best Practice, that recommends what should be done. Compliance to a guideline is not normally enforced.

Help Desk

(Service Operation) A Help Desk is an information and assistance resource that troubleshoots problems with computers or similar products. Corporations often provide help desk support to their customers via a toll-free number, Web site and/or email. There are also in-house help desks geared toward providing the same kind of help for employees only. Some schools offer classes in which they perform similar tasks as a help desk. In the Information Technology Infrastructure Library, within companies adhering to ISO/IEC 20000 or seeking to implement IT Service Management best practice, a help desk may offer a wider range of user centric services and be part of a larger Service Desk.

Hierarchic Escalation

(Service Operation) Informing or involving more senior levels of management to assist in an Escalation.

High Availability

(Service Design) An approach or Design that minimises or hides the effects of Configuration Item Failure on the Users of an IT Service. High Availability solutions are Designed to achieve an agreed level of Availability and make use of techniques such as Fault Tolerance, Resilience and fast Recovery to reduce the number of Incidents, and the Impact of Incidents.

Help Desk

It manages, co-ordinates, and resolve incidents as quickly as possible.

Hot Standby

Synonym for Fast Recovery or Immediate Recovery.

Identity

(Service Operation) A unique name that is used to identify a User, person or Role. The Identity is used to grant Rights to that User, person, or Role. Example identities might be the username SmithJ or the Role "Change manager".

Immediate Recovery

(Service Design) A Recovery Option which is also known as Hot Standby. Provision is made to Recover the IT Service with no loss of Service. Immediate Recovery typically uses mirroring, load balancing and split site technologies.

Impact

(Service Operation) (Service Transition) A measure of the effect of an Incident, Problem or Change on Business Processes. Impact is often based on how Service Levels will be affected. Impact and Urgency are used to assign Priority.

Incident

(Service Operation) An incident is any event which is not part of the standard operation of a service and which causes, or may cause, an interruption to, or a reduction in, the quality of service. The stated ITIL objective is to restore normal operations as quickly as possible with the least possible impact on either the business or the user, at a cost-effective price.

ICT Infrastructure Management

ICT Infrastructure Management processes recommend best practice for requirements analysis, planning, design, deployment and ongoing operations management and technical support of an ICT Infrastructure. ("ICT" is an acronym for "Information and Communication Technology".)

Improvements

It is the outcome that is once compared to the earlier state, which shows a computable increase in a desirable metric or decrease in an undesirable metric.

ICT Deployment

ICT Deployment provides a framework for the successful management of design, build, test, and roll-out (deploy) projects within an overall ICT program. It includes many project management disciplines in common with PRINCE2, but has a broader focus to include the necessary integration of Release Management and both functional and non functional testing.

ICT Design and Planning

ICT Design and Planning provides a framework and approach for the Strategic and Technical Design and Planning of ICT infrastructures. It includes the necessary combination of Business (and overall IS) strategy, with technical design and architecture. ICT Design and Planning drives both the Procurement of new ICT solutions through the production of Statements of Requirement ("SOR") and Invitations to Tender ("ITT") and is responsible for the initiation and management of ICT Program for strategic business change.

Incident Management

(Service Operation) Incident Management is used to restore normal service operation as quickly as possible and minimize the adverse effects on either the business or the user, at a cost-effective price, thus ensuring that the best possible levels of service quality and availability are maintained. 'Normal service operation' is defined here as service operation within Service Level Agreement (SLA) limits.

ICT Operations Management

ICT Operations Management provides the day-to-day technical supervision of the ICT infrastructure. Often confused with the role of Incident Management from Service Support, Operations is more technical and is concerned not solely with Incidents reported by users, but with Events generated by or recorded by the Infrastructure.

ICT Technical Support

ICT Technical Support is the specialist technical function for infrastructure within ICT. Primarily as a support to other processes, both in Infrastructure Management and Service Management, Technical Support provides a number of specialist functions

Incident Record

(Service Operation) A Record containing the details of an Incident. Each Incident record documents the Lifecycle of a single Incident.

Indirect Cost

(Service Strategy) A Cost of providing an IT Service which cannot be allocated in full to a specific Customer. For example Cost of providing shared Servers or software licenses. Also known as Overhead.

Information Security Management (ISM)

(Service Design) The Process that ensures the Confidentiality, Integrity and Availability of an Organisation's Assets, information, data and IT Services. Information Security Management usually forms part of an Organisational approach to Security Management which has a wider scope than the IT Service Provider, and includes handling of paper, building access, phone calls etc., for the entire Organisation.

Information Security Management System (ISMS)

Service Design) The framework of Policy, Processes, Standards, Guidelines and tools that ensures an Organisation can achieve its Information Security Management Objectives.

Information Security Policy

(Service Design) The Policy that governs the Organisation's approach to Information Security Management.

Information Technology (IT)

The use of technology for the storage, communication or processing of information. The technology typically includes computers, telecommunications, Applications and other software. The information may include Business data, voice, images, video, etc. Information Technology is often used to support Business Processes through IT Services.

Infrastructure Service

An IT Service that is not directly used by the Business, but is required by the IT Service Provider so they can provide other IT Services. For example Directory Services, naming services, or communication services.

Insourcing

Synonym for Internal Sourcing.

Integrity

(Service Design) A security principle that ensures data and Configuration Items are only modified by authorised personnel and Activities. Integrity considers all possible causes of modification, including software and hardware Failure, environmental Events, and human intervention.

Interactive Voice Response (IVR)

(Service Operation) A form of Automatic Call Distribution that accepts User input, such as key presses and spoken commands, to identify the correct destination for incoming Calls.

Intermediate Recovery

(Service Design) A Recovery Option which is also known as Warm Standby. Provision is made to Recover the IT Service in a period of time between 24 and 72 hours. Intermediate Recovery typically uses a shared Portable or Fixed Facility that has computer Systems and network Components. The hardware and software will need to be configured, and data will need to be restored, as part of the IT Service Continuity Plan.

Internal Customer

A Customer who works for the same Business as the IT Service Provider.

IT Facilities Management

IT Facilities Management is used to manage the physical environment where the IT infrastructure is located. It includes all aspects of managing the physical environment, for example power and cooling, building access management, and environmental monitoring. It is part of Service Operation and the owner of IT Facilities Management is the IT Facilities Manager.

IT Financial Management

IT Financial Management is the discipline of ensuring that the IT infrastructure is obtained at the most effective price (which does not necessarily mean cheapest) and calculating the cost of providing IT services so that an organization can understand the costs of its IT services. Costs are divided into costing units: Equipment; Software; Organization (staff, overtime; accommodation; transfer costs (costs of 3rd party service providers). These costs are divided into Direct and Indirect costs and may be Capital or Ongoing. These costs may then be recovered from the customer of the service.

Internal Metric

A Metric that is used within the IT Service Provider to Monitor the Efficiency, Effectiveness or Cost Effectiveness of the IT Service Provider's internal Processes. Internal Metrics are not normally reported to the Customer of the IT Service. See External Metric.

Internal Rate of Return (IRR)

(Service Strategy) A technique used to help make decisions about Capital Expenditure. IRR calculates a figure that allows two or more alternative investments to be compared. A larger IRR indicates a better investment.

Internal Service Provider

(Service Strategy) An IT Service Provider which is part of the same Organisation as their Customer. An IT Service Provider may have both Internal Customers and External Customers.

Internal Sourcing

(Service Strategy) Using an Internal Service Provider to manage IT Services.

International Organization for Standardization (ISO)

The International Organization for Standardization (ISO) is the world's largest developer of Standards. ISO is a non-governmental organization which is a network of the national standards institutes of 156 countries.

International Standards Organisation

See International Organization for Standardization (ISO)

Internet Service Provider (ISP)

An External Service Provider that provides access to the Internet. Most ISPs also provide other IT Services such as web hosting.

Intervene

It is used for monitoring and measuring to identify a point of intervention including successive changes and corrective actions.

Invocation

(Service Design) Initiation of the steps defined in a plan. For example initiating the IT Service Continuity Plan for one or more IT Services.

Ishikawa Diagram

(Service Operation) (Continual Service Improvement) Ishikawa diagrams are also called fishbone diagrams or cause-and-effect diagrams. They are diagrams that show the causes of a certain event. Common uses of the Ishikawa diagram are product design and quality defect prevention, to identify potential factors causing an overall effect. Each cause or reason for imperfection is a source of variation. Causes are usually grouped into major categories to identify these sources of variation.

ISO 9000

A generic term that refers to a number of international Standards and Guidelines for Quality Management Systems.

ISO 9001

An international Standard for Quality Management Systems.

ISO/IEC 17799

(Continual Service Improvement) ISO Code of Practice for Information Security Management.

ISO/IEC 20000

ISO Specification and Code of Practice for IT Service Management. ISO/IEC 20000 is aligned with ITIL Best Practice.

ISO/IEC 27001

(Service Design) (Continual Service Improvement) ISO Specification for Information Security Management. The corresponding Code of Practice is ISO/IEC 17799.

IT Architecture Management

IT Architecture Management is used to define a blueprint for the future development of the technological landscape, taking into account the service strategy and newly available technologies. It is part of Service Design and the owner of IT Architecture Management is the IT Architect. A well-defined architecture blueprint is very important for IT organizations.

IT Directorate

(Continual Service Improvement) Senior Management within a Service Provider, charged with developing and delivering IT services. Most commonly used in UK Government departments.

IT Infrastructure

All of the hardware, software, networks, facilities etc. that are required to Develop, Test, deliver, Monitor, Control or support IT Services. The term IT Infrastructure includes all of the Information Technology but not the associated people, Processes and documentation.

IT Operations

(Service Operation) Activities carried out by IT Operations Control, including Console Management, Job Scheduling, Backup and Restore, and Print and Output Management.

IT Operations Control

(Service Operation) The Function responsible for Monitoring and Control of the IT Services and IT Infrastructure.

IT Operations Management

Service Operation) The Function within an IT Service Provider which performs the daily Activities needed to manage IT Services and the supporting IT Infrastructure. IT Operations Management includes IT Operations Control and Facilities Management.

IT Service

A Service provided to one or more Customers by an IT Service Provider. An IT Service is based on the use of Information Technology and supports the Customer's Business Processes. An IT Service is made up from a combination of people, Processes and technology and should be defined in a Service Level Agreement.

IT Service Management

IT Service Management (ITSM) is a discipline for managing Information Technology (IT) systems, philosophically centered on the customer's perspective of IT's contribution to the business. ITSM stands in deliberate contrast to technology-centered approaches to IT management and business interaction.

IT Service Continuity Management (ITSCM)

(Service Design) IT Service Continuity Management is the process by which plans are put in place and managed to ensure that IT Services can recover and continue should a serious incident occur. It is not just about reactive measures, but also about proactive measures - reducing the risk of a disaster in the first instance. Continuity Management is very important in the sense that many organizations will not do business with IT service providers if contingency planning is not practiced within the service provider's organization.

IT Service Continuity Plan

(Service Design) A Plan defining the steps required to Recover one or more IT Services. The Plan will also identify the triggers for Invocation, people to be involved, communications etc. The IT Service Continuity Plan should be part of a Business Continuity Plan.

IT Service Management (ITSM)

The implementation and management of Quality IT Services that meet the needs of the Business. IT Service Management is performed by IT Service Providers through an appropriate mix of people, Process and Information Technology.

IT Service Management Forum (itSMF)

The IT Service Management Forum is an independent Organisation dedicated to promoting a professional approach to IT Service Management. The itSMF is a not-for-profit membership Organisation with representation in many countries around the world (itSMF Chapters). The itSMF and its membership contribute to the development of ITIL and associated IT Service Management Standards.

IT Service Provider

(Service Strategy) A Service Provider that provides IT Services to Internal Customers or External Customers.

IT Steering Group (ISG)

The IT Steering Group (ISG) is a formal group that is accountable for ensuring that the Business and the IT Service provider strategies and plans are very much associated with each other. It takes in senior representatives from the Business and the IT Service provider. IT Steering Group (ISG) sets the direction and strategy for IT Services. It includes members of senior management from business and IT. It reviews the business and IT strategies in order to make sure that they are aligned. It also sets priorities of service development programs/ projects.

ITIL

A set of Best Practice guidance for IT Service Management. ITIL is owned by the OGC and consists of a series of publications giving guidance on the provision of Quality IT Services, and on the Processes and facilities needed to support them. See http://www.itil.co.uk/ for more information.

Justify

It is used for monitoring and measuring to justify with realistic evidence or proof that a course of action is needed.

Job Description

A Document which defines the Roles, responsibilities, skills and knowledge required by a particular person. One Job Description can include multiple Roles, for example the Roles of Configuration Manager and Change Manager may be carried out by one person.

Job Scheduling

(Service Operation) Planning and managing the execution of software tasks that are required as part of an IT Service. Job Scheduling is carried out by IT Operations Management, and is often automated using software tools that run batch or online tasks at specific times of the day, week, month or year.

Kano Model

(Service Strategy) A Model developed by Noriaki Kano that is used to help understand Customer preferences. The Kano Model considers Attributes of an IT Service grouped into areas such as Basic Factors, Excitement Factors, Performance Factors etc.

Kepner & Tregoe Analysis

(Service Operation) (Continual Service Improvement) A structured approach to Problem solving. The Problem is analysed in terms of what, where, when and extent. Possible causes are identified. The most probable cause is tested. The true cause is verified.

Key Performance Indicators (KPIs)

(Continual Service Improvement) Key Performance Indicators (KPIs) are a measure of performance. Such measures are commonly used to help an organization define and evaluate how successful it is, typically in terms of making progress towards its long term organizational goals. KPIs can be specified by answering the question, "What is really important for different stakeholders?" KPIs may be monitored using Business Intelligence techniques to assess the present state of the business and to assist in prescribing a course of action. The act of monitoring KPIs in real-time is known as Business Activity Monitoring (BAM).

Knowledge Base

(Service Transition) A logical database containing the data used by the Service Knowledge Management System.

Knowledge Management

(Service Transition) Knowledge Management is used to gather, analyze, store, and share knowledge and information within an organization. The primary purpose of Knowledge Management is to improve efficiency by reducing the need to rediscover knowledge. It is part of Service Transition and the owner of Knowledge Management is the Knowledge Manager. ITIL V3, however, defines Knowledge Management as the one central process responsible for providing knowledge to all other IT Service Management processes.

Known Error

(Service Operation) A Problem that has a documented Root Cause and a Workaround. Known Errors are created and managed throughout their Lifecycle by Problem Management. Known Errors may also be identified by Development or Suppliers.

Known Error Database (KEDB)

(Service Operation) A database containing all Known Error Records. This database is created by Problem Management and used by Incident and Problem Management. The Known Error Database is part of the Service Knowledge Management System.

Known Error Record

(Service Operation) A Record containing the details of a Known Error. Each Known Error Record documents the Lifecycle of a Known Error, including the Status, Root Cause and Workaround. In some implementations a Known Error is documented using additional fields in a Problem Record.

Lifecycle

The various stages in the life of an IT Service, Configuration Item, Incident, Problem, Change etc. The Lifecycle defines the Categories for Status and the Status transitions that are permitted.

Line of Service (LOS)

(Service Strategy) A Core Service or Supporting Service that has multiple Service Level Packages. A line of Service is managed by a Product Manager and each Service Level Package is designed to support a particular market segment.

Local Service Desk

It is used to meet local business needs. It is practical only until multiple locations requiring support services are involved.

Live

(Service Transition) Refers to an IT Service or Configuration Item that is being used to deliver Service to a Customer.

Live Environment

(Service Transition) A controlled Environment containing Live Configuration Items used to deliver IT Services to Customers.

Maintainability

(Service Design) A measure of how quickly and Effectively a Configuration Item or IT Service can be restored to normal working after a Failure. Maintainability is often measured and reported as MTRS. Maintainability is also used in the context of Software or IT Service Development to mean ability to be Changed or Repaired easily.

Major Incident

(Service Operation) The highest Category of Impact for an Incident. A Major Incident results in significant disruption to the Business.

Managed Services

(Service Strategy) A perspective on IT Services which emphasizes the fact that they are managed. The term Managed Services is also used as a synonym for Outsourced IT Services.

Minor release

It integrates a number of fixes for known problems into the baseline, or trusted state, of an item. A minor release typically increments the version number at the first decimal place. For example, version 7.10 will change to version 7.20.

Major release

It typically introduces new capabilities/functions. A major release might accumulate all the changes from preceding minor releases. Major releases advance the version number by a full increment. For example, from version 7.70 to version 8.

Management Information

Information that is used to support decision making by managers. Management Information is often generated automatically by tools supporting the various IT Service Management Processes.

Management Information often includes the values of KPIs such as "Percentage of Changes leading to Incidents", or "first time fix rate".

Management of Risk (MoR)

The OGC methodology for managing Risks. MoR includes all the Activities required to identify and Control the exposure to Risk which may have an impact on the achievement of an Organisation's Business Objectives.

Management System

The framework of Policy, Processes and Functions that ensures an Organisation can achieve its Objectives.

Manual Workaround

A Workaround that requires manual intervention. Manual Workaround is also used as the name of a Recovery Option in which The Business Process Operates without the use of IT Services. This is a temporary measure and is usually combined with another Recovery Option.

Marginal Cost

(Service Strategy) The Cost of continuing to provide the IT Service. Marginal Cost does not include investment already made, for example the cost of developing new software and delivering training.

Market Space

(Service Strategy) All opportunities that an IT Service Provider could exploit to meet business needs of Customers. The Market Space identifies the possible IT Services that an IT Service Provider may wish to consider delivering.

Maturity

(Continual Service Improvement) A measure of the Reliability, Efficiency and Effectiveness of a Process, Function, Organisation etc. The most mature Processes and Functions are formally aligned to Business Objectives and Strategy, and are supported by a framework for continual improvement.

Maturity Level

A named level in a Maturity model such as the Carnegie Mellon Capability Maturity Model Integration.

Mean Time Between Failures (MTBF)

(Service Design) Mean Time Between Failures (MTBF) is the predicted elapsed time between inherent failures of a system during operation. MTBF can be calculated as the arithmetic mean time between failures of a system. MTBF is typically part of a model that assumes the failed system is immediately repaired, as a part of a renewal process. This is in contrast to the Mean Time To Failure (MTTF), which measures average time between failure with the modeling assumption that the failed system is not repaired.

Mean Time Between Service Incidents (MTBSI)

(Service Design) Mean Time Between Service Incidents (MTBSI) is a metric used to measure and report reliability. MTBSI is the mean time starting from when a system or IT service fails, until it next fails. MTBSI is equivalent to MTBF + MTRS. Mean Time Between Service Incidents (MTBSI) is used in Service Design of ITIL.

Mean Time To Failure

Mean Time To Failure (MTTF) is an approximate of the average, or mean time until a component's first failure, or disruption in the operation of the product, process, procedure, or design takes place. MTTF presumes that the product CANNOT be repaired and the product CANNOT continue any of its regular operations.

In many designs and components, MTTF is especially near to the MTBF, which is a bit longer than MTTF. This is due to the fact that MTBF adds the repair time of the designs or components. MTBF is the average time between failures to include the average repair time, or MTTR.

Mean Time To Repair (MTTR)

Mean Time To Repair (MTTR) is the average time taken to repair a Configuration Item or IT Service after a failure. It represents the average time required to repair a failed component or device. Expressed mathematically, it is the total corrective maintenance time divided by the total number of corrective maintenance actions during a given period of time. It generally does not include lead time for parts not readily available or other Administrative or Logistic Downtime (ALDT).

MTTR is often part of a maintenance contract, where a system whose MTTR is 24 hours is generally more valuable than for one of 7 days if mean time between failures is equal, because its Operational Availability is higher. MTTR is every now and then incorrectly used to mean Mean Time to Restore Service.

Mean Time to Restore Service (MTRS)

The average time taken to Restore a Configuration Item or IT Service after a Failure. MTRS is measured from when the CI or IT Service fails until it is fully Restored and delivering its normal functionality.

Metric

(Continual Service Improvement) Something that is measured and reported to help manage a Process, IT Service or Activity.

Middleware

(Service Design) Software that connects two or more software Components or Applications. Middleware is usually purchased from a Supplier, rather than developed within the IT Service Provider.

Mission Statement

The Mission Statement of an Organisation is a short but complete description of the overall purpose and intentions of that Organisation. It states what is to be achieved, but not how this should be done.

Model

A representation of a System, Process, IT Service, Configuration Item etc. that is used to help understand or predict future behaviour.

Modelling

A technique that is used to predict the future behaviour of a System, Process, IT Service, Configuration Item etc. Modelling is commonly used in Financial Management, Capacity Management and Availability Management.

Monitor Control Loop

(Service Operation) Monitoring the output of a Task, Process, IT Service or Configuration Item; comparing this output to a predefined norm; and taking appropriate action based on this comparison.

Monitoring

(Service Operation) Repeated observation of a Configuration Item, IT Service or Process to detect Events and to ensure that the current status is known.

Near-Shore

(Service Strategy) Provision of Services from a country near the country where the Customer is based. This can be the provision of an IT Service, or of supporting Functions such as Service Desk.

Net Present Value (NPV)

(Service Strategy) A technique used to help make decisions about Capital Expenditure. NPV compares cash inflows to cash outflows. Positive NPV indicates that an investment is worthwhile.

Notional Charging

(Service Strategy) An approach to Charging for IT Services. Charges to Customers are calculated and Customers are informed of the charge, but no money is actually transferred. Notional Charging is sometimes introduced to ensure that Customers are aware of the Costs they incur, or as a stage during the introduction of real Charging.

Objective

The defined purpose or aim of a Process, an Activity or an Organisation as a whole. Objectives are usually expressed as measurable targets. The term Objective is also informally used to mean a Requirement.

Off the Shelf

Synonym for Commercial Off the Shelf.

Office of Government Commerce (OGC)

OGC owns the ITIL brand (copyright and trademark). OGC is a UK Government department that supports the delivery of the government's procurement agenda through its work in collaborative procurement and in raising levels of procurement skills and capability with departments. It also provides support for complex public sector projects.

Office of Public Sector Information (OPSI)

OPSI license the Crown Copyright material used in the ITIL publications. They are a UK Government department who provide online access to UK legislation, license the re-use of Crown copyright material, manage the Information Fair Trader Scheme, maintain the Government's Information Asset Register and provide advice and guidance on official publishing and Crown copyright.

Off-shore

(Service Strategy) Provision of Services from a location outside the country where the Customer is based, often in a different continent. This can be the provision of an IT Service, or of supporting Functions such as Service Desk.

On-shore

(Service Strategy) Provision of Services from a location within the country where the Customer is based. See Off-shore, Near-shore.

Operate

To perform as expected. A Process or Configuration Item is said to Operate if it is delivering the Required outputs. Operate also means to perform one or more Operations. For example, to Operate a computer is to do the day-to-day Operations needed for it to perform as expected.

Operation

(Service Operation) Day-to-day management of an IT Service, System, or other Configuration Item. Operation is also used to mean any pre-defined Activity or Transaction. For example loading a magnetic tape, accepting money at a point of sale, or reading data from a disk drive.

Operational

The lowest of three levels of Planning and delivery (Strategic, Tactical, Operational). Operational Activities include the day-to-day or short term Planning or delivery of a Business Process or IT Service Management Process. The term Operational is also a synonym for Live.

Operational Cost

Cost resulting from running the IT Services. Often repeating payments. For example staff costs, hardware maintenance and electricity (also known as "current expenditure" or "revenue expenditure").

Operational Expenditure (OPEX)

Synonym for Operational Cost.

Operational Level Agreement (OLA)

(Service Design) (Continual Service Improvement) An Operational Level Agreement (OLA) defines the interdependent relationships among the internal support groups of an organization working to support a Service Level Agreement. The agreement describes the responsibilities of each internal support group toward other support groups, including the process and timeframe for delivery of their services. The objective of the OLA is to present a clear, concise, and measurable description of the service provider's internal support relationships.

Operations Bridge

(Service Operation) A physical location where IT Services and IT Infrastructure are monitored and managed.

Operations Control

Synonym for IT Operations Control.

Operations Management

Synonym for IT Operations Management.

Opportunity Cost

(Service Strategy) A Cost that is used in deciding between investment choices. Opportunity Cost represents the revenue that would have been generated by using the Resources in a different way. For example the

Opportunity Cost of purchasing a new Server may include not carrying out a Service Improvement activity that the money could have been spent on. Opportunity cost analysis is used as part of a decision making processes, but is not treated as an actual Cost in any financial statement.

Optimise

Review, Plan and request Changes, in order to obtain the maximum Efficiency and Effectiveness from a Process, Configuration Item, Application etc.

Organisation

A company, legal entity or other institution. Examples of Organisations that are not companies include International Standards Organisation or itSMF. The term Organisation is sometimes used to refer to any entity which has People, Resources and Budgets. For example a Project or Business Unit.

Outcome

The result of carrying out an Activity; following a Process; delivering an IT Service etc. The term Outcome is used to refer to intended results, as well as to actual results.

Outsourcing

(Service Strategy) Using an External Service Provider to manage IT Services.

Overhead

Synonym for Indirect cost

Pain Value Analysis

(Service Operation) A technique used to help identify the Business Impact of one or more Problems. A formula is used to calculate Pain Value based on the number of Users affected, the duration of the Downtime, the Impact on each User, and the cost to the Business (if known).

Pareto Principle

(Service Operation) A technique used to prioritise Activities. The Pareto Principle says that 80% of the value of any Activity is created with 20% of the effort. Pareto Analysis is also used in Problem Management to prioritise possible Problem causes for investigation.

Partnership

A relationship between two Organisations which involves working closely together for common goals or mutual benefit. The IT Service Provider should have a Partnership with the Business, and with Third Parties who are critical to the delivery of IT Services.

Passive Monitoring

(Service Operation) Monitoring of a Configuration Item, an IT Service or a Process that relies on an Alert or notification to discover the current status. See Active Monitoring.

Pattern of Business Activity (PBA)

(Service Strategy) A Workload profile of one or more Business Activities. Patterns of Business Activity are used to help the IT Service Provider understand and plan for different levels of Business Activity.

Percentage utilization

(Service Design) The amount of time that a Component is busy over a given period of time. For example, if a CPU is busy for 1800 seconds in a one hour period, its utilisation is 50%

Performance

A measure of what is achieved or delivered by a System, person, team, Process, or IT Service.

Performance Anatomy

(Service Strategy) An approach to Organisational Culture that integrates, and actively manages, leadership and strategy, people development, technology enablement, performance management and innovation.

Performance Management

(Continual Service Improvement) The Process responsible for day-to-day Capacity Management Activities. These include Monitoring, Threshold detection, Performance analysis and Tuning, and implementing Changes related to Performance and Capacity.

Pilot

(Service Transition) A limited Deployment of an IT Service, a Release or a Process to the Live Environment. A Pilot is used to reduce Risk and to gain User feedback and Acceptance.

Plan

A detailed proposal which describes the Activities and Resources needed to achieve an Objective. For example a Plan to implement a new IT Service or

Process. ISO/IEC 20000 requires a Plan for the management of each IT Service Management Process.

Plan-Do-Check-Act

(Continual Service Improvement) A four stage cycle for Process management, attributed to Edward Deming. Plan-Do-Check-Act is also called the Deming Cycle.

Planned Downtime

(Service Design) Agreed time when an IT Service will not be available. Planned Downtime is often used for maintenance, upgrades and testing.

Planning

An Activity responsible for creating one or more Plans. For example, Capacity Planning.

PMBOK

A Project management Standard maintained and published by the Project Management Institute. PMBOK stands for Project Management Body of Knowledge. See http://www.pmi.org/ for more information.

Policy

Formally documented management expectations and intentions. Policies are used to direct decisions, and to ensure consistent and appropriate development and implementation of Processes, Standards, Roles, Activities, IT Infrastructure etc.

Portable Facility

(Service Design) A prefabricated building, or a large vehicle, provided by a Third Party and moved to a site when needed by an IT Service Continuity Plan.

Post Implementation Review (PIR)

A Review that takes place after a Change or a Project has been implemented. A PIR determines if the Change or Project was successful, and identifies opportunities for improvement.

Practice

A way of working, or a way in which work must be done. Practices can include Activities, Processes, Functions, Standards and Guidelines.

Prerequisite for Success (PFS)

An Activity that needs to be completed, or a condition that needs to be met, to enable successful implementation of a Plan or Process. A PFS is often an output from one Process that is a required input to another Process.

Pricing

(Service Strategy) The Activity for establishing how much Customers will be Charged.

PRINCE2

The standard UK government methodology for Project management.

Problem Control

The Problem Control Process aims to handle problems in an efficient way. Problem control identifies the root cause of incidents and reports it to the service desk.

Priority

(Service Transition) (Service Operation) A Category used to identify the relative importance of an Incident, Problem or Change. Priority is based on Impact and Urgency, and is used to identify required times for actions to be taken. For example the SLA may state that Priority2 Incidents must be resolved within 12 hours.

Proactive Monitoring

(Service Operation) Monitoring that looks for patterns of Events to predict possible future Failures.

Proactive Problem Management

(Service Operation) Part of the Problem Management Process. The Objective of Proactive Problem Management is to identify Problems that might otherwise be missed. Proactive Problem Management analyses Incident Records, and uses data collected by other IT Service Management Processes to identify trends or significant Problems.

Problem

(Service Operation) A cause of one or more Incidents. The cause is not usually known at the time a Problem Record is created, and the Problem Management Process is responsible for further investigation.

Problem Management

(Service Operation) Problem Management is used to resolve the root cause of incidents, and thus to minimize the adverse impact of incidents and problems on business that are caused by errors within the IT infrastructure, and to prevent recurrence of incidents related to these errors. A problem is an unknown underlying cause of one or more incidents, and a known error is a problem that is successfully diagnosed and for which either a work-around or a permanent resolution has been identified.

Problem Management Process

The Problem Management Process is intended to reduce the number and severity of incidents and problems of the business, and report it in documentation to be available for the first-line and second line of the help desk. The proactive process identifies and resolves problems before incidents occur.

Problem Record

(Service Operation) A Record containing the details of a Problem. Each Problem Record documents the Lifecycle of a single Problem.

Procedure

A Document containing steps that specify how to achieve an Activity. Procedures are defined as part of Processes.

Processes

Processes provide transformation towards a goal. They make use of feedback for self-reinforcing and self-counteractive action to function as closed-loop systems. It is important to consider the complete process or how one process fits into another. Process definitions describe actions, dependencies, and sequence.

Process metrics

These are used in the form of CSFs, KPIs, and activity metrics for the service management processes. These metrics are used to find out the overall health of a process. KPIs can assist to answer four key questions that are about quality, performance, value, and compliance of following the process. CSI can use these metrics as input in identifying improvement opportunities for every process.

Problem Manager

The Problem Manager takes on research for the core causes of Incidents, and therefore he ensures the durable elimination of interruptions. If possible, he makes short-term solutions (Workarounds) available to Incident Management. The Problem Manager develops ultimate solutions for Known Errors. He also engages in the prevention of interruptions (Pro-active Problem Management), i.e. via a trend-analysis of vital services or historical Incidents.

Process Control

The Activity of planning and regulating a Process, with the Objective of performing the Process in an Effective, Efficient, and consistent manner.

Process Evaluation

Process Evaluation is used to evaluate processes on a regular basis. This includes identifying areas where the targeted process metrics are not reached, and holding regular bench markings, audits, maturity assessments, and reviews. It is part of Continual Service Improvement and the owner of Process Evaluation is the Process Manager.

Process Manager

The Process Manager is responsible for planning and coordinating all Process Management activities. He supports all parties involved in managing and improving processes, in particular the Process Owners. This role will also coordinate all Changes to processes, thereby making sure that all processes cooperate in a seamless way.

Process management

Process management is the ensemble of activities of planning and monitoring the performance of a process. Especially in the sense of business process, often confused with reengineering. Process Management is the application of knowledge, skills, tools, techniques and systems to define, visualize, measure, control, report, and improve processes with the goal to meet customer requirements profitably. Some people are of view that it is different from Program Management in the sense that Program Management is concerned with managing a group of inter-dependent projects. However, from another view point, Process Management includes Program Management.

Process Owner

The Process Owner executes the crucial role of process champion, design lead, supporter, instructor, and protector. The Process Owner should be a senior level manager with credibility, influence, and authority across the various areas impacted by the activities of the process. The Process Owner must have the ability to influence and make sure compliance to the policies and procedures put in place across the cultural and departmental silos of the IT organization.

Production Environment

Synonym for Live Environment.

Profit Centre

(Service Strategy) A Business Unit which charges for Services provided. A Profit Centre can be created with the objective of making a profit, recovering Costs, or running at a loss. An IT Service Provider can be run as a Cost Centre or a Profit Centre.

Packaged Release

It is a combination of many changes. For example, an operating system image which also contains specific applications.

pro-forma

A template, or example Document containing example data that will be replaced with the real values when these are available.

Programme

A number of Projects and Activities that are planned and managed together to achieve an overall set of related Objectives and other Outcomes.

Project

A temporary Organisation, with people and other Assets required to achieve an Objective or other Outcome. Each Project has a Lifecycle that typically includes initiation, Planning, execution, Closure etc. Projects are usually managed using a formal methodology such as PRINCE2.

Project management

Project management is the discipline of planning, organizing, and managing resources to bring about the successful completion of specific project goals and objectives. It is often closely related to and sometimes conflated with program management.

A project is a temporary endeavor, having a defined beginning and end, undertaken to meet particular goals and objectives, usually to bring about beneficial change or added value. In practice, the management of these two systems is often found to be quite different, and as such requires the development of distinct technical skills and the adoption of separate management.

Projected Service Outage (PSO)

(Service Transition) A Document that identifies the effect of planned Changes, maintenance Activities and Test Plans on agreed Service Levels.

PRojects IN Controlled Environments (PRINCE2)

See PRINCE2

Qualification

(Service Transition) An Activity that ensures that IT Infrastructure is appropriate, and correctly configured, to support an Application or IT Service.

Quality

The ability of a product, Service, or Process to provide the intended value. For example, a hardware Component can be considered to be of high Quality if it performs as expected and delivers the required Reliability. Process Quality also requires an ability to monitor Effectiveness and Efficiency, and to improve them if necessary.

Quality Assurance (QA)

(Service Transition) The Process responsible for ensuring that the Quality of a product, Service or Process will provide its intended Value.

Quality Management System (QMS)

(Continual Service Improvement) The set of Processes responsible for ensuring that all work carried out by an Organisation is of a suitable Quality to reliably meet Business Objectives or Service Levels.

Quick Win

(Continual Service Improvement) An improvement Activity which is expected to provide a Return on Investment in a short period of time with relatively small Cost and effort.

RACI

(Service Design) (Continual Service Improvement) A Model used to help define Roles and Responsibilities. RACI stands for Responsible, Accountable, Consulted and Informed.

Reactive Monitoring

(Service Operation) Monitoring that takes action in response to an Event. For example submitting a batch job when the previous job completes, or logging an Incident when an Error occurs.

Reciprocal Arrangement

(Service Design) A Recovery Option. An agreement between two Organisations to share resources in an emergency. For example, Computer Room space or use of a mainframe.

Record

A Document containing the results or other output from a Process or Activity. Records are evidence of the fact that an Activity took place and may be paper or electronic. For example, an Audit report, an Incident Record, or the minutes of a meeting.

Recovery

(Service Design) (Service Operation) Returning a Configuration Item or an IT Service to a working state. Recovery of an IT Service often includes recovering data to a known consistent state. After Recovery, further steps may be needed before the IT Service can be made available to the Users (Restoration).

Recovery Option

(Service Design) A Strategy for responding to an interruption to Service. Commonly used Strategies are Do Nothing, Manual Workaround, Reciprocal Arrangement, Gradual Recovery, Intermediate Recovery, Fast Recovery, Immediate Recovery. Recovery Options may make use of dedicated facilities, or Third Party facilities shared by multiple Businesses.

Recovery Point Objective (RPO)

(Service Operation) The maximum amount of data that may be lost when Service is Restored after an interruption. Recovery Point Objective is expressed as a length of time before the Failure. For example a Recovery Point Objective of one day may be supported by daily Backups, and up to 24 hours of data may be lost. Recovery Point Objectives for each IT Service should be negotiated, agreed and documented, and used as Requirements for Service Design and IT Service Continuity Plans.

Recovery Time Objective (RTO)

(Service Operation) The maximum time allowed for recovery of an IT Service following an interruption. The Service Level to be provided may be less than normal Service Level Targets. Recovery Time Objectives for each IT Service should be negotiated, agreed and documented.

Responsibility Assignment Matrix

A Responsibility Assignment Matrix (RAM), (also known as RACI matrix or Linear Responsibility Chart (LRC)), describes the participation by various roles in completing tasks or deliverables for a project or business process. It is especially useful in clarifying roles and responsibilities in cross-functional/departmental projects and processes.

Redundancy

Synonym for Fault Tolerance. The term Redundant also has a generic meaning of obsolete, or no longer needed.

Relationship

A connection or interaction between two people or things. In Business Relationship Management it is the interaction between the IT Service Provider and the Business. In Configuration Management it is a link between two Configuration Items that identifies a dependency or connection between them. For example Applications may be linked to the Servers they run on, IT Services have many links to all the CIs that contribute to them.

Relationship Processes The ISO/IEC 20000 Process group that includes Business Relationship Management and Supplier Management.

Release

(Service Transition) A collection of hardware, software, documentation, Processes or other Components required to implement one or more approved Changes to IT Services. The contents of each Release are managed, Tested, and Deployed as a single entity.

Release and Deployment Management

(Service Transition) The Process responsible for both Release Management and Deployment.

Release Identification

(Service Transition) A naming convention used to uniquely identify a Release. The Release Identification typically includes a reference to the Configuration Item and a version number. For example ISEB Office 2003 SR2.

Release Management

(Service Transition) Release Management is used for platform-independent and automated distribution of software and hardware, including license controls across the entire IT infrastructure. Proper software and hardware control ensures the availability of licensed, tested, and version-certified software and hardware, which functions as intended when introduced into existing infrastructure. Quality control during the development and implementation of new hardware and software is also the responsibility of Release Management. This guarantees that all software meets the demands of the business processes.

Release Process

The name used by ISO/IEC 20000 for the Process group that includes Release Management. This group does not include any other Processes. Release Process is also used as a synonym for Release Management Process.

Release Record

(Service Transition) A Record in the CMDB that defines the content of a Release. A Release Record has Relationships with all Configuration Items that are affected by the Release.

Release Unit

(Service Transition) Components of an IT Service that are normally Released together. A Release Unit typically includes sufficient Components to perform a useful Function. For example one Release Unit could be a Desktop PC, including Hardware, Software, Licenses, Documentation etc. A different Release Unit may be the complete Payroll Application, including IT Operations Procedures and User training.

Release Window

Synonym for Change Window.

Reliability

(Service Design) (Continual Service Improvement) A measure of how long a Configuration Item or IT Service can perform its agreed Function without interruption. Usually measured as MTBF or MTBSI. The term Reliability can also be used to state how likely it is that a Process, Function etc. will deliver its required outputs.

Remediation

(Service Transition) Recovery to a known state after a failed Change or Release.

Repair

(Service Operation) The replacement or correction of a failed Configuration Item.

Request for Change (RFC)

(Service Transition) A formal proposal for a Change to be made. An RFC includes details of the proposed Change, and may be recorded on paper or electronically. The term RFC is often misused to mean a Change Record, or the Change itself.

Request for Change (RFC): It is a form used to record details of a request for a change and is sent as an input to Change Management by the Change Requestor.

Return On Investment (ROI)

It is the difference between the benefit achieved and the amount spent to achieve that benefit, it is expressed as a percentage.

Request Fulfilment

(Service Operation) The Process responsible for managing the Lifecycle of all Service Requests.

Requirement

(Service Design) A formal statement of what is needed. For example a Service Level Requirement, a Project Requirement or the required Deliverables for a Process.

Resilience

(Service Design) The ability of a Configuration Item or IT Service to resist Failure or to Recover quickly following a Failure. For example, an armoured cable will resist failure when put under stress.

Resolution

(Service Operation) Action taken to repair the Root Cause of an Incident or Problem, or to implement a Workaround. In ISO/IEC 20000, Resolution Processes is the Process group that includes Incident and Problem Management.

Resolution Processes

The ISO/IEC 20000 Process group that includes Incident Management and Problem Management.

Resources

(Service Strategy) Resources are types of assets and they are direct inputs for production. Organizations use them to create value in the form of goods and services. Management, organization, people, and knowledge are used to transform resources. It is comparatively easy to obtain resources compared to capabilities.

Response Time

A measure of the time taken to complete an Operation or Transaction. Used in Capacity Management as a measure of IT Infrastructure Performance, and in Incident Management as a measure of the time taken to answer the phone, or to start Diagnosis.

Responsiveness

A measurement of the time taken to respond to something. This could be Response Time of a Transaction, or the speed with which an IT Service Provider responds to an Incident or Request for Change etc.

Restoration of Service

See Restore.

Restore

(Service Operation) Taking action to return an IT Service to the Users after Repair and Recovery from an Incident. This is the primary Objective of Incident Management.

Retire

(Service Transition) Permanent removal of an IT Service, or other Configuration Item, from the Live Environment. Retired is a stage in the Lifecycle of many Configuration Items.

Retired services

Retired services are not available for use by present customers. However, if the customers give a strong business case, the service providers can restore the phased out service. Although these services are fully terminated, information and data added while services were under operation are stored in the knowledge base of the company. Retiring the services is a normal event in a service lifecycle.

Return on Investment (ROI)

(Service Strategy) (Continual Service Improvement) A measurement of the expected benefit of an investment. In the simplest sense it is the net profit of an investment divided by the net worth of the assets invested.

Return to Normal

(Service Design) The phase of an IT Service Continuity Plan during which full normal operations are resumed. For example, if an alternate data centre has been in use, then this phase will bring the primary data centre back into operation, and restore the ability to invoke IT Service Continuity Plans again.

Review

An evaluation of a Change, Problem, Process, Project etc. Reviews are typically carried out at predefined points in the Lifecycle, and especially after Closure. The purpose of a Review is to ensure that all Deliverables have been provided, and to identify opportunities for improvement.

Rights

(Service Operation) Entitlements, or permissions, granted to a User or Role. For example the Right to modify particular data, or to authorize a Change.

Risk

A possible Event that could cause harm or loss, or affect the ability to achieve Objectives. A Risk is measured by the probability of a Threat, the Vulnerability of the Asset to that Threat, and the Impact it would have if it occurred.

Risk Assessment

The initial steps of Risk Management. Analysing the value of Assets to the business, identifying Threats to those Assets, and evaluating how Vulnerable each Asset is to those Threats. Risk Assessment can be quantitative (based on numerical data) or qualitative.

Risk Management

Risk Management is used to identify, assess, and control risks. It includes analyzing the value of assets to the business, identifying threats to those assets, and evaluating how vulnerable each asset is to those threats. Risk Management is part of Service Design and the owner of the Risk Management is the Risk Manager.

Risks are addressed within several processes in ITIL V3; however, there is no dedicated Risk Management process. ITIL V3 calls for "coordinated risk assessment exercises", so at IT Process Maps we decided to assign clear responsibilities for managing risks.

Role

A set of responsibilities, Activities and authorities granted to a person or team. A Role is defined in a Process. One person or team may have multiple Roles, for example the Roles of Configuration Manager and Change Manager may be carried out by a single person.

Rollout

(Service Transition) Synonym for Deployment. Most often used to refer to complex or phased Deployments or Deployments to multiple locations.

Root Cause

(Service Operation) The underlying or original cause of an Incident or Problem.

Root Cause Analysis (RCA)

(Service Operation) An Activity that identifies the Root Cause of an Incident or Problem. RCA typically concentrates on IT Infrastructure failures.

Running Costs

Synonym for Operational Costs

Scalability

The ability of an IT Service, Process, Configuration Item etc. to perform its agreed Function when the Workload or Scope changes.

Scope

The boundary, or extent, to which a Process, Procedure, Certification, Contract etc. applies. For example the Scope of Change Management may include all Live IT Services and related Configuration Items, the Scope of an ISO/IEC 20000 Certificate may include all IT Services delivered out of a named data centre.

Second-line Support

(Service Operation) The second level in a hierarchy of Support Groups involved in the resolution of Incidents and investigation of Problems. Each level contains more specialist skills, or has more time or other Resources.

Security

See Information Security Management

Security Management

Synonym for Information Security Management. Security Management describes the structured fitting of information security in the management organization. ITIL Security Management is based on the code of practice for information security management also known as ISO/IEC 17799.

Security Policy

Synonym for Information Security Policy

Separation of Concerns (SoC)

(Service Strategy) An approach to Designing a solution or IT Service that divides the problem into pieces that can be solved independently. This approach separates "what" is to be done from "how" it is to be done.

Server

(Service Operation) A computer that is connected to a network and provides software Functions that are used by other computers.

Service

A service is a way of delivering value to customers by facilitating outcome that customers wish to get without the control of specific costs and risks. It is a series of activities designed to enhance the level of customer satisfaction.

Outcomes are probable from the performance of tasks and are limited by the existence of certain constraints. A service facilitates outcomes by enhancing the performance and by reducing the clutch of constraints. The result is an increase in the possibility of desired outcomes. Its importance varies by product, industry and customer; defective or broken merchandise can be exchanged, often only with a receipt and within a specified time frame.

Service Acceptance Criteria (SAC)

(Service Transition) A set of criteria used to ensure that an IT Service meets its functionality and Quality Requirements and that the IT Service Provider is ready to Operate the new IT Service when it has been Deployed.

Service metrics

These metrics are the results of the end-to-end service. Component metrics are used to compute the service metrics.

Service Analytics

(Service Strategy) A technique used in the Assessment of the Business Impact of Incidents. Service Analytics Models the dependencies between Configuration Items, and the dependencies of IT Services on Configuration Items.

Service Asset

Any Capability or Resource of a Service Provider.

Service Asset and Configuration Management (SACM)

(Service Transition) Service Asset and Configuration Management is used to maintain information about Configuration Items (CI) required to deliver an IT service, including their relationships. It is part of Service Transition and the owner of Service Asset and Configuration Management is the Configuration Manager. Activities and process objectives of the Service Asset and Configuration Management process are broadly identical in ITIL V3 and V2. ITIL V3 introduces the "Configuration Management System (CMS)" as a logical data model, encompassing several Configuration Management Databases (CMDB).

Service Capacity Management (SCM)

(Service Design) (Continual Service Improvement) The Activity responsible for understanding the Performance and Capacity of IT Services. The Resources used by each IT Service and the pattern of usage over time are collected, recorded, and analysed for use in the Capacity Plan.

Six Sigma

Six Sigma is a business management strategy, initially implemented by Motorola. As of 2009 it enjoys widespread application in many sectors of industry, although its application is not without controversy. Six Sigma seeks to improve the quality of process outputs by identifying and removing the causes of defects and variability in manufacturing and business processes. It uses a set of quality management methods, including statistical methods, and creates a special infrastructure of people within the organization ("Black Belts", "Green Belts", etc.) who are experts in these methods. Each Six Sigma project carried out within an organization follows a defined sequence of steps and has quantified financial targets (cost reduction or profit increase).

Service Catalogue

(Service Design) A service catalog is a list of services that an organization provides, often to its employees or customers. Each service within the catalog typically includes the following:

- A description of the service

- Timeframes or Service Level Agreement (SLA) for fulfilling the service

- Who is entitled to request/view the service

- Costs (if any)

- How to fulfill the service

Service Catalogue Management

Service Catalogue Management is used to ensure that a Service Catalogue is produced and maintained, containing accurate information on all operational services and those being prepared to be run operationally. It provides vital information for all other Service Management processes: Service details, current status, and the services' interdependencies. It is part of Service Design and the owner of Service Catalogue Management is the Service Catalogue Manager.

Service Continuity Management

Synonym for IT Service Continuity Management.

Service Contract

(Service Strategy) A Contract to deliver one or more IT Services. The term Service Contract is also used to mean any Agreement to deliver IT Services, whether this is a legal Contract or an SLA.

Service Culture

A Customer oriented Culture. The major Objectives of a Service Culture are Customer satisfaction and helping the Customer to achieve their Business Objectives.

Service Design

(Service Design) Service Design provides good practice guidance on the design of IT services, processes, and other aspects of the service management effort. It covers design principles and methods for converting strategic objectives into portfolios of services and service assets. The scope of Service Design is not limited to new services. Significantly, design within ITIL is understood to encompass all elements relevant to technology service delivery, rather than focusing solely on design of the technology itself.

Service Design Package

(Service Design) Document(s) defining all aspects of an IT Service and its Requirements through each stage of its Lifecycle. A Service Design Package is produced for each new IT Service, major Change, or IT Service Retirement.

Service Delivery

Service Delivery is primarily concerned with proactive services the ICT must deliver to provide adequate support to business users. It focuses on the business as the customer of the ICT services (compare with: Service Support).

Service Desk

(Service Operation) Service Desk is a primary IT capability called for in IT Service Management (ITSM) as defined by the Information Technology Infrastructure Library (ITIL). It is intended to provide a Single Point of Contact ("SPOC") to meet the communication needs of both Users and IT, and to satisfy both Customer and IT Provider objectives. ("User" refers to the actual user of the service, while "Customer" refers to the entity that is paying for service)

Service Evaluation

Service Evaluation is used to evaluate service quality on a regular basis. This includes identifying areas where the targeted service levels are not reached and holding regular talks with business to make sure that the agreed service levels are still in line with business needs. It is part of Continual Service Improvement and the owner of Service Evaluation is the CSI Manager.

Service Failure Analysis (SFA)

(Service Design) An Activity that identifies underlying causes of one or more IT Service interruptions. SFA identifies opportunities to improve the IT Service Provider's Processes and tools, and not just the IT Infrastructure. SFA is a time constrained, project-like activity, rather than an ongoing process of analysis. See Root Cause Analysis.

Request Fulfillment

Request Fulfillment is added as a new process to ITIL V3 with the aim to have a dedicated process dealing with Service Requests. This was motivated by a clear distinction in ITIL V3 between Incidents (Service Interruptions) and Service Requests (standard requests from users, e.g. password resets). In ITIL V2, Service Requests were fulfilled by the Incident Management process. There are no sub-processes specified for Request Fulfillment according to ITIL V3.

Service Hours

(Service Design) (Continual Service Improvement) An agreed time period when a particular IT Service should be Available. For example, "Monday-Friday 08:00 to 17:00 except public holidays". Service Hours should be defined in a Service Level Agreement.

Service Improvement Plan (SIP)

(Continual Service Improvement) The Service Improvement Plan (SIP) refers to the steps that must be taken if there is a major gap in the projected delivery quality of a service and the actual delivery. SIP is a model that belongs to the Service Level Management (SLM) process. SLM is mainly defined in the Service Design of ITIL v3, but like many processes in v3, SLM is also documented in other volumes. SIP is particularly documented in Continual Service Improvement (CSI). SIP is also referred to when capital budgeting is being discussed with reference to preference decisions.

Service Knowledge Management System (SKMS)

(Service Transition) A set of tools and databases that are used to manage knowledge and information. The SKMS includes the Configuration Management System, as well as other tools and databases. The SKMS stores, manages, updates, and presents all information that an IT Service Provider needs to manage the full Lifecycle of IT Services.

Service Level

Measured and reported achievement against one or more Service Level Targets. The term Service Level is sometimes used informally to mean Service Level Target.

Service Level Agreement (SLA)

(Service Design) (Continual Service Improvement) Service Level Agreement (frequently abbreviated as SLA) is a part of a service contract where the level of service is formally defined. In practice, the term SLA is sometimes used to refer to the contracted delivery time (of the service) or performance.

Service Level Manager

The Service Level Manager is responsible for negotiating Service Level Agreements and ensuring that these are met. He makes sure that all IT Service Management processes, Operational Level Agreements, and Underpinning Contracts are appropriate for the agreed service level targets. The Service Level Manager also monitors and reports on service levels.

Service Level Management (SLM)

(Service Design) (Continual Service Improvement) Service Level Management provides for continual identification, monitoring and review of the levels of IT services specified in the service level agreements (SLAs). It ensures that arrangements are in place with internal IT Support Providers and external suppliers in the form of Operational Level Agreements (OLAs) and Underpinning Contracts (UCs). The process involves assessing the impact of change upon service quality and SLAs. The Service Level Management process is in close relation with the operational processes to control their activities. The central role of Service Level Management makes it the natural place for metrics to be established and monitored against a benchmark.

Service Level Package (SLP)

(Service Strategy) A defined level of Utility and Warranty for a particular Service Package. Each SLP is designed to meet the needs of a particular Pattern of Business Activity.

Service Level Requirement (SLR)

(Service Design) (Continual Service Improvement) A Customer Requirement for an aspect of an IT Service. SLRs are based on Business Objectives and are used to negotiate agreed Service Level Targets.

Service Level Target (Service Design)

(Continual Service Improvement) A commitment that is documented in a Service Level Agreement. Service Level Targets are based on Service Level Requirements, and are needed to ensure that the IT Service design is Fit for Purpose. Service Level Targets should be SMART, and are usually based on KPIs.

Service Maintenance Objective

(Service Operation) The expected time that a Configuration Item will be unavailable due to planned maintenance Activity.

Service Management

Service Management is a set of specialized organizational capabilities for providing value to customers in the form of services.

Service Management Lifecycle

An approach to IT Service Management that emphasizes the importance of coordination and Control across the various Functions, Processes, and Systems necessary to manage the full Lifecycle of IT Services. The Service Management Lifecycle approach considers the Strategy, Design, Transition, Operation and Continuous Improvement of IT Services.

Service Manager

A manager who is responsible for managing the end-to-end Lifecycle of one or more IT Services. The term Service Manager is also used to mean any manager within the IT Service Provider. Most commonly used to refer to a Business Relationship Manager, a Process Manager, an Account Manager or a senior manager with responsibility for IT Services overall.

Service Operation

(Service Operation) Service Operation is the best practice for achieving the delivery of agreed levels of services both to end-users and the customers (where "customers" refer to those individuals who pay for the service and negotiate the SLAs). Service Operation is the part of the lifecycle where the services and value are actually directly delivered. Also, the monitoring of problems and balance between service reliability and cost, etc. are considered.

Service Owner

(Continual Service Improvement) The Service Owner is responsible for a specific service such as Infrastructure, Application, or Professional Service within an organization despite of where the underpinning technology components, processes, or professional capabilities are located. However, in order to ensure that a service is managed with a business focus, the definition of a single point of responsibility is absolutely necessary to give the level of attention and focus required for its delivery. Service ownership is as critical to service management as establishing ownership for processes which cross multiple vertical silos or departments.

Service Package

(Service Strategy) A detailed description of an IT Service that is available to be delivered to Customers. A Service Package includes a Service Level Package and one or more Core Services and Supporting Services.

Service Pipeline

(Service Strategy) The service pipeline is one of the three phases of Service Portfolio. It is a future based concept that defines the strategic future direction for the service provider. It is the concept that defines the variety of services that are currently under development in Service Portfolio. The pipeline is an excellent indicator on the overall strength of the service provider, as it shows the services that are under development for customers or markets.

Service Portfolio

(Service Strategy) Service Portfolio represents a complete list of the services managed by a service provider; some of these services are visible to the customers, while others are not. It contains present contractual commitments, new service development, and ongoing service improvement plans initiated by Continual Service Improvement. It also includes third-party services, which are an integral part of service offerings to customers.

Service Portfolio Management (SPM)

(Service Strategy) Service Portfolio Management is used to decide on a strategy to serve customers, and to develop the service provider's offerings and capabilities. It is part of Service Strategy. The Owner of Service Portfolio Management Process is the Service Portfolio Manager. Managing services as a portfolio is a new concept in ITIL V3. ITIL V3 introduces strategic thinking about how the Service Portfolio should be developed in the future.

Service Potential

(Service Strategy) The total possible value of the overall Capabilities and Resources of the IT Service Provider.

Service Provider

(Service Strategy) An Organisation supplying Services to one or more Internal Customers or External Customers. Service Provider is often used as an abbreviation for IT Service Provider.

Service Provider Interface (SPI)

(Service Strategy) An interface between the IT Service Provider and a User, Customer, Business Process, or a Supplier. Analysis of Service Provider Interfaces helps to coordinate end-to-end management of IT Services.

Service Provisioning Optimization (SPO)

(Service Strategy) Analysing the finances and constraints of an IT Service to decide if alternative approaches to Service delivery might reduce Costs or improve Quality.

Service Reporting

(Continual Service Improvement) The Process responsible for producing and delivering reports of achievement and trends against Service Levels. Service Reporting should agree the format, content and frequency of reports with Customers.

Service Request

(Service Operation) A Service Request is a request from a user for information, advice, a standard change, or access to an IT service. For example, to reset a password, or to provide standard IT services for a new user. Service Requests are usually handled by a service desk or a request fulfillment group, and do not require an RFC to be submitted.

Service Request Management

Service Request Management (SRM) is the underlying workflow and processes that enable an IT procurement or service request to be reliably submitted, routed, approved, monitored, and delivered. SRM is the process of managing a service request through its lifecycle from submission through delivery and follow-up.

Service Sourcing

(Service Strategy) The Strategy and approach for deciding whether to provide a Service internally or to Outsource it to an External Service Provider. Service Sourcing also means the execution of this Strategy.

Service Strategy

(Service Strategy) Service Strategy is the center and origin point of the ITIL Service Lifecycle. It provides guidance on how to design, develop, and implement service management not only as an organizational capability but also as a strategic asset. Service Strategy provides guidance on clarification and prioritization of service provider investments in services. More generally, Service Strategy focuses on helping IT organizations improve and develop over the long term. In both cases, Service Strategy relies largely upon a market-driven approach.

Service Support

Service Support is one of the two disciplines that comprise ITIL Service Management. It is focused on users of the ICT services and is primarily concerned with ensuring that they have access to the appropriate services to support the business functions. To a business, customers, and users are the entry point to the process model.

Service Transition

(Service Transition) Service Transition relates to the delivery of services required by the business into live/operational use, and often encompasses the "project" side of IT rather than Business As Usual (BAU). It provides guidance for the development and improvement of capabilities for transitioning new and changed services into operations. Service Transition provides assistance on how the necessities of Service strategy determined in Service design, thus the necessities are effectively understood in Service operation while controlling the risks of failure and disruption.

Service Utility

(Service Strategy) The Functionality of an IT Service from the Customer's perspective. The Business value of an IT Service is created by the combination of Service Utility (what the Service does) and Service Warranty (how well it does it).

Service Validation and Testing

(Service Transition) Service Validation and Testing is used to ensure that deployed releases and the resulting services meet customer expectations, and to verify that IT operations are able to support the new service. It is part of Service Transition and the owner of Service Validation and Testing is the Test Manager. Service Validation and Testing is a new process in ITIL V3. It includes details on the various testing stages during Service Transition and descriptions of the corresponding testing approaches.

Service Valuation

(Service Strategy) A measurement of the total Cost of delivering an IT Service, and the total value to the Business of that IT Service. Service Valuation is used to help the Business and the IT Service Provider agree on the value of the IT Service.

Service Warranty

(Service Strategy) Assurance that an IT Service will meet agreed Requirements. This may be a formal Agreement such as a Service Level Agreement or Contract, or may be a marketing message or brand image. The Business value of an IT Service is created by the combination of Service Utility (what the Service does) and Service Warranty (how well it does it).

Serviceability

(Service Design) (Continual Service Improvement) The ability of a Third Party Supplier to meet the terms of their Contract. This Contract will include agreed levels of Reliability, Maintainability or Availability for a Configuration Item.

Shift

(Service Operation) A group or team of people who carry out a specific Role for a fixed period of time. For example there could be four shifts of IT Operations Control personnel to support an IT Service that is used 24 hours a day.

Simulation modelling

(Service Design) (Continual Service Improvement) A technique that creates a detailed Model to predict the behaviour of a Configuration Item or IT Service. Simulation Models can be very accurate but are expensive and time consuming to create. A Simulation Model is often created by using the actual Configuration Items that are being modelled, with artificial Workloads or Transactions. They are used in Capacity Management when accurate results are important. A simulation model is sometimes called a Performance Benchmark.

Single Point of Contact

(Service Operation) Providing a single consistent way to communicate with an Organisation or Business Unit. For example, a Single Point of Contact for an IT Service Provider is usually called a Service Desk.

Single Point of Failure (SPOF)

(Service Design) Any Configuration Item that can cause an Incident when it fails, and for which a Countermeasure has not been implemented. A SPOF may be a person, or a step in a Process or Activity, as well as a Component of the IT Infrastructure.

SLAM Chart

(Continual Service Improvement) A Service Level Agreement Monitoring Chart is used to help monitor and report achievements against Service Level Targets. A SLAM Chart is typically colour coded to show whether each agreed Service Level Target has been met, missed, or nearly missed during each of the previous 12 months.

SMART

(Service Design) (Continual Service Improvement) An acronym for helping to remember that targets in Service Level Agreements and Project Plans should be Specific, Measurable, Achievable, Relevant and Timely.

Snapshot

(Service Transition) The current state of a Configuration as captured by a discovery tool.

Source

See Service Sourcing.

Software Asset Management

Software Asset Management (SAM) is the practice of integrating people, processes and technology to allow software licenses and usage to be systematically tracked, evaluated, and managed. The goal of SAM is to reduce IT expenditures, human resource overhead and risks inherent in owning and managing software assets.

Specification

A formal definition of Requirements. A Specification may be used to define technical or Operational Requirements, and may be internal or external. Many public Standards consist of a Code of Practice and a Specification. The Specification defines the Standard against which an Organisation can be Audited.

Stakeholder

All people who have an interest in an Organisation, Project, IT Service etc. Stakeholders may be interested in the Activities, targets, Resources, or Deliverables. Stakeholders may include Customers, Partners, employees, shareholders, owners, etc. See RACI.

Standard

A mandatory Requirement. Examples include ISO/IEC 20000 (an international Standard), an internal security Standard for Unix configuration, or a government Standard for how financial Records should be maintained. The term Standard is also used to refer to a Code of Practice or Specification published by a Standards Organisation such as ISO or BSI.

Standard Change

(Service Transition) A pre-approved Change that is low Risk, relatively common and follows a Procedure or Work Instruction. For example password reset or provision of standard equipment to a new employee. RFCs are not required to implement a Standard Change, and they are logged and tracked using a different mechanism, such as a Service Request.

Standard Operating Procedures (SOP)

(Service Operation) Procedures used by IT Operations Management.

Standby

(Service Design) Used to refer to Resources that are not required to deliver the Live IT Services, but are available to support IT Service Continuity Plans. For example a Standby data centre may be maintained to support Hot Standby, Warm Standby or Cold Standby arrangements.

Statement of requirements (SOR)

(Service Design) A Document containing all Requirements for a product purchase, or a new or changed IT Service.

Status

The name of a required field in many types of Record. It shows the current stage in the Lifecycle of the associated Configuration Item, Incident, Problem etc.

Status Accounting

(Service Transition) The Activity responsible for recording and reporting the Lifecycle of each Configuration Item.

Storage Management

(Service Operation) The Process responsible for managing the storage and maintenance of data throughout its Lifecycle.

Strategic

(Service Strategy) The highest of three levels of Planning and delivery (Strategic, Tactical, Operational). Strategic Activities include Objective setting and long term Planning to achieve the overall Vision.

Strategy

(Service Strategy) A Strategic Plan designed to achieve defined Objectives.

Super User

(Service Operation) A User who helps other Users, and assists in communication with the Service Desk or other parts of the IT Service Provider. Super Users typically provide support for minor Incidents and training.

Service Desk

It not only handles incidents, problems and questions but also provides an interface for other activities such as change requests, maintenance contracts, software licenses, service level management, configuration management, availability management, Financial Management, and IT Services Continuity Management.

Supplier

(Service Strategy) (Service Design) A Third Party responsible for supplying goods or Services that are required to deliver IT services. Examples of suppliers include commodity hardware and software vendors, network and telecom providers, and Outsourcing Organisations.

Supplier and Contract Database (SCD)

(Service Design) A database or structured Document used to manage Supplier Contracts throughout their Lifecycle. The SCD contains key Attributes of all Contracts with Suppliers, and should be part of the Service Knowledge Management System.

Supplier Management

(Service Design) Supplier Management is used to ensure that all contracts with suppliers support the needs of the business, and that all suppliers meet their contractual commitments. It is part of the Service Design. The owner of Supplier Management is the Supplier Manager. In ITIL V3, Supplier Management is part of the Service Design process to allow for a better integration into the Service Lifecycle.

Supply Chain

(Service Strategy) The Activities in a Value Chain carried out by Suppliers. A Supply Chain typically involves multiple Suppliers, each adding value to the product or Service.

Support Group

(Service Operation) A group of people with technical skills. Support Groups provide the Technical Support needed by all of the IT Service Management Processes.

Support Hours

(Service Design) (Service Operation) The times or hours when support is available to the Users. Typically this is the hours when the Service Desk is available. Support Hours should be defined in a Service Level Agreement, and may be different from Service Hours. For example, Service Hours may be 24 hours a day, but the Support Hours may be 07:00 to 19:00.

Supporting Service

(Service Strategy) A Service that enables or enhances a Core Service. For example a Directory Service or a Backup Service.

SWOT Analysis

(Continual Service Improvement) A technique that reviews and analyses the internal strengths and weaknesses of an Organisation and the external opportunities and threats which it faces SWOT stands for Strengths, Weaknesses, Opportunities and Threats.

System

A number of related things that work together to achieve an overall Objective.

System Management

The part of IT Service Management that focuses on the management of IT Infrastructure rather than Process.

Tactical

The middle of three levels of Planning and delivery (Strategic, Tactical, Operational). Tactical Activities include the medium term Plans required to achieve specific Objectives, typically over a period of weeks to months.

Tag

(Service Strategy) A short code used to identify a Category. For example tags EC1, EC2, EC3 etc. might be used to identify different Customer outcomes when analysing and comparing Strategies. The term Tag is also used to refer to the Activity of assigning Tags to things.

Technical Management

(Service Operation) The Function responsible for providing technical skills in support of IT Services and management of the IT Infrastructure. Technical Management defines the Roles of Support Groups, as well as the tools, Processes and Procedures required.

Technical Observation (TO)

(Continual Service Improvement) A technique used in Service Improvement, Problem investigation and Availability Management. Technical support staff meet to monitor the behaviour and Performance of an IT Service and make recommendations for improvement.

Technical Service

Synonym for Infrastructure Service.

Technical Service Catalogue

Technical Service Catalogue includes details of all the IT services delivered to customers. It also includes the IT services together with relationship to the supporting services, shared services, components, and Configuration Items (CIs). Technical Service Catalogue is the technical perspective of the Service Catalogue and is not available to customers.

Technical Support

Synonym for Technical Management.

Tension Metrics   (Continual Service Improvement) A set of related Metrics, in which improvements to one Metric have a negative effect on another. Tension Metrics are designed to ensure that an appropriate balance is achieved.

Terms of Reference (TOR)

(Service Design) A Document specifying the Requirements, Scope, Deliverables, Resources and schedule for a Project or Activity.

Test

(Service Transition) An Activity that verifies that a Configuration Item, IT Service, Process, etc. meets its Specification or agreed Requirements.

Test Environment

(Service Transition) A controlled Environment used to Test Configuration Items, Builds, IT Services, Processes etc.

Third Party

A person, group, or Business who is not part of the Service Level Agreement for an IT Service, but is required to ensure successful delivery of that IT Service. For example a software Supplier, a hardware maintenance company, or a facilities department. Requirements for Third Parties are typically specified in Underpinning Contracts or Operational Level Agreements.

Third-line Support

(Service Operation) The third level in a hierarchy of Support Groups involved in the resolution of Incidents and investigation of Problems. Each level contains more specialist skills, or has more time or other Resources.

Threat

Anything that might exploit a Vulnerability. Any potential cause of an Incident can be considered to be a Threat. For example a fire is a Threat that could exploit the Vulnerability of flammable floor coverings. This term is commonly used in Information Security Management and IT Service Continuity Management, but also applies to other areas such as Problem and Availability Management.

Technology metrics

These are often associated with component and application-based metrics.

Threshold

The value of a Metric which should cause an Alert to be generated, or management action to be taken. For example "Priority1 Incident not solved within 4 hours", "more than 5 soft disk errors in an hour", or "more than 10 failed changes in a month".

Throughput

(Service Design) A measure of the number of Transactions, or other Operations, performed in a fixed time. For example 5000 emails sent per hour, or 200 disk I/Os per second.

Total Cost of Ownership (TCO)

(Service Strategy) A methodology used to help make investment decisions. TCO assesses the full Lifecycle Cost of owning a Configuration Item, not just the initial Cost or purchase price.

Total Cost of Utilization (TCU)

(Service Strategy) A methodology used to help make investment and Service Sourcing decisions. TCU assesses the full Lifecycle Cost to the Customer of using an IT Service.

Total Quality Management (TQM)

(Continual Service Improvement) A methodology for managing continual Improvement by using a Quality Management System. TQM establishes a Culture involving all people in the Organisation in a Process of continual monitoring and improvement.

Transaction

A discrete Function performed by an IT Service. For example transferring money from one bank account to another. A single Transaction may involve numerous additions, deletions and modifications of data. Either all of these complete successfully or none of them is carried out.

Transition

(Service Transition) A change in state, corresponding to a movement of an IT Service or other Configuration Item from one Lifecycle status to the next.

Transition Planning and Support

(Service Transition) The Process responsible for Planning all Service Transition Processes and co-ordinating the resources that they require. These Service Transition Processes are Change Management, Service Asset and Configuration Management, Release and Deployment Management, Service Validation and Testing, Evaluation, and Knowledge Management.

Trend Analysis

(Continual Service Improvement) Analysis of data to identify time related patterns. Trend Analysis is used in Problem Management to identify common Failures or fragile Configuration Items, and in Capacity Management as a Modelling tool to predict future behaviour. It is also used as a management tool for identifying deficiencies in IT Service Management Processes.

Tuning

The Activity responsible for Planning Changes to make the most efficient use of Resources. Tuning is part of Performance Management, which also includes Performance Monitoring and implementation of the required Changes.

Type I Service Provider

(Service Strategy) An Internal Service Provider that is embedded within a Business Unit. There may be several Type I Service Providers within an Organisation.

Type II Service Provider

(Service Strategy) An Internal Service Provider that provides shared IT Services to more than one Business Unit.

Type III Service Provider

(Service Strategy) A Service Provider that provides IT Services to External Customers.

Underpinning Contract (UC)

(Service Design) Underpinning Contract (UC) is a contract between an IT service provider and a third party. In another way, it is an agreement between the IT organization and an external provider about the delivery of one or more services. The third party provides services that support the delivery of a service to a customer. The Underpinning Contract defines targets and responsibilities that are required to meet agreed Service Level targets in an SLA.

Unit Cost

(Service Strategy) The Cost to the IT Service Provider of providing a single Component of an IT Service. For example the Cost of a single desktop PC, or of a single Transaction.

Urgency

(Service Transition) (Service Design) A measure of how long it will be until an Incident, Problem or Change has a significant Impact on the Business. For example a high Impact Incident may have low Urgency, if the Impact will not affect the Business until the end of the financial year. Impact and Urgency are used to assign Priority.

Usability

(Service Design) The ease with which an Application, product, or IT Service can be used. Usability Requirements are often included in a Statement of Requirements.

Use Case

(Service Design) A technique used to define required functionality and Objectives, and to Design Tests. Use Cases define realistic scenarios that describe interactions between Users and an IT Service or other System.

User

A person who uses the IT Service on a day-to-day basis. Users are distinct from Customers, as some Customers do not use the IT Service directly.

User Profile (UP)

(Service Strategy) A pattern of User demand for IT Services. Each User Profile includes one or more Patterns of Business Activity.

Utility

(Service Strategy) Functionality offered by a Product or Service to meet a particular need. Utility is often summarised as "what it does".

Validation

(Service Transition) An Activity that ensures a new or changed IT Service, Process, Plan, or other Deliverable meets the needs of the Business.

Validation ensures that Business Requirements are met even though these may have changed since the original Design.

Validate

It is used for monitoring and measuring to validate earlier decisions.

Value Chain

(Service Strategy) A sequence of Processes that creates a product or Service that is of value to a Customer. Each step of the sequence builds on the previous steps and contributes to the overall product or Service.

Value for Money

An informal measure of Cost Effectiveness. Value for Money is often based on a comparison with the Cost of alternatives.

Value Network

(Service Strategy) A complex set of Relationships between two or more groups or organisations. Value is generated through exchange of knowledge, information, goods or Services.

Value on Investment (VOI)

(Continual Service Improvement) A measurement of the expected benefit of an investment. VOI considers both financial and intangible benefits.

Variable Cost

(Service Strategy) A Cost that depends on how much the IT Service is used, how many products are produced, the number and type of Users, or something else that cannot be fixed in advance.

Variable Cost Dynamics

(Service Strategy) A technique used to understand how overall Costs are impacted by the many complex variable elements that contribute to the provision of IT Services.

Virtual Service Desk

It is used for organizations having multi-country locations. It can be situated and accessed from anywhere in the world due to advances in network performance and telecommunications, reducing operational costs and improving usage of available resources.

Value On Investment (VOI)

It is the extra value produced by establishment of benefits that include long-term outcomes. ROI is a sub-component of VOI.

Variance

The difference between a planned value and the actual measured value. Commonly used in Financial Management, Capacity Management and Service Level Management, but could apply in any area where Plans are in place.

Verification

(Service Transition) An Activity that ensures a new or changed IT Service, Process, Plan, or other Deliverable is complete, accurate, Reliable and matches its Design Specification.

Verification and Audit

(Service Transition) The Activities responsible for ensuring that information in the CMDB is accurate and that all Configuration Items have been identified and recorded in the CMDB. Verification includes routine checks that are part of other Processes. For example, verifying the serial number of a desktop PC when a User logs an Incident. Audit is a periodic, formal check.

Version

(Service Transition) A Version is used to identify a specific Baseline of a Configuration Item. Versions typically use a naming convention that enables the sequence or date of each Baseline to be identified. For example Payroll Application Version 3 contains updated functionality from Version 2.

Vision

A description of what the Organisation intends to become in the future. A Vision is created by senior management and is used to help influence Culture and Strategic Planning.

Vital Business Function (VBF)

(Service Design) A Function of a Business Process which is critical to the success of the Business. Vital Business Functions are an important consideration of Business Continuity Management, IT Service Continuity Management and Availability Management.

Vulnerability

A weakness that could be exploited by a Threat. For example an open firewall port, a password that is never changed, or a flammable carpet. A missing Control is also considered to be a Vulnerability.

Warm Standby

Synonym for Intermediate Recovery.

Warranty

(Service Strategy) A promise or guarantee that a product or Service will meet its agreed Requirements.

See Service Validation and Testing, Service Warranty.

Work in Progress (WIP)

A Status that means Activities have started but are not yet complete. It is commonly used as a Status for Incidents, Problems, Changes etc.

Work Instruction

A Document containing detailed instructions that specify exactly what steps to follow to carry out an Activity. A Work Instruction contains much more detail than a Procedure and is only created if very detailed instructions are needed.

Workaround

(Service Operation) A workaround is a bypass of a known problem in a system. A workaround is a temporary fix that implies that a genuine solution to the problem is needed. Frequently workarounds are as creative as true solutions, involving outside the box thinking in their creation.

They are considered weak in that they will not respond well to further pressure from a system beyond the original design. In implementing a workaround it is important to flag the change so as to later implement a proper solution. Placing pressure on a workaround may result in later failures in the system.

Workload

The Resources required to deliver an identifiable part of an IT Service. Workloads may be Categorised by Users, groups of Users, or Functions within the IT Service. This is used to assist in analysing and managing the Capacity, Performance and Utilisation of Configuration Items and IT Services. The term Workload is sometimes used as a synonym for Throughput.

ISEB Certifications

The **Information Systems Examinations Board** (**ISEB**) is an examination awarding body and a part of BCS, The Chartered Institute for IT. Initially started as a collaboration between the National Computing Centre (NCC) and BCS for the creation of the 'Certificate in Systems Analysis and Design' for the then Systems Analysis Examination Board. In 1989 a new qualification in Project Management was developed. This was the start of an expansion of the portfolio of qualifications and therefore the Systems Analysis Examination Board made the decision to change its name to Information Systems Examination Board (ISEB). ISEB provides the following ITIL certifications:

Foundation (ITIL® V2)

ITIL® / IT Service Management (V2) qualifications at Foundation level:

- IT Service Management (V2)

Other Foundation Qualifications

Other IT Service Management qualifications at Foundation level:

- ISO/IEC 20000: IT Service Management

- Problem & Incident Management (Kepner Tregoe®)

Intermediate (ITIL® V3)

ITIL® / IT Service Management (V3) qualifications at Intermediate level:

- Foundation Bridge (from V2 to V3)

- Lifecycle Modules

- Capability Modules

Practitioner (ITIL® V2)

ITIL® / IT Service Management (V2) qualifications at Practitioner level:

- Availability Management

- Capacity Management

- Change Management

- Configuration Management

- Financial Management for IT Services

- IT Service Continuity Management

- Problem Management

- Release and Control

- Release Management

- Service Desk and Incident Management

- Service Level Management

Specialist Qualifications in IT Service Management

The new Specialist Qualifications in IT Service Management are a series of qualifications that focus on a single IT Service Management job role and present detailed knowledge and information on how each particular job role operates within an organisation, based on industry good practice. They offer a framework for obtaining detailed knowledge of the operation of each of the individual processes within the set of service management processes. There are six subject areas covered with each qualification being based on industry 'good practice' from ITIL, COBIT, ISO/IEC 20000, and SFIA.

- Service Desk and Incident Management

- Change Management

- Service Level Management

- Business Relationship Management

- Problem Management

- Supplier Management

Higher (ITIL® V3)

ITIL® / IT Service Management (V3) qualifications at Higher level:

- Managers Bridge (from V2 to V3)

- Managing Across the Lifecycle

Higher (ITIL® V2)

ITIL® / IT Service Management (V2) qualifications at Higher level:

- IT Service Management (V2)

Software Testing

Software Testing certification is available from BCS at Foundation, Intermediate, Advanced, and Practitioner levels. It is used to support software testing professionals educational requirements at each stage of their career path.

Qualifications in software testing will offer an insight in to the different types of testing and the techniques and tools, which can be used to execute and manage testing.

The Software Testing qualifications available from BCS offer an international benchmark of skills and experience for software testers. The exams offers a stepping stone from Foundation through Intermediate and Advanced. This assists testers with their career development every step of the way.

Foundation

- Software Testing

Intermediate

- Software Testing

Advanced

- Advanced Level Certification

Practitioner

- Test Analysis

- Test Management

Sustainable IT

BCS is widely involved with various green initiatives, including extensive work through the BCS Ethics Forum, the Carbon Footprint Working Group, and the Data Centre Specialist Group. BCS has developed the ISEB Foundation Certificate in Green IT. This is intended for anyone interested in, or affected by, issues surrounding Green IT.

ISEB currently developing more qualifications in the field of sustainability and energy efficiency, including a Practitioner Certificate for data centre operators. This follows the publication of the EU Code of Conduct for data centres and BCS's recent work to encourage the IT industry to address the issues of energy cost, power consumption and carbon emissions.

The qualification will set an international standard for IT professionals in understanding energy efficiency irrespective of what regulation they practice within the industry.

Foundation

- Green IT

Intermediate

- EU Code of Conduct on Data Centres

Business Analysis / Change

A range of qualifications at all ISEB levels covering the subject of business analysis, change management, and consultancy. The qualifications can permit IT professionals to gain an understanding of the business context for IT, by studying one of the individual certificate modules or the Foundation qualifications.

Foundation

- Business Analysis

- IT Enabled Business Change

Practitioner

- Benefits Management & Business Acceptance

- Business Analysis Essentials

- Modelling Business Processes

- Organisational Context

- Requirements Engineering

Higher

- Business Analysis Diploma

- IS Consultancy Practice

Solution Development

This subject area includes analysis, modelling, design, implementation, and architecture, in addition to areas, such as configuration and release management. Some features of ISEB Solution Development qualifications are as follows:

- Modular approach to certification

- Full Diploma for specialists

- Incorporates Agile, object-oriented (UML) and structured approaches

- Links to Business Analysis, Software Testing and Service Management

- Examination approach designed for flexibility

Foundation

- Systems Development

Intermediate

- Enterprise and Solution Architecture

Practitioner

- Enterprise and Solution Architecture

- Integrating Off-the-Shelf Software Solutions

- Systems Design & Implementation Techniques

- Systems Development Essentials

- Systems Modelling Techniques

Higher

- Solution/SystemsDevelopment Diploma

Project Management and Support

This subject area provides a range of qualifications at different ISEB levels covering the subjects of Project Management and Project Support Office. ISEB qualifications in this area provide techniques to support best practice taking into account the particular needs of IS.

The foundation level qualification covers the area of Project Management, Programme Management, Risk, and Project Support. Some of the features offered by the ISEB qualifications in this area are below:

- The only Project Management qualifications devoted to IS and for those working in or managing Project Support Offices.

- Qualifications for new entrants, experienced employees, and short courses embedded into post graduate courses.

- The Project Management qualifications are complementary to PRINCE2 specific qualifications and accounting for other approaches.

Foundation

- IS Project Management

- Programme & Project Support Office Essentials

Practitioner

- Programme & Project Support Office

Higher

- IS Project Management

IT Governance, Information, and Security

ISEB qualifications in this area cover a range of aspects of Information Security with specific emphasis on managing risk.

Information Security affects the whole of an organisation and its skill to function effectively. Therefore, a qualification in this area of IT can be extremely beneficial in today's security conscious world.

ISEB qualifications are internationally recognised and have been developed in line with widely accepted and proven best practices. They are aligned to the ISO/IEC 20000 series standards.

The ISEB Information Security qualifications cover the complete range of skills required for an organisation to implement information security effectively.

The security principles course covers confidentiality, integrity, and availability. It provides a grounding in information security management.

Foundation

- Information Security Management Principles

Practitioner

- Business Continuity Management

- Data Protection

- Freedom of Information

- Information Risk Management

IT Assets and Infrastructure

ISEB qualifications in this area think about the relationship between the acquisition and management of IT assets and their employ through IT services to the business.

Practitioner qualifications cover the complete range of IT assets including data, software, applications, IT infrastructure and the competencies of staff needed to use these.

The Foundation certificate considers the acquisition and management of a range of IT assets including Applications, Data, Infrastructure, and Software.

The ISEB approach pays particular interest to the relationship between this area and that of IT Service Management.

Foundation

- IT Assets & Infrastructure

- Software Asset Management Essentials

Practitioner

- Application Management Essentials

- Data Management Essentials

- Software Asset Management

Higher

- ITIL® Infrastructure Management

Certificate in IT for Insurance Professionals (CITIP)

The Certificate in IT for Insurance Professionals is the only qualification intended particularly to cover IT issues and responsibilities in the insurance industry.

It is developed jointly by The Chartered Insurance Institute (CII) and BCS, it provides support of a broad understanding of the principles and make use of IT in insurance, independent of any particular software/hardware platform.

Things to Practice: A Final Checklist

The ISEB (ITIL V3) Foundation Certificate in IT Service Management BH0-006 exam is aimed at raising an individual's understanding of, and competence in, IT Service Management as described in the ITIL Service Strategy, ITIL Service Design, ITIL Service Transition, ITIL Service Operation, ITIL Continual Service Improvement, ITIL Introduction, and ITIL Glossary publications. Candidates for the ISEB (ITIL V3) Foundation Certificate in IT Service Management (BH0-006) exam have to practice all the 40 Things to successfully pass the examination.

1. Describe the concept of Good Practice.

2. Define and explain the concept of a Service.

3. Define and explain the concept of Service Management.

4. Define Functions and Processes.

5. Explain the process model and the characteristics of processes.

6. Describe the structure, scope, components, and interfaces of the Service Lifecycle.

7. Account for the main goals and objectives of Service Strategy.

8. Account for the main goals and objectives of Service Design.

9. Briefly explain what value Service Design provides to the business.

10. Account for the main goals and objectives of Service Transition.

11. Briefly explain what value Service Transition provides to the business.

12. Account for the main goals and objectives of Service Operations.

13. Briefly explain what value Service Operation provides to the business.

14. Account for the main goals and objectives of Continual Service Improvement.

15. Define Utility and Warranty.

16. Define Resources, Capabilities, and Assets.

17. Define Service Portfolio and Service Catalogue.

18. Define the role of IT Governance across the Service Lifecycle.

19. Define Business Case and Risk.

20. Define Service Provider, Supplier, Service Level Agreement (SLA), and Operational Level Agreement (OLA).

21. Define Contract, Service Design Package, Service Knowledge Management System (SKMS), and Availability.

22. Define Configuration Item (CI) and Configuration Management System.

23. Define Service Change, Change types, Definitive Media Library (DML), and Release Unit.

24. Define the concept of Seven R's of Change Management; no requirement to learn list Event.

25. Define Alert (SO Glossary).

26. Define Incident, Impact, Urgency, and Priority.

27. Define Service Request and Problem.

28. Define Workaround, Known Error, and Known Error Data Base (KEDB).

29. Define the role of communication in Service Operation.

30. Define Service Assets and Release policy.

31. Define key Principles and models of Service Strategy, Service Design, and Continual Service Improvement.

32. Define Service Strategy and Service Design processes.

33. Define Service Transition and Service Operation processes.

34. Explain the role, objectives, and organizational structures for the Service Desk function.

35. State the role, objectives, and organizational overlap of the Technical Management function.

36. State the role, objectives, and organizational overlap of the Application Management function.

37. State the role, objectives, and organizational overlap of the IT Operations Management function.

38. Account for the role and the responsibilities of the Process owner and Service owner.

39. Recognize the RACI model and explain its role in determining organizational structure.

40. Understand how Service Automation assists with Integrating Service Management processes.

uCertify Test Prepration Software for ISEB Exam BH0-006

uCertify test preparation simulation software (PrepKit) is designed to efficiently help you pass the ISEB Exam BH0-006. Each PrepKit contains hundreds of practice questions modeled on real world scenarios. Each exam objective is covered with full explanations of key concepts and numerous study aids such as study guides, pop quizzes and flash cards help reinforce key concepts.

Installation is simple and no internet connection is required once you have installed the PrepKit. To download a free trial please visit:

Download link:

http://www.ucertify.com/exams/ITIL/BH0-006.html

At the core of every uCertify Prepkit is our powerful PrepEngine that allows for a sophisticated level of customized learning. The folks at uCertify, understand that your time is important. We have created a unique blend of learning and test preparation, the foundation of which is working smarter. Years of experience has gone into the creation of detailed reference material that ensure your learning and practice questions that closely simulate real life technical problems to test your understanding of the subject. Our time tested and continuously improving methodology instantly gives you the benefit of separating the fluff from the real deal. Anticipating your needs and customizing the material to your strengths and weaknesses is at the core of our unique engine. We help you gain the skills you need not just to pass the test, but to actually use them on the job!

uCertify's Prepkits have numerous built-in Study Aids such as Flash Cards, Study Notes, Tagging and more reduce the burden of trying to determine how to sift through vast study material by providing refresher or quick reference at any time. Studies have shown this raises the confidence level of students. The student can on the fly, customize Practice tests and learning, such that the content meets their current levels of knowledge. Immediate, Gap analysis reports tell the student what they need to learn to perform better in a particular subject area. Context sensitive study material and tips help enhance a student's knowledge of a subject area, helping them truly learn the material. This helps improve student performance and productivity on the job for employees. The platform also has the capability for subject matter expertise to be captured and communicated in a consistent manner.

Top 12 features of our Award Winning Prepkits

- Simple, intuitive, user-friendly interface

- One click dashboard makes it easy to find what you need

- Guided learning steps you through the process of learning and test preparation, including crucial information about the exam format and test preparation tips

- Reference Notes and Study Guides organized according to the actual test objectives

- Numerous study aids, including study notes, flash cards, pop Pop Quiz and more

- Useful Technical Articles section contains information written by industry experts and How To's that help for easy look up to specific questions

- Collaboration

- Exhaustive practice questions and tests, starting with Diagnostic tests to determine your initial level

- Learning and test modes

- Customize your tests – decide how many questions, combine one or more topics of your choice, quiz yourself on a study note, increase the level of difficulty based on your performance at any point in time, even create a test based on the amount of time you have to take a test!

- Feedback and assessment when you need it, including Gap Analysis that clearly indicate your areas of strength and weakness

- Full length Final Practice test that closely simulates those on the certification exam to gauge your preparation level for the actual exam

Contact us

- **Fax:** 209 231 3841

- **US:** 800 796 3062

- **International:** 1 415 513 1125

- **India:** 532 244 0503

- **Sales:** sales@ucertify.com

- **Support:** support@ucertify.com

Useful Links

- **uCertify USA:** http://www.ucertify.com/

- **Download PrepKits:** http://www.ucertify.com/download/

- **PrepEngine Features:** http://www.prepengine.com/

- **uCertify Blog:** http://www.ucertify.com/blog

- **uCertify Forum:** http://www.ucertify.com/forum

- **uCertify Certification Wiki:** http://www.ucertify.com/wiki

Useful Links

- **uCertify – The Fastest way to IT Certification:**
  http://www.ucertify.com/

- **BCS, The Chartered Institute for IT:**
  http://www.bcs.org/

- **Official ITIL® Website:**
  http://www.itil-officialsite.com/home/home.asp

- **The Itil Community Forum:**
  http://www.itilcommunity.com/

- **uCertify – The Fastest way to IT Certification:**
  http://www.ucertify.in/

- **Itil Forums:**
  http://www.itilforums.com/

- **The Itil Open Guide:**
  http://www.itlibrary.org/

Made in the USA
Lexington, KY
19 November 2010